To LOAD FORGO____ DECK
RESET
LOAD
   Typewriter will remind you to log, then start,

READER NO FEED will be lit.
RESTART READER

PROGRAM DECK
PUT C C Card first
  RESET
  INSERT
  RELEASE
  START

Basic Programming Concepts
and
The IBM 1620 Computer

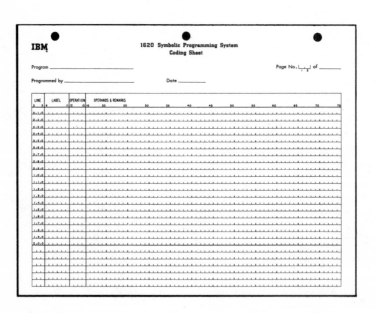

BASIC PROGRAMMING CONCEPTS

AND

THE IBM 1620 COMPUTER

Daniel N. Leeson

Donald L. Dimitry

HOLT, RINEHART AND WINSTON, INC.

New York   Chicago   San Francisco   Toronto   London

We acknowledge with thanks the cooperation of the International Business Machines Corporation in assisting us with materials for the publication of this book. Their kindness in allowing us to use certain copywritten materials is greatly appreciated.

For
Rosanne and Helen

Preface

Construction of a text on computers usually takes one of two directions: (1) general computer philosophy stressing engineering design, scientific-commercial applications, and a variety of related subjects such as Boolean algebra, switching circuit theory, and so forth, or (2) the total organization of a single computer (possibly an imaginary one) with the tacit assumption that one learns an entire range of computers by studying a particular one.

There is a variety of excellent books on general computer philosophy (see "Reading Reference"). However, we have decided to take the latter tack and generate a book on one specific computer whose popularity makes its choice a logical one.

Authorities on computing and computers differ in their opinions as to how material of this nature should be taught. An example of this is the disagreement about the necessity of flow charting, the distinction between coding and programming, and so forth. At this early stage of computing education there is far too little experience to rely upon, and consequently, each individual expresses his beliefs as he feels them to be correct.

The materials in this text are what we believe to be a satisfactory approach to the pedagogical problem of computer education. Perhaps, with the passage of time, our opinions will change as computers develop towards goals now considered in the realm of fantasy.

For the following two reasons, the machine chosen for this total organization study is the IBM 1620 computer: First, the 1620 is a physically small machine of good computing power whose size makes its availability to a university, and subsequently to a student, more practical; second, the 1620 is a computer that uses the decimal system of arithmetic. It is our belief that a "first" machine should be decimal in its internal arithmetic. This is not to say that a decimal machine is superior to a machine using another arithmetic system, or that the converse is true. There is much to be said for each one. However, the problems of learning basic machine concepts are difficult enough without confusing the situation by adding the complexities of a new or less commonly used type of arithmetic.

It is also our belief that adequate study of this single computer prepares one for further study on a whole host of other machines, including computers using binary arithmetic internally.

There is a general concept, romantically propagated by the uninformed, which assumes that programmers are deep, silent thinkers given only to esoteric intellectual pursuits. Such is not the case at all. The qualities that make for a competent programmer are too elusive to pinpoint. There is, however, one quality that is common to all programmers: an astonishing ability to absorb repeated failure. This is because the "first-time correct" program is extremely rare, and the word "first" can be changed to "second," "third," and "fourth" with the statement still true.

Each person becomes proficient in his art by a study of the classic problems pertaining to his field. The Euclidian geometry has had its theorems proven time and again by students of mathematics. The budding musician masters his art by practicing scales. The beginning programmer obtains one form of proficiency by analysis and coding of certain "classic" problems. Many of these have been incorporated here in a chapter consisting solely of problems.

There are many techniques that make a program not only run, but run efficiently, and one of the tasks of the novice programmer is to discover these tricks for himself. To the professional programmer, the old saw, "Time is money," takes on a whole universe of meaning.

We make no assumptions about the educational background of the reader, nor do we assume that a 1620 is available for program testing. It is quite possible, and in some machine installations most practical, for the programmer never to see or physically operate the computer. Although it is desirable to see the results of one's efforts in operation, it is not mandatory for instruction purposes.

It is true that the majority of the examples in the chapter of problems assume some technical background, and the chapters dealing with floating point and Fortran also imply a scientific utilization of the machine. However, the computer may be studied for commercial applications as well as scientific with equal facility. The text, because of the subject matter, must be technical in its presentation, but the nonscientifically oriented reader should be able to assimilate the material.

The student is to be constantly reminded of two "theorems" associated with computer programming which, unfortunately, have more truth than humor: Theorem 1. Every program has at least one error. Theorem 2. Every program can be shortened.

It is difficult to describe how many people have assisted us in the preparation of this book, and to thank each of them in the manner that they deserve would require at least one additional volume.

However, we would be remiss in our responsibilities if we did not mention those individuals whose tireless efforts reached Herculean proportions. These people are: Edward Sinanian and Charles Stewart of IBM General Products Division, San Jose, California, for their review of the manuscript and their particular attention to the chapters on symbolic programming and Fortran; Frank Beckman and Kenneth King for encouraging the use of this book in a classroom situation at the Watson Scientific Computing Laboratories, Columbia University; Sarah Snook, IBM, New York, Guy Magnuson, IBM, Chicago, and

Richard King, IBM, Los Angeles for their suggestions based upon geographical needs; James W. Perry, Numerical Analysis Laboratory, University of Arizona, Alfred T. Chen, Engineering Mathematics Department, University of Louisville, and Frederick Way, III, Associate Director of Computing Center, Case Institute, for their professional and much needed comments on the original manuscript; Frances Perrone for her typing, and typing, and typing, and typing.

To all of these people we say simply "Thank you very much."

FAIR LAWN, NEW JERSEY   D. N. LEESON

JULY 4, 1962   D. L. DIMITRY

Table of Contents

PAGE

PREFACE vii

INTRODUCTION
TO DATA PROCESSING SYSTEMS .... CHAPTER 1   7

Data processing and data processing systems. The computer and its
relationship to the productivity of man. Development of the stored
program computer. Basic considerations of data processing. Entering
and recording of data. General requirements of a storage media. The
data processing system's control center. Philosophy of the stored
program. Data recording on cards and paper tape. General and
elementary computer characteristics.

INTRODUCTION TO THE
1620 DATA PROCESSING SYSTEM .... CHAPTER 2   10

General description. The representation of data in core storage. Functions of the flag bit. Field and record definitions. Internal modes of data
representation. The structure and operation of magnetic core storage.

BASIC PROGRAMMING CONCEPTS .... CHAPTER 3   22

Computer instruction categories. Instruction format. List of instructions and codes. P-address description. Q-address description. Immediate instructions. Two-address instruction system. One-over-one
address system. Internal machine indicators. Execution-time-formula
abbreviations.

THE ALGORITHMS OF ARITHMETIC .... CHAPTER 4   26

Principle of the hand calculator. Subtraction, multiplication, and division as functions of addition. The addition and multiplication tables.
Carry propagation in addition. Insertion of high-order zeros. Subtraction. Carry propagation in subtraction. Multiplication. Caution in
indiscriminate use of arithmetic table areas.

THE ARITHMETIC INSTRUCTIONS .... CHAPTER 5   33

Importance of arithmetic commands. Division methods. Add. Subtract.
Multiply. Compare. Add Immediate. Subtract Immediate. Multiply
Immediate. Compare Immediate. Problems.

xi

PAGE

INTERNAL DATA TRANSMISSION .... CHAPTER 6   53
Necessity for data transmission. Transmit Digit. Transmit Field. Trans-
mit Record. Transmit Digit Immediate. Transmit Field Immediate.
Problems.

BRANCH INSTRUCTIONS .... CHAPTER 7   60
Deviation from sequential program execution. Branch. Looping. Closed
subroutines. Branch and Transmit. Branch and Transmit Immediate.
Branch Back. Branch on Digit. Branch no Flag. Branch no Record
Mark. Branch Indicator. Branch no Indicator. Problems.

INPUT-OUTPUT .... CHAPTER 8   74
Input-output devices. Read Numerically. Real Alphamerically. Write
Numerically. Write Alphamerically. Dump Numerically. Problems.

MISCELLANEOUS INSTRUCTIONS .... CHAPTER 9   82
Set Flag. Clear Flag. Halt. Debugging feature of the Halt command.
No Operation. Control. Problems.

INTRODUCTION TO A
SYMBOLIC PROGRAMMING SYSTEM .... CHAPTER 10   88
Necessity for a symbolic system. Construction of an operation code
translator. Elements of a translating system. Total translation of certain
specialized instructions. List of all operations and associated unique
mnemonics. Dictionary concept. Information sentences for a processor.
Origin counting. Choice of useful mnemonics. Complete program
translation. Declaratives and instructions. Labeling concepts. Processor
definition. Assembly system.

THE SYMBOLIC PROGRAMMING SYSTEM ..... CHAPTER 11   100
Instructions and declaratives. The SPS coding form. Construction of
labels. Operands and remarks. Types of operands. Arithmetic allowable
on operands. DORG. DEND. DS. DC. DSS. DSC. DAS. DAC.
DSA. DSB. TCD. TRA. HEAD. DNB. SEND. Additional processor
information. Error detection in the source program.

FLOATING POINT ARITHMETIC .... CHAPTER 12   148
Difficulties arising in fixed-point calculation. Number scaling. Floating
point. Scientific notation. Characteristic. Mantissa. Normalization.
Range of floating-point numbers. Flag requirements. Overflow and
underflow conditions. Excess fifty notation. Problems.

MACRO INSTRUCTIONS .... CHAPTER 13   155
Open subroutines. Closed subroutines. Macro instructions. Linkage

systems. Floating Add. Floating Subtract. Floating Multiply. Float-
ing Divide. Fixed Divide. Floating Square Root. Floating Sine Cosine. Floating Arctangent. Floating Exponential. Floating Logarithm.
Floating Transmit Field. Floating Branch and Transmit. Restrictions
and general information about macro instructions. Function of the
subroutine Pick. Normalization, noise, and filling digits.

INTRODUCTION TO FORTRAN .... CHAPTER 14 170

Advances in computer technology. Advances in programming systems.
Efficiency. Fortran. Make-up of the Fortran system. Compilation.

BASIC 1620 FORTRAN .... CHAPTER 15 174

Definitions. Fixed and floating-point constants. Fixed and floating-
point point variables. Basic operations. Expression definition. Types
of Fortran statements. Arithmetic-type statements. Numbering of
statements. Unconditional Go To. Computed Go To. If. If Sense
Switch. Input-output and Format. Pause. Stop. End. The subscription of variables. Dimension. Do. Continue. Library functions. Comments. Examples. General information.

PROBLEMS .... CHAPTER 16 221

Problems for absolute coding. Macroless symbolic problems. Full symbolic problems. Basic Fortran problems.

ADDITIONAL INSTRUCTIONS .... APPENDIX I 233

Move flag. P-field meaning for Strip and Fill instructions. Double-
digit conversion. Transfer Numerical Strip. Transfer Numerical Fill.
Problems.

DIRECT DIVIDE .... APPENDIX II 239

Automatic division. Dividend, divisor, and quotient size. Load Dividend. Load Dividend Immediate. Divide. Method of successive subtraction. Divide Immediate. Incorrect division positioning. Summary
of division rules. Problems.

INDIRECT ADDRESSING .... APPENDIX III 248

Purpose of indirect addressing. Direct addressing. Indirect addressing.
Form of an indirect address. Allowable indirect instruction operands.
Examples.

FLOATING POINT HARDWARE .... APPENDIX IV 253

Advantages of floating-point hardware. Mantissa size. Characteristic
range. Restrictions. Floating Add. Floating Subtract. Floating Multi-

ply. Floating Divide. Floating Transmit Field. Field Branch and Transmit. Floating Shift Right. Floating Shift Left. General information on floating-point hardware.

THE INPUT-OUTPUT DEVICES .... APPENDIX V   262

The paper-tape reader. The paper-tape punch. Specialized error conditions. Loading the paper-tape punch. The card reader and punch. Buffering. The card reader. Specialized error conditions. Card reader component description. The card punch. Specialized error conditions. Card punch component description. Operating lights for card read-punch unit. Error restart procedures. The console typewriter.

THE 1620 CONSOLE .... APPENDIX VI   281

The console panel. Instruction and execute cycle panel. Control gates. Input-output. Operation register. Multiplier. Sense and branch. Memory buffer register. Memory data register. Digit register. Memory address register. Memory address register display selector. Parity check switch and indicator lights. Input-output check switch and indicator lights. Overflow check switch and indicator light. Program switches. Power-on switch and light. Power-ready light. Reset key. Thermal light. Punch no feed light. Reader no feed light. Display MAR key. Save key and light. Insert key and light. Release key. Start key. Automatic light. Manual light. Stop key. Instant stop key. Check stop light. Emergency-off switch.

CONSOLE OPERATING PROCEDURES .... APPENDIX VII   296

Instructing the computer from the typewriter. Clearing core storage to zeros. Program entry from the typewriter. Printing core storage data on the typewriter. Program alteration and/or data entry. Single instruction execution of a program. Procedure to turn off thermal light. Assembling an SPS source program (tape). Error detection in source program. Procedure for handling errors. Running the object program. Error messages at object time. Compiling a Fortran program (tape). Errors in the source program. The Fortran trace feature. Running the object program. Typewriter entry of data. Error messages at object time. Assembling an SPS program (card). Error detection in the source program. Procedures for handling errors. Running the object program. Error messages at object time. Compiling a Fortran program (card). Errors in the source program. Sequence checking the Fortran compiler and subroutine decks. Fortran trace features. Running the object program. Typewriter entry of data. Error messages at object time.

THE INTERNAL ORGANIZATION
OF BASIC 1620 FORTRAN .... APPENDIX VIII   326

The table of symbols. Locating an encountered operation. Locating
the addresses of encountered symbols. FAC. Determining the category
of Fortran statements. Events that occur before the determination of
category. Categories 1 and 2. Nonrelocatable subroutines. The
manipulation of algebraic statements. Polish notation. Scanning techniques. Linkage to relocatable subroutines. The unary minus. Dimension. Go to. Pause. Stop. If Sense Switch. If floating point. If fixed
point. If expression. Computed go to. Do. Continue. Input-output
and format. Problems.

GLOSSARY   354

READING REFERENCE   359

INDEX   363

Chapter 1

Introduction to Data Processing Systems

Data processing is a series of planned actions and operations upon information to achieve a desired result. The operations are performed according to precise and strict rules of procedure. The procedures and devices used are what constitute a data processing system. Recently, "data processing" has become a generic term for "computing."

The computer offers to man a means to increase his productivity. This is accomplished in five ways. (1) Computers through their speed alone enable man to increase his output per hour. (2) Computers enable man to make use of many mathematical methods that were previously impractical due to the lengthy and time-consuming calculations involved. Imagine attempting to solve a system of 50 simultaneous linear equations on a desk calculator. The computer solves this problem in minutes. (3) Computers have enabled man to develop new mathematical techniques to solve problems previously thought to be beyond the realm of practical mathematics. (4) Computers increase accuracy. Extensive analysis has shown that the human will make at least 5 errors in 100 hand calculations, making him at best 95 percent effective. The computer closely approaches 100 percent accuracy (99.99+ percent). When an error does occur, it is usually sensed, and its presence is indicated to the operator. (5) Computers increase productivity by encouraging intelligent planning.

The need for data processing systems is widespread. Technological growth and advances have been increasing at a rapid and frantic pace. The demands for information are enormous. The aircraft industry, manned missiles, an invulnerable defense network, and design engineering all require an amount of data processing that staggers the imagination.

The 1940's were a great development period for data processing systems. The principles of electronics were applied to data processing equipment, and the first "stored program" computer was developed. At the start, data processing machines were directed by machine instructions that were programmed on interchangeable control panels, cards, or paper tapes. Detailed instructions telling the machine what to do next had to be wired in or read in as the work progressed. Data put into the machine were processed according to the instructions contained in these preset devices. Only in a limited fashion could the computer deviate from the fixed sequence of its program.

It soon became apparent that these programming techniques inhibited the speed and performance of the computer. To give the computer greater latitude in working problems without operator assistance, scientists proposed that the computer store its program in a high-speed internal memory or storage unit. Thus, it would have immediate access to instructions as it called for them. With an internal storage system, the computer could process a program in much the same way that it processed data. It could even be made to modify its own instructions as dictated by developing stages of work. To meet this requirement, high-speed storage devices were developed and the "stored program" computer was born.

All data processing involves at least three basic considerations: (1) the data or *input* to the system, (2) the orderly planned processing of the input within the system, and (3) the end result or *output* from the system.

The input may consist of any type of data: commercial, scientific, statistical, engineering, etc. Processing is carried out by a pre-established sequence of instructions that are followed automatically by a computer. These instructions are the result of an analysis of the desired output by a programmer. He then originates a series of instructions to the computer to produce the end result. The processing terminates with the end result, which is recorded for further processing or for reports or data files.

To meet these three basic considerations, data processing systems are composed of four types of functional units: input, output, storage, and processing devices. They are designed to process business and scientific data at electronic speeds. In addition automatic self-checking devices insure great accuracy. The key element of these systems is the processing unit, a high speed electronic computer.

INPUT AND OUTPUT DEVICES

The data processing system requires, as a necessary part of its information handling ability, devices that can enter data and instructions into the system and record data from the system. These functions are performed by input-output devices linked directly to the system.

Input devices read or sense the coded data or instructions that are recorded on a prescribed medium and make this information available to the computer. Output devices record or write information from the computer on an output medium. Specific input-output devices relating to the 1620 Data Processing System, will be discussed in Appendix V.

STORAGE (MEMORY)

Storage devices are capable of receiving information, retaining information, and making this information available. All data and instructions must be placed in storage before they can be processed by the computer. Each storage location holds a specific unit of data. Information is read into storage by an input device and is then available for processing. Each location, position, or section of storage is numbered so that the stored data or instructions can be readily located by the computer as needed.

When information enters a storage location, it replaces the previous contents of that location. However, when information is taken from a storage location, the contents remain unaltered. Thus, once located in storage, the same data may be used many times. The computer requires time to locate and transfer information to and from storage. This is called *access* time.

The size or capacity of storage determines the amount of information that can be held within the system at any one time.

CENTRAL PROCESSING UNIT

The central processing unit is the control center of the entire data processing system. It is divided into two parts: (1) the arithmetic-logical unit and (2) the control section.

The arithmetic-logical unit performs such operations as addition, subtraction, multiplication, division, comparing, transferring, and storing. It also has logical ability—the ability to test various conditions encountered during processing and to take one of two or more alternate paths, depending on the result of the test.

The control section directs and coordinates the entire computer system as a single multipurpose machine. These functions involve controlling the input-output units and the arithmetic-logical operation of the central processing unit. This section directs the system according to the procedure (stored program) developed by its human programmer.

STORED PROGRAMS

Each data processing system is designed to perform only a specific number and class of operations. It is directed to perform each operation by an instruction. The instruction defines a basic operation to be performed and identifies the data, device, or mechanism needed to carry out the operation. The entire series of instructions required to complete a given procedure is known as a *program*.

For example, the computer may have the operation of multiplication built into its circuits in much the same way that the ability to add is built into a simple desk calculator. There must be some means of directing the computer to perform multiplication just as the adding machine is directed by depressing keys. There must also be a way to instruct the computer where in storage it can find the factors which are to be multiplied.

Further, the comparatively simple operation of multiplication implies other activity that must precede and follow the calculation. The multiplicand and multiplier must be read into storage by an input device. Once the calculation is performed, the product may be recorded by an output device.

Any calculation, therefore, implies reading in data, locating factors in storage, perhaps adjusting the result, and perhaps writing out the completed result. Even the simplest portion of a procedure involves a number of planned steps that must be precisely specified to the computer if the procedure is to be accomplished.

An entire procedure is composed of these individual steps grouped in a sequence that directs the computer to produce a desired result. Thus, a complex problem must first be reduced to a series of basic machine operations before it can be solved. Each of these operations is coded as an instruction in a form that can be interpreted by the computer. An instruction in this form is called a "machine language instruction." The instructions are placed *in toto*, in the storage unit as a stored program.

The possible variations of a stored program provide the data processing system with almost unlimited flexibility. One computer can be applied to a great number of different procedures by simply reading in or loading the proper program into storage.

DATA REPRESENTATION

Communication with a computer system requires that data be reduced to a set of symbols that can be read and interpreted by data processing machines. The symbols differ from those easily recognizable by man, because the information to be represented must conform to the design and operation of the computer. The choice of these symbols and their meaning is a matter of convention on the part of the designers. The important fact is that information can be represented by symbols, which become the language for communication between people and machines.

Information to be used for computer systems can be recorded on various media. We shall discuss two of them, cards and paper tape. Data are represented on cards by the presence or absence of holes in specific locations of the card. In a similar manner, small holes along a paper tape represent data.

CARDS

The punched card is the most widely used media for communication with machines. Information is recorded as small holes punched in specific locations in a card of standard size.[1] Information represented (coded) by the presence or absence of holes in specific locations can be read or sensed as the card is moved through a card-reading device. Reading or sensing the card is basically a process of automatically converting data recorded as holes to an electronic language and entering the data into the computer.

The punched card provides 80 vertical columns with 12 punching positions in each column. The 12 punching positions form 12 horizontal rows across the card. One or more punches in a single column represent a character. The number of columns used depends on the amount of data to be represented. The standard card code uses one or more of the 12 possible punching positions of a vertical column to represent a numeric, alphabetic, or special character. The 12 punching positions are divided into two areas, numeric and zone. The first 9 punching positions from the bottom of the card are the numeric punching positions and have an assigned value of 9, 8, 7, 6, 5, 4, 3, 2, and 1, respectively. The remaining 3 positions, 0, 11 (synonymously termed X), and 12, are the zone positions. The 0 position is considered to be both a numeric and zone position.

The numeric characters 0 through 9 are represented by a single punch in a vertical column. For example, 0 is represented by a single punch in the 0 zone position of the column. A numeric 5 is represented by a single punch in the 5 position of the column.

The alphabetic characters are represented by two punches in a single

[1] The standard-size card is 7⅜ by 3¼in.

vertical column, one numeric punch and one zone punch. The alphabetic characters A through I use the 12 zone punch and a numeric punch 1 through 9. In this fashion the letter A is punched as 12-1, B as 12-2 . . . I as 12-9. The alphabetic characters J through R use the 11 zone punch and a numeric punch 1 through 9, respectively. The alphabetic characters S through Z use the 0 zone punch and the numeric characters 2 through 9, respectively (see Fig. 1.1).

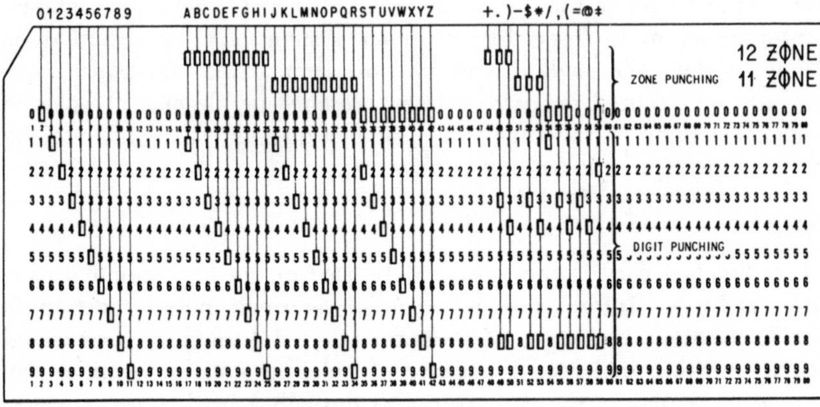

Fig. 1.1 Standard Punched Card Codes.

Special characters are represented by one, two, or three punches in a single column of the card and consist of punch configurations not used to represent numeric or alphabetic data.

PAPER TAPE

Punched paper tape serves much the same purpose as the punched cards. Data are recorded as a special arrangement of punched holes along the length of a paper tape. Paper tape is a continuous recording medium as compared to cards which are fixed in length.

Reading or sensing paper tape is basically a process of automatically converting data recorded as holes to an electronic language and entering the data into the computer.

Data are recorded (punched) and read as holes located in eight parallel channels along the length of the paper tape. One column of the eight possible punching positions (one for each channel) across the width of the tape is used to code numeric, alphabetic, special, and functional characters.

The lower four channels of the tape (excluding the feed holes) are labeled 1, 2, 4, and 8, and are used to record numeric characters. The numeric characters 1 through 9 are represented as a punch or punches in these four positions and the character "0" is represented as a punch in the zero position. The sum of the positional values indicates the numeric value of the character. For example, a hole in channel 1 is used to represent a numeric 1; a combination of a 1 and 2 punch represents a numeric 3. The X and 0 channels are similar to the zone punches in cards. These channels are used in combination with the numeric channels to record alphabetic and special characters (see Fig. 1.2).

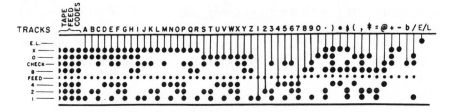

Fig. 1.2.   Character Coding for Eight-Channel Paper Tape.

To check that each character is recorded correctly, each column of the tape is punched with an odd number of holes. A check hole must be present in any column whose basic code (X, 0, 8, 4, 2, 1) consists of an even number of holes. Internal checking devices in the 1620 investigate each vertical array of punches to assure that this condition has been satisfied.

A punch in the E/L (end-of-line) channel is a specific function character used to mark the end of a record on the tape. The tape feed code consists of punches in the X, 0, C, 8, 4, 2, and 1 channels and is used to indicate blank character positions. A paper tape reader automatically skips over areas of tape punched with the tape feed code.

Figure 1.2 shows the 1620 coding for all characters on an 8-channel paper tape.

COMPUTER CHARACTERISTICS

MACHINE CYCLES

All computer operations take place in fixed time intervals called *machine cycles.* These time intervals are measured by pulses from an electronic clock in the system. Within a machine cycle, the computer can perform a specific machine operation. The number of machine cycles required to execute a single instruction depends on the nature and function of the instruction.

SERIAL AND PARALLEL OPERATION

Computers are classified as either serial or parallel depending on the method the computer uses to perform arithmetic. Essentially, all arithmetic is performed by addition.

In a serial computer, numbers to be added are considered one position at a time (the units position, tens position, hundreds, and so on) in the same way that addition is done with paper and pencil. Whenever a carry is developed, it is retained temporarily and then added to the sum of the next higher order position.

The time required for serial operation depends on the number of digits in the factors to be added. Serial addition is shown in Table 1.1.

Table 1.1

	1ST STEP	2ND STEP	3RD STEP	4TH STEP
Augend	1234	1234	1234	1234
Addend	2459	2459	2459	2459
Carry	1	1		
Sum	3	93	693	3693

In a parallel computer, addition is performed on complete data words (a "word" is made up of two or more storage positions). The words are combined in one operation, including carries. Any two data words, regardless of the magnitude of the numbers contained in the words, can be added in the same time. Table 1.2 shows parallel addition.

Table 1.2

Augend	00564213
Addend	00000824
Carry	1
Final Result	00565037

FIXED AND VARIABLE WORD LENGTH

"Fixed word length" and "variable word length" are terms used to describe the unit of data that can be addressed (referenced) and processed by a computer system.

In fixed word length operation, information is handled and addressed in units or words containing a predetermined number of positions. The size of a word is designed into the system and normally corresponds to the smallest unit of information that can be addressed for processing in the central processing unit. Records, fields, characters, or factors are all manipulated in parallel as words.

In variable word length operations, data-handling circuitry is designed to process information serially as single characters. Records, fields, or factors may be of any practical length within the capacity of the storage unit. Information is available by character instead of by word.

Operation within a given data processing system may be entirely of a fixed word nature, entirely variable, or a combination of both. In the 1620 Data Processing System, data are stored and processed as single characters. All arithmetic and data-handling operations are done serially, character by character.

Chapter 2

Introduction to the 1620 Data Processing System

The 1620 Data Processing System (Fig. 2.1) is an electronic digital computer designed for technological and commercial applications. The heart of the system is the 1620 Central Processing Unit (Fig. 2.2) which houses the arithmetic and logical units, the magnetic core storage (20,000 positions), and the console panel and typewriter. The central processing unit is augmented by the 1622 Card Read-Punch and/or the 1621 Paper Tape Reader and the 1624 Paper Tape Punch, depending on whether the system is to process punched cards, paper tape, or both.

Expansion of the basic system is possible by increasing the size of the magnetic core storage in increments of 20,000 positions until a maximum of 60,000 positions is reached (Fig. 2.3). A variety of special devices and additional instructions is available to increase the power and flexibility of the system.

Data and instructions entered into the system are placed in core storage as decimal digits. Each core storage position can be referred to individually and can store one digit of information. The addressing system provides for the selection of any digit or group of digits in storage. The 1620 can also process alphabetic characters and special characters such as $, *, −, +, etc.

The arithmetic and logical section of the computer is directed by the stored program. The 1620 has more than 30 different operations in its

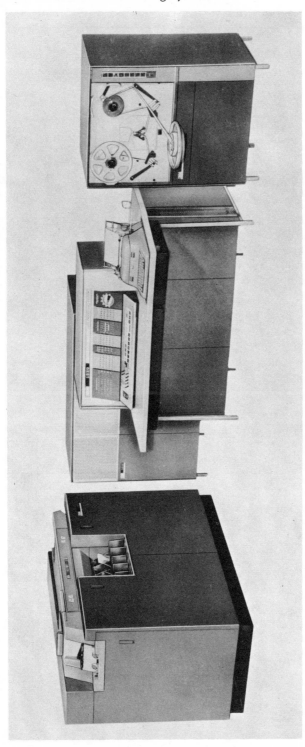

Fig. 2.1. The 1620 Data Processing System.

Fig. 2.2.   The 1620 Central Processing Unit.

Fig. 2.3.   Additional Core Module with Housing.

repertoire. Among these is a powerful set of branching instructions that make logical decisions based on the results of tests performed on a system of indicators and switches.

Addition, subtraction, and multiplication operations are performed by a table look-up method described in Chapter 4. Addition and multiplication tables are stored in specified areas of storage and are automatically referred to when one of the arithmetic operations is being performed. Division is accomplished by a division simulating program or by an *automatic division feature.*

The 1620 is a variable field computer in the complete sense of the term. Not only can data fields be of different lengths, but these same variable length fields can also be factors in all arithmetic operations without editing for size or position. Accuracy of results is insured by automatic internal checking that operates when data is being entered, read out, or processed by the system.

The console of the 1620 consists of control keys, switches, indicator panel, and typewriter. The control keys and switches are used for manual or automatic operation of the system. The console panel provides a visual indication of the status of various registers and control circuitry within the computer. The typewriter is used as an output device, for direct entry of data and instructions into core storage, and for permanent logging of the operator's intervention during the execution of a program.

Information is entered into the system by the input devices: the 1621 Paper Tape Reader, the 1622 Card Read-Punch, and the typewriter. Eighty-column cards are read at the rate of 250 cards per minute. The paper tape reader reads an 8-channel paper tape at the rate of 150 characters per second. Speed of typewriter information entry depends upon the operator's ability.

The recording of processed information is accomplished by the output devices; the 1622 Card Read-Punch, the 1624 Paper Tape Punch, and the typewriter. Cards are punched at the rate of 125 80-column cards per minute; the tape punch punches information in an 8-channel paper tape at the rate of 15 characters per second; and the typewriter types at the rate of 10 characters per second.

Program preparation is simplified by the use of two major programming systems. These are the Symbolic Programming System (SPS) and Fortran (from "formula translation"), both of which will be discussed in detail.

SPS, which simplifies program writing by reducing the clerical work involved, assembles a program written in mnemonic or symbolic notation by converting the symbols to machine language instructions and assigning locations in core storage for both data and instructions.

Fortran translates a problem expressed as a series of algebraic statements into a complete machine language program, generating the step-by-step instructions necessary to solve the problem. A program written in Fortran for the 1620, after minor modifications, can also be translated and executed on other computers such as the IBM 7090, 1401, and many others.

INTERNAL DATA REPRESENTATION

DIGITS

Each core storage position in the 1620 has a unique address and can store one digit of information. Each digit is in a binary coded decimal (BCD) form represented by a 6-bit numeric code. In this code, six positions of binary notation (0 or 1) are used and each of these positions is called a bit (binary digit). Each position has one of two conditions: either a bit is present represented by a "1" or it is not present represented by a "0." The six positions are divided into three groups: one check bit (C bit), one flag bit (F bit), and four numeric bits with the assigned values of 8, 4, 2, and 1 (table 2.1).

Table 2.1

CHECK BIT	FLAG BIT	NUMERICAL BITS			
C	F	8	4	2	1

The value of a decimal digit is the sum of the bits present in the numeric portion of the 6-bit code. Only bit combinations whose sum is 9 or less are used. Using the notation that a "1" indicates the presence of a bit and a "0" indicates the absence of a bit, we would represent the decimal digit 6 as 0110 considering only the numeric positions. The digit 8 is represented as 1000.

The check bit is used for parity checking purposes. A parity check is a built-in method of checking the validity of coded information. This code checking occurs automatically within the computer as the data processing operations are carried out. Each character in the computer represented in the 6-bit numeric code must consist of an odd number of bits. During processing, a character with an even number of bits causes the machine to signal a parity error. When a digit is read into the computer by an input device, it is automatically converted to the

6-bit numeric code and the check bit is automatically added if it is required. The flag bit, to be discussed shortly, is counted in parity checking. The check bit alone represents the digit 0.

Table 2.2 shows the 6-bit numeric coding of the decimal digits 0 through 9.

Table 2.2
CHARACTER CODING

	C	F	8	4	2	1
0	1	0	0	0	0	0
1	0	0	0	0	0	1
2	0	0	0	0	1	0
3	1	0	0	0	1	1
4	0	0	0	1	0	0
5	1	0	0	1	0	1
6	1	0	0	1	1	0
7	0	0	0	1	1	1
8	0	0	1	0	0	0
9	1	0	1	0	0	1

The flag bit is used in three ways:

1. Field Definition: The high-order position of a numeric field is defined by the presence of a flag (the terms "flag" and "flag bit" are used synonymously). Thus the number 537 would appear in storage with a flag bit in the core position containing the 5. A flag is denoted by a horizontal line above a digit, $\overline{5}37$.

2. Sign Control: The presence of a flag in the units position of a numeric field indicates that the field is negative. If no flag is present in the units position of a field, the field is taken to be positive. The number −537 would appear in storage as $\overline{5}3\overline{7}$.

3. Carries: Flags present in certain digits of the addition table (see Chapter 4) are interpreted as carries in arithmetic operations.

A record mark character (‡) is a nondecimal digit with C-8-2 or F-8-2 coding. It is primarily used in input and output operations and in record transmission within the computer. The novice programmer will find that a good portion of his errors occur in attempting to do arithmetic operations on record marks.

A numeric blank has C-8-4 coding. It is used for the control of blank columns when cards are being punched, and, like the record mark, cannot be used in arithmetic operations. Unlike the record mark, it may not even be present in an instruction.

Alphabetic information is represented in the computer in a double-digit form. Two core storage locations are required to represent one alphamerical character. The two digits are referred to as the zone digit and the numerical digit. The two digits representing one alphamerical character must be located in adjacent core positions, and the zone digit must always occupy an even-numbered core position.

Table 2.3 shows the double-digit representation of all the alphameric characters.

Table 2.3
ALPHAMERIC DATA REPRESENTATION

┌Zone Digit
│ ┌Numerical Digit
│ │ ┌Character

Zone+Numerical Digit	Character	Zone+Numerical Digit	Character
0‡	‡	53	L
00	b (blank)	54	M
03	.	55	N
04	)	56	O
10	+	57	P
13	$	58	Q
14	★	59	R
20	−	62	S
21	/	63	T
23	,	64	U
24	(	65	V
33	=	66	W
34	@	67	X
41	A	68	Y
42	B	69	Z
43	C	70	0
44	D	71	1
45	E	72	2
46	F	73	3
47	G	74	4
48	H	75	5
49	Ī	76	6
50	0̄	77	7
51	J	78	8
52	K	79	9

FIELDS

A field consists of a number of consecutive digits which are considered as a group in arithmetic and internal data transmission instructions. A field is always addressed (referenced) by its low-order digit, which occupies the highest numbered core storage position of the field. A field is processed serially from right to left into successively lower core storage positions until a digit with a flag is sensed. The digit with the flag is treated as part of the field, but no more digits are processed.

The absence of a flag in the low-order position of a field (the addressed digit) is unconditionally interpreted as a positive field of data.

One-digit fields of data are not allowed. The smallest allowable data field is two digits.

Figure 2.4 illustrates the processing of a field.

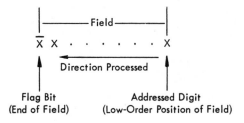

Fig. 2.4.   Field Processing.

RECORDS

A record consists of a field or fields of data related to input-output operations. A record is addressed at its high-order digit, which occupies the lowest core storage position of the record. Records are processed

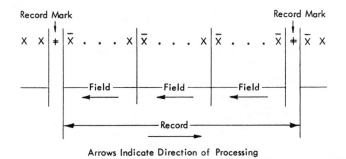

Arrows Indicate Direction of Processing

Fig. 2.5.   Record Processing.

serially from left to right (high-order to low-order digits). A record mark (‡) defines the end of a record and is located in the highest numbered core location.

Figure 2.5 illustrates the processing of a record as compared to the processing of a field.

NUMERICAL AND ALPHAMERICAL MODES

The input-output instructions of the 1620 cause data to be read or written in either a numerical or alphamerical mode. The 1620 has no way to determine if an element entering the system is being entered as numeric data or alphabetic data unless the appropriate mode is indicated in the input-output instruction.

In the numeric input mode each character read in is represented in storage by *one* decimal digit. Alphabetic and special characters will not enter storage correctly as they require a double-digit representation. Only the record mark (‡), numeric blank, and the digits 0 through 9 will be represented in storage correctly. In the numeric output mode each character in storage is represented as a single character on the output medium. Data in storage in the double-digit code will *not* be converted to its single character representation.

In the alphameric input mode each input character is automatically converted to its double-digit representation and is stored in memory as two decimal digits. In the alphameric output mode the double-digit representation of data is automatically converted to single characters which are then written on the output medium.

MAGNETIC CORE STORAGE

The storage medium utilized by the 1620 Data Processing System is magnetic core storage. A magnetic core is a tiny ring of ferromagnetic material a few hundredths of an inch in diameter. The outstanding characteristic of the core is that it can be easily magnetized, and, unless deliberately changed, it retains its magnetism indefinitely.

Many of these cores are strung on a screen of wires to form what is called a core plane (Fig. 2.6).

By sending *half* the amount of current necessary to magnetize a core through each of the two wires passing through the core in question we can magnetize it. Note that no other core in the plane becomes magnetized by the current flowing through the two wires. Furthermore, by reversing the flow of current through the wires, we can magnetize the core in the other direction. Thus, depending upon the direction of the current flow, a core can be either positively or negatively magnetized.

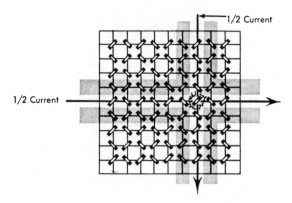

Fig. 2.6.   A Standard Core Plane.

Cores then can be controlled in two ways: by selecting a specific pair of wires, we can decide which core is to be affected; and by controlling the direction of current flow, we can determine whether it is to be positively or negatively magnetized. We can now adopt a convention and say that when a core is positively magnetized it is "on" or contains a bit. If a core is negatively magnetized it is "off" and does not contain a bit.

If we stacked six core planes vertically so that a vertical column contained six cores, we could represent the 6-bit numeric coding used by the 1620 for internal data representation. Each of the six core planes assumes a specific value—one plane would be the C-bit plane, another plane would be the F-bit plane, and another plane would be the 8-bit plane, etc. Thus six vertical cores form a core storage position and can represent any decimal digit through the 6-bit numeric code signified by the status of the cores (positive or negative).

In the 1620, core storage is made up of 12 core planes. Thus one vertical column contains two core storage positions. The top six core planes represent all the even-numbered addresses, and the bottom six core planes represent all the odd-numbered core addresses. Figure 2.7 shows the core array in the 1620.

Since all 12 core planes are read out simultaneously, any single core storage address affects two adjacent core storage positions, one with an even-numbered address and one with an odd-numbered address. Those cores with a positive charge are read into a Memory Buffer Register (MBR). The MBR is a two-position register into which both the odd and even addressed digits are read from core. If the digit in core position 00500 were addressed, the MBR would receive the digits from core positions 00500 and 00501. If the digit in core position 00501 were ad-

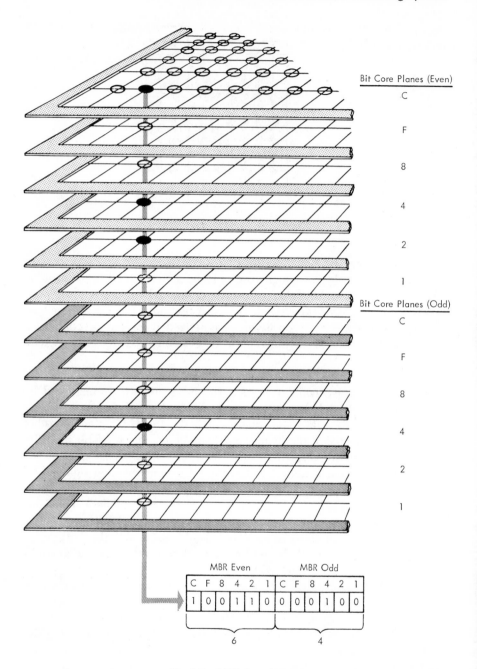

Fig. 2.7.   1620 Core Array.

dressed, the MBR would again receive the digits from core positions 00500 and 00501.

Core storage positions are addressed sequentially from 00000 to the highest numbered core storage address: 19999, 39999, or 59999. Addressing is cyclical in that position 00000 follows the highest allowable address when incrementing, and precedes the highest allowable address when decrementing.

Chapter *3*

Basic Programming Concepts

Contrary to some popular belief, the digital computer is not a "brain." It does not yet possess the intelligence to think. The computer can do nothing of its own volition, but must rely upon instructions supplied by humans to perform a given task. Thus a communication between man and computer is necessary. This communication takes the form of a set of formal instructions with which we command the computer and to which the computer responds. Once the computer has received its instructions, it can perform its task at speeds measured in microseconds. The combination of the human thought process and the fantastic speeds at which computers operate form a powerful tool for industry and research.

Chapters 5 through 9 are devoted to a complete detailed description of all basic 1620 instructions. These instructions fall into five general categories:

1. Arithmetic
2. Internal Data Transmission
3. Branch
4. Input-Output
5. Miscellaneous

The 1620 digital computer utilizes a 12-digit instruction which is divided into three parts: a 2-digit operation (OP) code, a 5-digit P address (P Operand), and a 5-digit Q address (Q Operand). Each of the 12 digits making up an instruction is assigned a unique notation so that easy reference may be made to any part of an instruction. The two digits forming the operation code will be referenced as O_0 and O_1. The five digits comprising the P address will be referenced as P_2, P_3, P_4, P_5, and P_6. Similarly, the five digits comprising the Q address will be referenced as Q_7, Q_8, Q_9, Q_{10}, and Q_{11}.

Fig. 3.1 illustrates the format of a 1620 instruction.

O_0	O_1	P_2	P_3	P_4	P_5	P_6	Q_7	Q_8	Q_9	Q_{10}	Q_{11}
OP Code		P Address					Q Address				

Fig. 3.1. Instruction Format.

The 2-digit operation code specifies which operation is to be executed. Table 3-1 is a chart of all *basic* 1620 operation codes and their associated mnemonics. Mnemonics refer to the alphabetic representation of operations codes used in the symbolic programming system (see Chapter 11).

The 5-digit P operand has many functions, depending on the instruction. It may represent the core location (1) that data is transmitted to, (2) that data is transmitted from, (3) that the program branches to, or (4) of data to be processed.

Likewise, the Q operand has many functions, depending on the instruction. It may represent (1) the address from which data is transmitted, (2) the input-output device that is employed, (3) the address of data to be processed, or (4) the indicator that is interrogated.

The 1620 has an extremely powerful and flexible instruction repertoire. Certain arithmetic and internal data transmission instructions are labeled *immediate*. These instructions use part of the instruction itself as a data field. The low-order position of the data field is the Q_{11} position of the instruction itself. The immediate instructions greatly facilitate programming and conserve storage locations by storing constants as part of instructions.

The instructions that direct the 1620 are stored in the magnetic core memory of the computer. The high-order digit (O_0) of an instruction must be located in an even-numbered core position. This restriction is imposed by the workings of the internal circuitry of the computer, with which we will not concern ourselves at this time. Suffice it to say that this restriction is easily complied with.

An instruction is referenced by the core location of its high-order digit (O_0). Thus if we refer to the instruction at core location 00012, the instruction we are referencing is made up of the digits in core locations 00012 to 00023, inclusive.

Table 3.1

	Mnemonic	Code
ARITHMETIC INSTRUCTIONS		
Add	A	21
Add Immediate	AM	11
Subtract	S	22
Subtract Immediate	SM	12
Multiply	M	23
Multiply Immediate	MM	13
Compare	C	24
Compare Immediate	CM	14
INTERNAL DATA TRANSMISSION INSTRUCTIONS		
Transmit Digit	TD	25
Transmit Digit Immediate	TDM	15
Transmit Field	TF	26
Transmit Field Immediate	TFM	16
Transmit Record	TR	31
BRANCH INSTRUCTIONS		
Branch	B	49
Branch No Flag	BNF	44
Branch No Record Mark	BNR	45
Branch on Digit	BD	43
Branch Indicator	BI	46
Branch No Indicator	BNI	47
Branch and Transmit	BT	27
Branch and Transmit Immediate	BTM	17
Branch Back	BB	42
INPUT-OUTPUT INSTRUCTIONS		
Read Numerically	RN	36
Write Numerically	WN	38
Dump Numerically	DN	35
Read Alphamerically	RA	37
Write Alphamerically	WA	39
MISCELLANEOUS INSTRUCTIONS		
Control	K	34
Set Flag	SF	32
Clear Flag	CF	33
Halt	H	48
No Operation	NOP	41

The 1620 uses a 2-address instruction system. During normal operation, program instructions are executed sequentially. For example, if we start at core location 00000, the instructions at 00000, 00012, 00024, 00036, and so forth, are executed in that order. This sequential execution of instructions can be altered by the use of the branch instructions discussed in Chapter 7.

In a 2-address system both addresses may reference data. The 2-address system is in contrast to a 1-over-1 addressing system, in which part of the instruction itself is used to indicate the location of the instruction to be executed next. The 2-address system is, in many ways, a much more powerful and flexible programming system.

In the discussion of the functions of the Q address, it was mentioned that indicators may be interrogated. The 1620 has internal machine indicators to facilitate the decision-making ability of the computer. The three indicators of greatest importance are the following:

1. *High Positive* (H/P). The High Positive indicator is turned on if the result of an arithmetic operation is positive and not zero.
2. *Equal/Zero* (E/Z). The Equal Zero indicator is turned on if the result of an arithmetic operation is zero.
3. *Overflow*. The Overflow indicator is turned on if certain overflow conditions exist.

A more detailed discussion of the on-off status of the indicators is made in the chapter on arithmetic instructions.

As each instruction is discussed, a formula for computing execution time will be given. The following abbreviations are used.

D_p = Number of digits, including high-order zeros, in the field at the P address.

D_q = Number of digits, including high-order zeros, in the field at the Q address.

D_z = Number of positions compared prior to detection of a digit other than zero.

R_q = Number of digits, including the record mark, in the record at the Q address.

Chapter 4

The Algorithms of Arithmetic

The heart of the hand calculator is the accumulator unit, which operates on the principle of the toothed gear. Addition is usually accomplished by rotating the gear in one direction. As the gear reaches a maximum position it flips an adjacent gear. In this way carries are propagated in the addition process. Subtraction is accomplished by rotating the gear in a direction opposite to that of addition. Multiplication can be considered as successive addition, and division as a process of iterative subtraction. The 1620 has no accumulator and does not operate on the principle of the toothed gear. Consequently, an alternate method of performing the basic functions of mathematics must be used. The basic operations of the 1620 are addition and multiplication, and certain areas of core storage are reserved for addition and multiplication tables. These operations are done serially, digit by digit, and the computer "looks up" the result of an operation in these tables. Subtraction utilizes the addition table but prepares the subtrahend digit before entry into the addition table. This preparation takes the form of tens or nines complementation. The process of division is discussed in a special chapter.

The addition table occupies core positions 00300–00399 (see Table 4.1). Looking at this table, the reader will notice that the number 7 appears at the following 8 locations: 00307, 00316, 00325, 000334, 00343, 00352, 00361, and 00370. The reader will also notice that a flagged 7 ($\overline{7}$) appears at core positions 00389 and 00398.

You have probably noticed that the sum of the digits in the units and tens positions of the address is the digit located in that core position.

Table 4.1

Add Table

High-Order Positions of Address	Units Position of Address									
	0	1	2	3	4	5	6	7	8	9
0030	0	1	2	3	4	5	6	7	8	9
0031	1	.2	3	4	5	6	7	8	9	$\bar{0}$
0032	2	3	4	5	6	7	8	9	$\bar{0}$	$\bar{1}$
0033	3	4	5	6	7	8	9	$\bar{0}$	$\bar{1}$	$\bar{2}$
0034	4	5	6	7	8	9	$\bar{0}$	$\bar{1}$	$\bar{2}$	$\bar{3}$
0035	5	6	7	8	9	$\bar{0}$	$\bar{1}$	$\bar{2}$	$\bar{3}$	$\bar{4}$
0036	6	7	8	9	$\bar{0}$	$\bar{1}$	$\bar{2}$	$\bar{3}$	$\bar{4}$	$\bar{5}$
0037	7	8	9	$\bar{0}$	$\bar{1}$	$\bar{2}$	$\bar{3}$	$\bar{4}$	$\bar{5}$	$\bar{6}$
0038	8	9	$\bar{0}$	$\bar{1}$	$\bar{2}$	$\bar{3}$	$\bar{4}$	$\bar{5}$	$\bar{6}$	$\bar{7}$
0039	9	$\bar{0}$	$\bar{1}$	$\bar{2}$	$\bar{3}$	$\bar{4}$	$\bar{5}$	$\bar{6}$	$\bar{7}$	$\bar{8}$

It is also obvious in the case of the two flagged 7's that the flag is present for the purpose of propagation of carries. Addition is accomplished in the 1620 by literally attaching data digits to a machine-generated address of 003XX to form a 5-digit add table address. The answer is then "looked up" in the add table.

As a further example note that the sum of the digits 4 and 2 is found at table address 00342 or 00324.

The addition of two numbers that generates a carry-over produces the following result: the addition table address generated by the adjacent digits will be increased by 1.

If a field containing n digits is added to a field containing $n + k$ digits ($k>0$), k zeros are inserted automatically to make the fields of equal length. These zeros are inserted one at a time by internal circuitry of the 1620. They do not alter the field permanently. (See Fig. 4.1.)

The process of subtraction is almost identical with that of addition. That is, an address of 003XX is generated with the data digits supplying the missing positions of the address. However, the subtrahend digit is inserted in the look-up address in its tens complement form on the first cycle and in its nines complement form thereafter. If the addition table yields a flagged digit, the address generated by the contiguous digits will be increased by 1 (see Fig. 4.2).

Multiplication in the 1620 is also accomplished by combining the digits

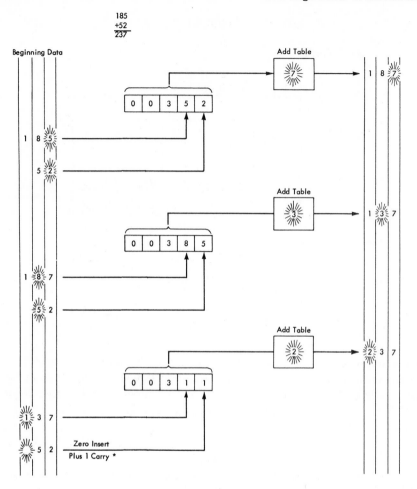

Fig. 4.1. Schematic Diagram of Add Operation.

to be multiplied into a table address. The multiplication table, which occupies core locations 00100–00299 (see Table 4.2), does not yield as obvious an algorithm as did the addition process.

The computer does not generate a base address of 001XX as might be expected. Instead, the base address is chosen to be 00XXX. The multiplicand digit is inserted into the tens position of the base address. The multiplier digit is routed through a special device called the *doubler*. The doubler is an internal device that doubles a digit. Although the multiplier digit enters the doubler as a single element, it leaves this unit as a 2-digit number (see Fig. 4.3). After exit from the doubler, the tens digit of the

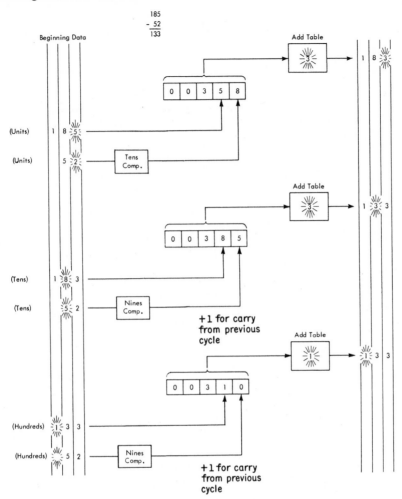

Fig. 4.2. Schematic Diagram of Subtract Operation.

number is incremented by 1 and is then routed to the hundreds digit
of the base address being formed. The units digit of the doubler's effort
is routed to the units digit of the base address, and this completes the
construction of the multiplication table look-up address.

Unlike the addition process, the multiplication table look-up process
yields not one but two digits as the product of any two elements. These
are found at the table look-up address and the adjacent odd address one
position higher in core. Internal machine operation causes these digits
to be reversed and routed out to a product generation area (see Fig. 4.3).

Table 4.2

Multiply Table

High-Order Positions of Address	Units Position of Address									
	0	1	2	3	4	5	6	7	8	9
0010	0	0	0	0	0	0	0	0	0	0
0011	0	0	1	0	2	0	3	0	4	0
0012	0	0	2	0	4	0	6	0	8	0
0013	0	0	3	0	6	0	9	0	2	1
0014	0	0	4	0	8	0	2	1	6	1
0015	0	0	5	0	0	1	5	1	0	2
0016	0	0	6	0	2	1	8	1	4	2
0017	0	0	7	0	4	1	1	2	8	2
0018	0	0	8	0	6	1	4	2	2	3
0019	0	0	9	0	8	1	7	2	6	3
0020	0	0	0	0	0	0	0	0	0	0
0021	5	0	6	0	7	0	8	0	9	0
0022	0	1	2	1	4	1	6	1	8	1
0023	5	1	8	1	1	2	4	2	7	2
0024	0	2	4	2	8	2	2	3	6	3
0025	5	2	0	3	5	3	0	4	5	4
0026	0	3	6	3	2	4	8	4	4	5
0027	5	3	2	4	9	4	6	5	3	6
0028	0	4	8	4	6	5	4	6	2	7
0029	5	4	4	5	3	6	2	7	1	8

To the novice, this may seem like a good deal of wind and very little storm. Popular belief may lead one to the idea that the computer is intelligent enough to add 2 and 3, or multiply 5 and 6, without extensive coaching. Unfortunately, in the present state of computer development, the thinking machine is semifantasy, semifiction.

Some computers have accumulating units, as do hand calculators. But the methods of arithmetic are generally performed by a cleverly arranged

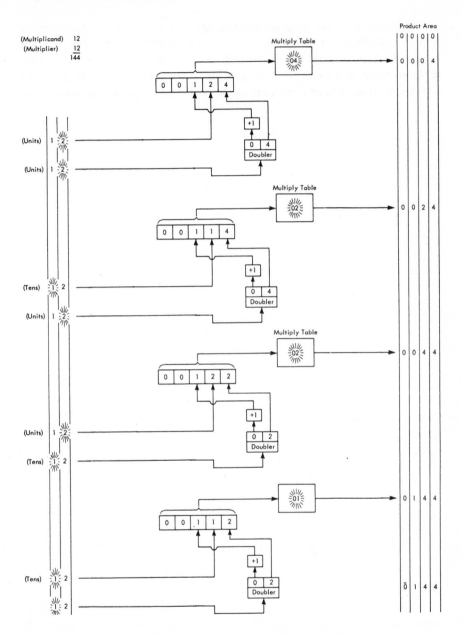

Fig. 4.3. Schematic Diagram of Multiply Operation.

sequence of electronic switching circuits rather than by the use of the toothed gear principle.

In general, it is not necessary for a programmer to know these arithmetic algorithms. In the 1620, however, care must be taken not to store information in the core area reserved for the addition and multiplication table sections of memory. **There is no internal circuitry to prevent entry into this area or destruction thereof during program operation.**

Chapter 5

The Arithmetic Instructions

Fundamentally, a computer is a calculator. Hence, the instructions that perform arithmetic are among the most important in the repertoire of commands. This chapter deals only with those arithmetic instructions that are common to all 1620's. Divide commands, which are not necessary for a machine installation, are discussed in a later chapter. Special division-simulating programs perform this operation in a variety of ways: successive subtraction; approximation of a reciprocal by series, followed by a multiplication; etc. The statement that "divide commands are not necessary" does not imply that one may not divide with the 1620. Circuitry, which performs division under command, may not be present in some machines, in which case one must resort to division simulators called *division subroutines*. The choice to have division command circuitry is made at each machine installation, and such a choice is generally made with consideration of two factors: necessity and funds. The difference between subroutine divide and command circuitry is only one of speed, *not* accuracy.

Although speed of calculation is not the only factor under consideration when one undertakes a computer survey, it is an extremely critical one. The reader will notice that all timings of operations are given in microseconds. It is this remarkable speed factor that makes a computer so valuable.

Instruction: Add
Operation Code: 21
Symbolic Name: A
Description:

The data[1] that is located at the Q address (Q field data) is added to the data that is located at the P address (P field data). The sum

---

[1] Unless otherwise specified, the term "data" refers to a single item.

replaces the P field data. The Q field data remains unchanged. A zero sum retains the sign of the P field data. A sum other than zero retains the sign of the larger valued field. If the number of digits in the Q field data is less than the number of digits in the P field data, high-order zeros are internally generated to make the fields of equal length. The generated zeros do not alter the Q field data.

The addition process is terminated by the sensing of the flag over the high-order digit of the P field data. The algebraic sign of the result is indicated by the presence or absence of a flag in the units position of the P field data after termination of the operation.

A correct answer may not be developed if the number of digits in the Q field data exceeds the number of digits in the P field data. Only the number of digits in the Q field data equal to the number of digits in the P field data is used in developing the result. An invalid addition is always obtained if the addition causes a carry beyond the high-order position of the initial P field data. The carry is lost and does not affect the field contiguous to the high-order digit of the P field data.

If either of the preceding two conditions is obtained, the Overflow indicator will be turned on. Processing does not necessarily terminate.

On the console of the 1620 there are many switches that have two settings: "on" and "off". One of these, the Overflow switch, causes the 1620 to halt if the Overflow indicator is on *and* the switch is in the "on" position. If the Overflow indicator is on and the switch is in the "off" position, processing continues. If the Overflow indicator is off, the switch setting has no effect upon machine operations.

If the result of the addition is positive, and not zero, the High/Positive (H/P) indicator will be turned on. The H/P indicator is turned off if the result of an addition is negative or zero. The Equal/Zero (E/Z) indicator is turned on if the result is zero and off if the result is not zero, regardless of sign.

Execution time of addition varies according to the number of digits in the P field data and also according to whether recomplementation is necessary. Recomplementation is necessary if *both* the following conditions exist:

1. The Q and P fields of data are of opposite sign.
2. The absolute value of the Q field data is greater than the absolute value of the P field data.

Basic Execution Time in Microseconds: $160 + 80D_p$

Recomplementation Time in Microseconds: $80 (D_p + 1)$

The following examples demonstrate (1) the proper form of the Add command, (2) the action as a result of the command, (3) which indicators are in the on status at the conclusion of the command, (4) the time of execution including, where applicable, recomplementation time, and (5) the validity of the algebraic result.

Example: 21 15002 10003

$\overline{1}2962$ ⟵————————⌐
Core location 15002
before addition

$\overline{4}007$ ⟵————————⌐
Core location 10003 before
and after addition

$\overline{1}6969$ ⟵————————⌐
Core location 15002
after addition

Indicator Condition: H/P on
Time of Execution: 560 microseconds
Arithmetic Result: Valid

Example: 21 00932 17962

$\overline{0}000010$ ⟵————————⌐
Core location 00932
before addition

$\overline{0}1526$ ⟵————————⌐
Core location 17962 before
and after addition

$\overline{0}001516$ ⟵————————⌐
Core location 00932
after addition

Indicator Condition: H/P on
Time of Execution: 1360 microseconds
Arithmetic Result: Valid

Example: 21 00917 01232

$\overline{0}1$ ⟵————————⌐
Core location 00917
before addition

$\overline{0}102$ ⟵————————⌐
Core location 01232 before
and after addition

$\overline{0}3$ ⟵————————⌐
Core location 00917
after addition

Indicator Condition: Overflow and H/P on
Time of Execution: 320 microseconds
Arithmetic Result: Invalid

Example: 21 10000 15000

0̄521 ◄────────────┐   52̄1 ◄────────────┐

Core location 10000   Core location 15000 before
before addition   and after addition

0̄000 ◄────────────┐

Core location 10000
after addition

Indicator Condition: E/Z on

Time of Execution: 480 microseconds

Arithmetic Result: Valid

Example: 21 18053 19999

9̄9999991 ◄────────────┐   0̄9 ◄────────────┐

Core location 18053   Core location 19999 before
before addition   and after addition

0̄0000000 ◄────────────┐

Core location 18053
after addition

Indicator Condition: Overflow and E/Z on

Time of Execution: 800 microseconds

Arithmetic Result: Invalid

Example: 21 15721 18982

0̄12 ◄────────────┐   0̄0003 ◄────────────┐

Core location 15721   Core location 18982 before
before addition   and after addition

0̄15 ◄────────────┐

Core location 15721
after addition

Indicator Condition: Overflow and H/P on

Time of Execution: 400 microseconds

Arithmetic Result: Valid

Example: 21 18999 17999

$\overline{0}0012$ ◄─────────┐
Core location 18999
before addition

$\overline{0}0010$ ◄─────────┐
Core location 18999
after addition

$\overline{0}000000002\overline{2}$ ◄─────┐
Core location 17999 before
and after addition

Indicator Condition: Overflow on

Time of Execution: 1040 microseconds

Arithmetic Result: Valid

Example: 21 00895 01026

$\overline{0}015$ ◄─────────┐
Core location 00895
before addition

$\overline{0}030$ ◄─────────┐
Core location 00895
after addition

$\overline{1}\overline{5}$ ◄─────────┐
Core location 01026 before
and after addition

Indicator Condition: All off

Time of Execution: 480 microseconds

Arithmetic Result: Valid

Instruction: Subtract
Operation Code: 22
Symbolic Name: S
Description:

The data that is located at the Q address (Q field data) is subtracted from the data that is located at the P address (P field data). The difference replaces the P field data. The Q field data remains unchanged. A zero result retains the sign of the P field data. The sign of a result, other than zero, is determined by algebraic analysis of the P and Q fields of data.

The rules concerning validity of result in the subtract operation are identical with those of addition. Execution time is also identical with that of addition. Recomplementation is necessary if *both* of the following conditions exist:

1. The Q and P fields of data are of like sign.
2. The absolute value of the Q field data is greater than that of the P field data.

Example: 22 00932 17932

$\overline{0}00001\overline{0}$ ◄───────┐

Core location 00932
before subtraction

$\overline{0}00153\overline{6}$ ◄───────┐

Core location 00932
after subtraction

$\overline{0}1526$ ◄───────┐

Core location 17932 before
and after subtraction

Indicator Condition: All off

Time of Execution: 720 microseconds

Arithmetic Result: Valid

Example: 22 15002 10003

$\overline{1}2962$ ◄───────┐

Core location 15002
before subtraction

$\overline{0}8955$ ◄───────┐

Core location 15002
after subtraction

$\overline{4}007$ ◄───────┐

Core location 10003 before
and after subtraction

Indicator Condition: H/P on

Time of Execution: 560 microseconds

Arithmetic Result: Valid

Example: 22 00917 01232

$\overline{0}1$ ◄───────┐

Core location 00917
before subtraction

$\overline{0}\overline{1}$ ◄───────┐

Core location 00917
after subtraction

$\overline{0}102$ ◄───────┐

Core location 01232 before
and after subtraction

Indicator Condition: Overflow on

Time of Execution: 560 microseconds

Arithmetic Result: Invalid

Example: 22 10000 15000

$\bar{0}521$ ←⎤

Core location 10000
before subtraction

$\bar{1}042$ ←⎤

Core location 10000
after subtraction

$\bar{0}52\bar{1}$ ←⎤

Core location 15000 before
and after subtraction

Indicator Condition: H/P on

Time of Execution: 480 microseconds

Arithmetic Result: Valid

Example: 22 18053 19999

$\bar{0}00000$ ←⎤

Core location 18053
before subtraction

$\bar{0}0000\bar{1}$ ←⎤

Core location 18053
after subtraction

$\bar{0}1$ ←⎤

Core location 19999 before
and after subtraction

Indicator Condition: All off

Time of Execution: 1200 microseconds

Arithmetic Result: Valid

Example: 22 17895 01888

$\bar{1}00\bar{0}$ ←⎤

Core location 17895
before subtraction

$\bar{0}00\bar{0}$ ←⎤

Core location 17895
after subtraction

$\bar{1}00\bar{0}$ ←⎤

Core location 01888 before
and after subtraction

Indicator Condition: E/Z on

Time of Execution: 480 microseconds

Arithmetic Result: Valid

Instruction: Multiplication
Operation Code: 23
Symbolic Name: M
Description:

The data that is located at the P address (P field data) is multiplied by the data that is located at the Q address (Q field data). The resultant product is placed in core storage beginning at position 00099 and extending through successively lower numbered core positions.

There are 20 locations in storage (positions 00080–00099) which, *in toto*, are referred to as the fixed product area. These positions are automatically cleared to zeros before formation of the product begins. The multiplication operation is terminated by the flag in the high-order position of the Q field data. A flag is placed over the high-order position of the product and the sign of the product is indicated by the presence or absence of a flag in position 00099.

A zero product may be either positive or negative depending upon the signs of the Q and P fields of data. The algebraic rules of sign manipulation are obeyed.

Since the fixed product area is cleared before multiplication begins, chain multiplications, without intermediate saving of results, are not possible.

The length of the product is the sum of the number of digits (high-order zeros included) in the Q and P fields of data. Although only 20 core positions are cleared to zero prior to the multiplication, a product may be formed whose length is limited only by the number of available core storage positions. Thus, the product of two 100-digit numbers (or greater) is quite possible in a 20,000-core-position 1620.

If the product to be developed exceeds 100 digits, the highest numbered core position below 00000 will contain the digit immediately following that contained in 00000. This feature is sometimes termed "wrap-around memory." Thus, a product of two 52-digit numbers will have its high-order digit at 19996 and its low-order digit at 00099 in a 20,000-core-position machine or 39996–00099 in a 40,000-core-position machine, and so forth.

It is the programmer's responsibility to clear any core locations below core position 00080 if he intends to use them in development of a product. Failure to do this may result in an invalid product.

The H/P and E/Z indicators are affected by multiplication in the same fashion as by addition and subtraction. However, it is not possible to obtain an overflow condition through multiplication.

Execution time varies according to the number of digits in the fields of data at the Q and P addresses.

Execution Time in Microseconds: $560 + 40D_q + 168D_qD_p$

Example: 23 15000 16000

$\overline{0}03$ ◄─────────────┐
Core location 15000 before
and after multiplication

$\overline{0}0002$ ◄─────────────┐
Core location 16000 before
and after multiplication

$\overline{0}0000006$ ◄───────┐
Core location 00099
after multiplication

Indicator Condition: H/P on

Execution Time: 3280 microseconds

Example: 23 19765 00897

$\overline{0}1\overline{2}$ ◄─────────────┐
Core location 19765 before
and after multiplication

$\overline{1}1$ ◄─────────────┐
Core location 00897 before
and after multiplication

$\overline{0}013\overline{2}$ ◄───────────┐
Core location 00099
after multiplication

Indicator Condition: All off

Execution Time: 1648 microseconds

Example: 23 15000 16000

$\overline{0}\overline{1}$ ◄─────────────┐
Core location 15000 before
and after multiplication

$\overline{0}\overline{1}$ ◄─────────────┐
Core location 16000 before
and after multiplication

$\overline{0}001$ ◄───────────┐
Core location 00099
after multiplication

Indicator Condition: H/P on

Execution Time: 1312 microseconds

Instruction: Compare
Operation Code: 24
Symbolic Name: C
Description:

The data that is located at the Q address (Q field data) is compared with the data that is located at the P address (P field data). This comparison is accomplished by subtracting the Q field data from the P field data and discarding the digits of the difference. However, this subtraction is performed by internal machine circuitry and does not affect the Q and P fields of data. If the number of digits in the Q field data is less than the number of digits in the P field data, high-order zeros are internally generated to make the fields of equal length. The generated zeros do not alter the Q field data.

The result of the comparison triggers indicators (H/P, E/Z, and Overflow) which may be interrogated at a later stage of the program. In no way is the sequence of the program altered by the act of comparison.

If the P field data is algebraically greater than the Q field data, the H/P indicator is turned on and the E/Z indicator is turned off. If the P field data is equal to the Q field data, the E/Z indicator is turned on and the H/P indicator is turned off. If the P field data is less than the Q field data, both the H/P and E/Z indicators are turned off. It is *a priori* obvious that both the H/P and E/Z indicators cannot be on simultaneously.

Comparison proceeds serially from low- to high-order positions of data (high- to low-core addresses) until terminated by the flag in the high-order digit of the P field data. If the number of digits (high-order zeros included) in the P field data is less than the number of digits (high-order zeros included) in the Q field data, the Overflow indicator is turned on and the comparison terminates with the high-order (flagged) digit of the P field data. The comparison up to that point will have been correct and the H/P and/or E/Z indicators affected accordingly.

If the signs of the two fields differ initially, comparison terminates when a digit other than zero is detected in either the P or Q fields of data. When two fields contain all zeros, the comparison disregards the sign and the E/Z indicator is turned on. In the comparison of two fields of unlike sign, the positive field is, of course, the greater.

The numerical sequence of comparison is, as would be expected, ascending from 0 through 9. In alphameric representation, the following is the sequential order from lowest to highest:

b [blank character with representation of 00] .) + $ ⋆ − / , (
= @ A B C D E F G H I 0̄ J K L M N O P Q R S T U V W
X Y Z 0 1 2 3 4 5 6 7 8 9

The record mark and numerical blank (see Chapter 2) are not usable in the compare instructions as they were also not usable as data in arithmetic instructions. Attempts to use them in such commands will result in memory address register check stop conditions (see Appendix VI). The computer halts with a MAR check indication at the console.

Execution time varies according to the number of digits (high-order zeros included) in the P field data if and only if the data fields are of like sign. The execution time for fields of unlike sign depends upon the number of digits compared before a nonzero digit is detected in either data field.

Basic Execution Time in Microseconds: $160 + 80D_p$

Execution Time in Microseconds for Fields of Unlike Sign: $200 + 80D_z$

Example: 24 10000 15000

$\overline{857}$ ◄────────────┐

Core location 10000 before
and after comparison

$\overline{4}9$ ◄────────────┐

Core location 15000 before
and after comparison

Indicator Condition: H/P on

Time of Execution: 400 microseconds

Example: 24 17862 00953

$\overline{9}9$ ◄────────────┐

Core location 17862 before
and after comparison

$\overline{0}0001$ ◄────────────┐

Core location 00953 before
and after comparison

Indicator Condition: Overflow and H/P on

Time of Execution: 320 microseconds

Example: 24 19823 19999

$\overline{1}52$ ◄────────────┐

Core location 19823 before
and after comparison

$\overline{1}009$ ◄────────────┐

Core location 19999 before
and after comparison

Indicator Condition: Overflow and H/P on

Time of Execution: 400 microseconds

Example: 24 12345 01976

$\overline{0}1000$ ◄────────────┐

Core location 12345 before
and after comparison

$\overline{1}000$ ◄────────────┐

Core location 01976 before
and after comparison

Indicator Condition: E/Z on

Time of Execution: 560 microseconds

Example: 24 18999 18001

$\overline{1}9\overline{2}$ ◄――――――――┐ $\overline{9}8765$ ◄――――――――┐

Core location 18999 before   Core location 18001 before
and after comparison   and after comparison

Indicator Condition: All off

Time of Execution: 280 microseconds

Example: 24 15000 16000

$\overline{1}\overline{5}\overline{0}$ ◄――――――――┐ $\overline{1}3\overline{8}$ ◄――――――――┐

Core location 15000 before   Core location 16000 before
and after comparison   and after comparison

Indicator Condition: All off

Time of Execution: 400 microseconds

――――――――――――――――――――

Instruction: Add Immediate

Operation Code: 11

Symbolic Name: AM

Description:

In the Add instruction, both the P and Q portions of the instruction reference core locations where the two data fields are to be found. In the Add Immediate instruction, only the P portion of the instruction references a data field. The instruction itself, beginning with the digit in position Q_{11}, is chosen as the field of data. Addition then proceeds in a fashion identical with that of the standard Add command: digit by digit serial addition extending through lower and lower core positions.

As will be remembered in the case of the Add command, both fields require flags to designate their high-order positions, and the high-order P field data digit terminates the operation. The rule is identical here, but since the Q_{11} digit defines the low-order position of the second data field, a flag should be present somewhere within the Add Immediate instruction to indicate the high-order position of the field. Without this flag, addition may proceed through the Q, P, and Operation portions of the instruction and into the contiguous instruction, not necessarily halting even there.

All other information pertaining to the Add Immediate command, including execution time, is identical with that of Add.

Example: 11 12345 000$\overline{1}$0

$\overline{3}$50 ←————————┐

Core location 12345 before
Add Immediate

$\overline{3}$60 ←————————┐

Core location 12345 after
Add Immediate

Indicator Condition: H/P on

Time of Execution: 400 microseconds

Arithmetic Result: Valid

Example: 11 19854 $\overline{0}$8000

$\overline{1}$78569 ←————————┐

Core location 19854 before
Add Immediate

$\overline{1}$86569 ←————————┐

Core location 19854 after
Add Immediate

Indicator Condition: H/P on

Time of Execution: 640 microseconds

Arithmetic Result: Valid

Example: 11 $\overline{0}$0500 00000

$\overline{5}$000000000 ←————————┐

Core location 00500 before
Add Immediate

$\overline{5}$050000000 ←————————┐

Core location 00500 after
Add Immediate

Indicator Condition: H/P on

Time of Execution: 960 microseconds

Arithmetic Result: Valid

Example: 11 18888 000$\overline{0}\overline{1}$

$\overline{0}500$ ⟵————————⌐

Core location 18888 before
Add Immediate

$\overline{0}499$ ⟵————————⌐

Core location 18888 after
Add Immediate

Indicator Condition: H/P on

Time of Execution: 480 microseconds

Arithmetic Result: Valid

Example: 11 14567 $\overline{0}1500\overline{0}$...

Example: 11 14567 $\overline{0}1500$

$\overline{0}1326$ ⟵————————⌐

Core location 14567 before
Add Immediate

$\overline{0}017\overline{4}$ ⟵————————⌐

Core location 14567 after
Add Immediate

Indicator Condition: All off

Time of Execution: 1040 microseconds

Arithmetic Result: Valid

Example: 11 15000 00100

$\overline{0}00100$ ⟵————————⌐

Core location 15000 before
Add Immediate

$\overline{0}00200$ ⟵————————⌐

Core location 15000 after
Add Immediate

Indicator Condition: Overflow and H/P on

Time of Execution: 640 microseconds

Arithmetic Result: Valid

———————————

Instruction: Subtract Immediate
Operation Code: 12
Symbolic Name: SM
Description:

The field beginning with the Q_{11} digit of the Subtract Immediate instruction is subtracted from the field referenced by the P address. The requirements pertaining to the use of the flag in Add Immediate are identical here. All other information, including execution time, is identical with that of Subtract.

Example: 12 12345 000$\overline{1}$0

$\overline{6}$10 ⟵——————————┐

Core location 12345 before
Subtract Immediate

$\overline{6}$00 ⟵——————————┐

Core location 12345 after
Subtract Immediate

Indicator Condition: H/P on

Time of Execution: 400 microseconds

Arithmetic Result: Valid

Example: 12 16543 0$\overline{0}$10$\overline{1}$

$\overline{1}$001 ⟵——————————┐

Core location 16543 before
Subtract Immediate

$\overline{1}$102 ⟵——————————┐

Core location 16543 after
Subtract Immediate

Indicator Condition: H/P on

Time of Execution: 480 microseconds

Arithmetic Result: Valid

Example: 12 09527 $\overline{0}$1000

$\overline{0}$0572 ⟵——————————┐

Core location 09527 before
Subtract Immediate

$\overline{0}$042$\overline{8}$ ⟵——————————┐

Core location 09527 after
Subtract Immediate

Indicator Condition: All off

Time of Execution: 1040 microseconds

Arithmetic Result: Valid

Example: 12 152̄2̄ 12345

Ī25 ←————————————┐
Core location 15222 before
Subtract Immediate

2̄2̄0̄ ←————————————┐
Core location 15222 after
Subtract Immediate

Indicator Condition: Overflow on

Time of Execution: 720 microseconds

Arithmetic Result: Invalid

Example: Ī2 10000 00000

0̄00000000000 ←————┐
Core Location 10000 before
Subtract Immediate

Ī2100000000̄0̄ ←————┐
Core location 10000 after
Subtract Immediate

Indicator Condition: All off

Time of Execution: 2160 microseconds

Arithmetic Result: Valid

Instruction: Multiply Immediate

Operation Code: 13

Symbolic Name: MM

Description:

The P field data is multiplied by the field beginning with the Q_{11} digit of the Multiply Immediate instruction. Multiplication is terminated by a flag in the high-order position of the multiplier. Since the low-order multiplier digit is Q_{11} of the Multiply Immediate instruction, the requirements concerning the use of the flag in previous Immediate-type instructions are also applicable here. All other information, including execution time, is identical with that of Multiply.

Example: 13 13243 0̄0100

$\overline{2}$5 ⟵⎯⎯⎯⎯⎯⎯⎯⎤

Core location 13243 before and
after Multiply Immediate

$\overline{0}$02500 ⟵⎯⎯⎯⎯⎯⎤

Core location 00099 after
Multiply Immediate

Indicator Condition: H/P on

Time of Execution: 2064 microseconds

Example: 13 00800 0̄00̄0$\overline{2}$

$\overline{0}$2 ⟵⎯⎯⎯⎯⎯⎯⎤

Core location 00800 before and
after Multiply Immediate

$\overline{0}$000$\overline{4}$ ⟵⎯⎯⎯⎯⎯⎤

Core location 00099 after
Multiply Immediate

Indicator Condition: All off

Time of Execution: 1688 microseconds

Example: 13 10000 0̄0̄0$\overline{1}$

$\overline{0}\overline{1}$ ⟵⎯⎯⎯⎯⎯⎯⎤

Core location 10000 before and
after Multiply Immediate

$\overline{0}$0001 ⟵⎯⎯⎯⎯⎯⎤

Core location 00099 after
Multiply Immediate

Indicator Condition: H/P on

Time of Execution: 1688 microseconds

Instruction: Compare Immediate

Operation Code: 14

Symbolic Name: CM

Description:

The P field data is compared with the field whose units position is at
the Q_{11} digit of the Compare Immediate instruction. The requirements

concerning the use of a flag in the previous Immediate instructions are also applicable here. All other information, including execution time, is identical with that of Compare.

Example: 14 15000 001̄23

     1̄35 ◄────────┐

Core location 15000 before and after Compare Immediate

Indicator Condition: H/P on

Time of Execution: 400 microseconds

Example: 14 17869 0̄0011̄

     0̄0000011̄ ◄────────┐

Core location 17869 before and after Compare Immediate

Indicator Condition: E/Z on

Time of Execution: 800 microseconds

Example: 14 15̄003 12354

     0̄0021789 ◄────────┐

Core location 15003 before and after Compare Immediate

Indicator Condition: All off

Time of Execution: 800 microseconds

Example: 14 12345 1̄0000

     0̄500 ◄────────┐

Core location 12345 before and after Compare Immediate

Indicator Condition: Overflow and H/P on

Time of Execution: 480 microseconds

Example: 14 13000 00000

     1̄41300000000 ◄────┐

Core location 13000 before and after Compare Immediate

Indicator Condition: Overflow and E/Z on

Time of Execution: 1120 microseconds

Problems

For all Problems, the following core content is assumed:

CORE LOCATION (LOW-ORDER DIGIT)	CONTENTS
00857	$3\bar{2}\bar{0}$
10000	$\bar{9}5$
12027	$\bar{1}562\bar{1}$
13056	$\bar{0}09102$
15007	$0\bar{1}$
16029	$\bar{0}0\bar{1}$
17926	$\bar{1}0$
18522	$\bar{9}87651$
19027	$\bar{9}812971$
19558	$\bar{2}87028$

State the following for all problems:
1. Result (Value and location).
2. Indicator conditions (In the case of multistep programs, state final indicator conditions).
3. Timings in microseconds.
4. Validity (In the case of multistep programs, state validity of final result).

The core content listed above is to be assumed for every problem and the results of any one problem are independent of all others.

1. 21 18522 15007	16. 21 12027 17926	
2. 21 10000 12027	22 12027 10000	
3. 21 12027 10000	17. 21 13056 12027	
4. 21 16029 16029	22 13056 19027	
5. 21 19027 19558	18. 21 19027 19558	
6. 21 17926 16029	21 16029 10000	
7. 21 13056 15007	22 19027 16029	
8. 22 18522 15007	19. 23 10000 15007	
9. 22 10000 12027	20. 23 17926 18522	
10. 22 12027 10000	21. 23 18522 17926	
11. 22 16029 16029	22. 23 13056 16029	
12. 22 19027 19558	23. 23 16029 13056	
13. 22 17926 16029	24. 22 10000 15007	
14. 22 13056 15007	21 16029 10000	
15. 21 12027 10000	23 16029 17926	
22 12027 17926	25. 22 19027 19558	

22 19027 15007

23 16029 19027

26. 21 16029 15007

21 10000 17926

23 16029 10000

27. 24 16029 17926

28. 24 18522 19558

29. 24 15007 16029

30. 24 00857 17926

31. 21 10000 15007

22 10000 17926

23 17926 17926

24 00099 10000

32. 23 00857 17926

24 12027 00099

33. 11 15007 $000\overline{0}1$

34. 11 17926 $000\overline{0}3$

35. 11 12027 $\overline{1}0000$

36. 11 $1305\overline{6}$ 10000

37. 22 00857 10000

11 10000 $000\overline{1}0$

22 00857 10000

38. 12 10000 $000\overline{1}0$

11 10000 $000\overline{0}1$

13 10000 $00\overline{1}00$

14 00099 $\overline{8}6000$

39. 21 13056 12027

22 13056 10000

13 13056 $\overline{0}1000$

24 00099 19027

40. 23 16029 16029

24 00099 15007

Chapter 6

Internal Data Transmission

The ability to move data from one internal location to another is fundamental to computer operations. For instance, it may be necessary to obtain the sum of two fields and retain both fields unaltered. Thus, one field must be moved to an alternate location and the addition process then accomplished.

The variety of ways that data may be internally transmitted distinguishes today's computers from those of five years ago. Computers of the future will undoubtedly have an even greater repertoire of data transmission instructions. The 1620 has five such commands in its basic repertoire.

Instruction: Transmit Digit

Operation Code: 25

Symbolic Name: TD

Description:

The content of the single core position referenced by Q_7 through Q_{11} is transmitted to the single core position referenced by P_2 through P_6. The digit at the Q address is not altered. If it contains a flag, the flag is transmitted also.

Execution Time in Microseconds: 200 (constant)

Example: 25 15000 10000

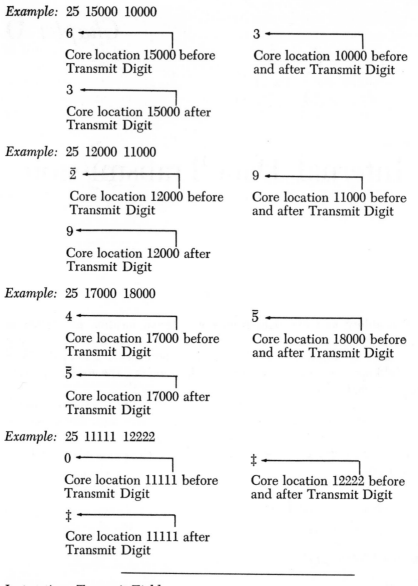

6 ←——————————┐
Core location 15000 before
Transmit Digit

3 ←——————————┐
Core location 15000 after
Transmit Digit

3 ←——————————┐
Core location 10000 before
and after Transmit Digit

Example: 25 12000 11000

$\bar{2}$ ←——————————┐
Core location 12000 before
Transmit Digit

9 ←——————————┐
Core location 12000 after
Transmit Digit

9 ←——————————┐
Core location 11000 before
and after Transmit Digit

Example: 25 17000 18000

4 ←——————————┐
Core location 17000 before
Transmit Digit

$\bar{5}$ ←——————————┐
Core location 17000 after
Transmit Digit

$\bar{5}$ ←——————————┐
Core location 18000 before
and after Transmit Digit

Example: 25 11111 12222

0 ←——————————┐
Core location 11111 before
Transmit Digit

‡ ←——————————┐
Core location 11111 after
Transmit Digit

‡ ←——————————┐
Core location 12222 before
and after Transmit Digit

Instruction: Transmit Field

Operation Code: 26

Symbolic Name: TF

Description:

The Q field data is transmitted serially to contiguous core locations beginning at the core position referenced by the P address of the Transmit Field instruction. Transmission proceeds from low- to high-order digits of the Q field data (high- to low-core addresses) and is terminated by the sensing of the flag in the high-order position of the Q field data.

The transmission of data is destructive in nature. That is, the data in locations P through $P - D_q + 1$ is destroyed by the transmission of the Q field data digits. The Q field data remains unchanged.

Execution Time in Microseconds: $160 + 40D_q$

Example: 26 15000 16000

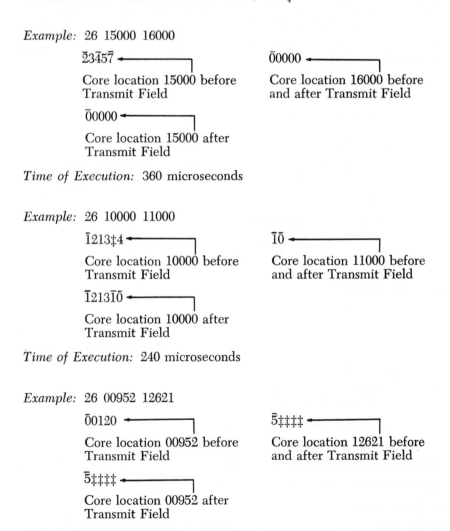

$\overline{2}3\overline{4}5\overline{7}$ ◄────────────┐

Core location 15000 before
Transmit Field

$\overline{0}0000$ ◄────────────┐

Core location 15000 after
Transmit Field

$\overline{0}0000$ ◄────────────┐

Core location 16000 before
and after Transmit Field

Time of Execution: 360 microseconds

Example: 26 10000 11000

$\overline{1}213\ddagger4$ ◄────────────┐

Core location 10000 before
Transmit Field

$\overline{1}213\overline{1}\overline{0}$ ◄────────────┐

Core location 10000 after
Transmit Field

$\overline{1}\overline{0}$ ◄────────────┐

Core location 11000 before
and after Transmit Field

Time of Execution: 240 microseconds

Example: 26 00952 12621

$\overline{0}0120$ ◄────────────┐

Core location 00952 before
Transmit Field

$\overline{5}\ddagger\ddagger\ddagger\ddagger$ ◄────────────┐

Core location 00952 after
Transmit Field

$\overline{5}\ddagger\ddagger\ddagger\ddagger$ ◄────────────┐

Core location 12621 before
and after Transmit Field

Time of Execution: 360 microseconds

Instruction: Transmit Record

Operation Code: 31

Symbolic Name: TR

Description:

The Q record data is transmitted serially to contiguous core locations beginning at the core position specified by the P address. Transmission proceeds from high- to low-order digits of the Q record data (low- to high-core addresses) and is terminated by the presence of a record mark in the Q record data. The record mark is transmitted as part of the record and the Q record data remains unchanged. Record transmission, like field transmission, is destructive in nature.

Execution Time in Microseconds: $160 + 40R_q$

Example: 31 15000 16000

$\overline{12}1\overline{345}\ldots$
Core location 15000 before Transmit Record

$4\overline{1}4\overline{2}4\overline{3}4\overline{4}0\overline{00}\ddagger$
Core location 16000 before and after Transmit Record

$4\overline{1}4\overline{2}4\overline{3}4\overline{4}0\overline{00}\ddagger$
Core Location 15000 after Transmit Record

Time of Execution: 640 microseconds

Example: 31 10000 15500

$1\ddagger3\ddagger5\overline{\ddagger}217\ddagger02\ldots$
Core location 10000 before Transmit Record

$\overline{2}1\overline{653}\ddagger$
Core location 15500 before and after Transmit Record

$\overline{2}1\overline{653}\ddagger217\ddagger02\ldots$
Core location 10000 after Transmit Record

Time of Execution: 400 microseconds

Instruction: Transmit Digit Immediate

Operation Code: 15

Symbolic Name: TDM

Description:

The digit located at Q_{11} of the Transmit Digit Immediate instruction is transmitted to the single core position referenced by P_2 through P_6.

The original Q_{11} digit is not altered. If the Q_{11} digit is flagged, the flag is also transmitted. Positions Q_7 through Q_{10} are not utilized.

Execution Time in Microseconds: 200 (constant)

Example: 15 10000 12345

6 ←————————————⌐

Core location 10000 before
Transmit Digit Immediate

5 ←————————————⌐

Core location 10000 after
Transmit Digit Immediate

Example: 15 11125 00$\overline{1}$2$\overline{3}$

‡ ←————————————⌐

Core location 11125 before
Transmit Digit Immediate

$\overline{3}$ ←————————————⌐

Core location 11125 after
Transmit Digit Immediate

Example: 15 00928 8888‡

$\overline{2}$ ←————————————⌐

Core location 00928 before
Transmit Digit Immediate

‡ ←————————————⌐

Core location 00928 after
Transmit Digit Immediate

Instruction: Transmit Field Immediate

Operation Code: 16

Symbolic Name: TFM

Description:

The field whose units position is the Q_{11} digit of the Transmit Field Immediate instruction is chosen as the data field and is serially transmitted to contiguous core locations beginning at the core position referenced by the P address. Transmission proceeds from low- to high-order digits of the data field (high- to low-core addresses) until terminated by the presence of a flag in the high-order position of the field. The requirements imposed by the necessity for a flag in the arithmetic Immediate instructions are identical here.

Execution Time in Microseconds: $160 + 40D_q$

Example: 16 19999 $\overline{1}$2345

       01$\overline{9}$86 ◂─────────┐
       Core location 19999 before
       Transmit Field Immediate

       $\overline{1}$2345 ◂─────────┐
       Core location 19999 after
       Transmit Field Immediate

Time of Execution: 360 microseconds

Example: 16 09$\overline{0}$00 00000

       $\overline{1}$1$\overline{1}$1$\overline{1}$1$\overline{1}$1 ◂─────────┐
       Core location 09000 before
       Transmit Field Immediate

       $\overline{0}$0000000 ◂─────────┐
       Core location 09000 after
       Transmit Field Immediate

Time of Execution: 480 microseconds

Example: 16 10000 $\overline{0}$‡‡‡‡

       9$\overline{8}$76$\overline{5}$ ◂─────────┐
       Core location 10000 before
       Transmit Field Immediate

       $\overline{0}$‡‡‡‡ ◂─────────┐
       Core location 10000 after
       Transmit Field Immediate

Time of Execution: 360 microseconds

Problems

For all problems the following core location and content is assumed:

CORE LOCATION (LOW-ORDER DIGIT)	CONTENTS
10000	$\bar{1}23\ddagger42$
11000	$\bar{6}00000$
12255	$\bar{2}7$
17956	$\bar{1}\bar{0}$

The core content listed above is to be assumed for every problem and the results of any one problem are independent of all others.

What and where will be the final arithmetic results for the following problems?

1. 25 11001 09998
    31 16995 10995
    21 17000 17956
    12 17000 $\bar{0}0010\bar{0}$

2. 15 12256 00000
    15 12257 00000
    15 12258 00000
    15 12259 00000
    26 17000 12259
    22 17000 17956

3. 16 12259 0$\bar{0}$000
    25 12256 11000
    26 17000 12259
    22 17000 17956

4. 26 12259 10998

    15 12256 00000
    26 17000 17956
    22 17000 17956

5. 31 10998 09995
    15 10998 00001
    11 11000 00$\bar{1}2\bar{3}$
    21 11000 12255
    12 11000 000$\bar{2}7$

6. 21 11000 09997
    25 19999 11000
    25 11000 10999
    25 10999 19999
    26 19999 11000
    11 19999 00$\bar{1}3\bar{2}$
    24 11000 19999

Chapter 7

Branch Instructions

The great power of a digital computer is derived not only from its microsecond speed, but also from its ability to make logical decisions and choose alternative paths. In fact, the ability to choose one of several alternate paths is what differentiates the computer from a high-speed calculator.

As previously stated, the 1620 executes the stored program instructions sequentially. Obviously, it is often desirable to deviate from sequential execution of instructions and to "branch" (go to) to some other part of the program for the next instruction. The question of whether to continue instruction execution sequentially or to branch to some other portion of the program requires the computer to make a decision that might be based on the result of a test. For example, if we were writing a program to calculate the real roots of a quadratic equation by the formula

$$X = \frac{-B \pm \sqrt{B^2 - 4AC}}{2A}$$

we would first find the value of $B^2 - 4AC$. If this value were positive we would want to continue and solve for X. However, if the result were negative we would not want to continue, but would want to go to another part of the program and perhaps type out an indication that no real roots existed. The 1620 can be programmed to make certain tests and to branch to a particular part of the stored program as determined by the results of the tests. Several tests may be made to effect more complex decisions.

This chapter is devoted to that class of instructions which enable the computer to deviate from a sequential instruction execution and to go to some other portion of the program for the next instruction. The 1620 has in its instruction repertoire 9 Branch instructions, 2 of which give the programmer the ability to test for any one of 28 conditions.

Branch instructions are of two types, unconditional branches and conditional branches. As the name implies, an unconditional branch will branch to a specified address for the next instruction no matter what conditions exist at the time. In contrast, a conditional branch will branch to another part of the program for the next instruction if and only if some specific condition exists.

UNCONDITIONAL BRANCH INSTRUCTIONS

Instruction: Branch
Operation Code: 49
Symbolic Name: B
Description:

The program branches unconditionally to the instruction specified by the P address. The P address must reference an even-numbered core location since it is the address of an instruction. The Q portion of the instruction is not utilized.

The Branch instruction may be used to return to the first of a series of instructions which are repeatedly executed, with variations in data each time, until certain conditions are satisfied. This is an iterative process known in data processing as *looping*. One execution of a loop is called a pass. As an example of looping, consider the flow chart of a program to sum the numbers from 1 to 100.

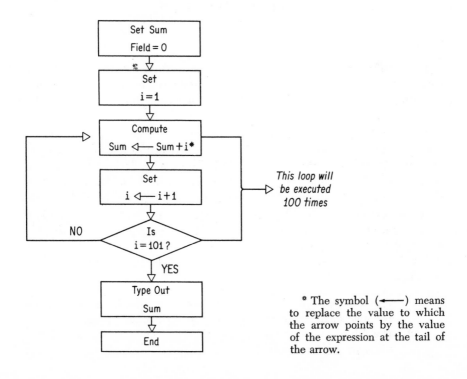

This loop will be executed 100 times

* The symbol (◄───) means to replace the value to which the arrow points by the value of the expression at the tail of the arrow.

The Branch instruction may also be used to return to the main program after an exception routine is completed or to start a program at any instruction in core storage.

Execution Time in Microseconds: 200 (constant)

Example: 49 07000 00000

> Branch to the instruction
> whose address is 07000

Example: 49 00402 89617

> Branch to location 00402 for
> the next instruction

Example: 49 08013 00000

> This instruction is incorrect
> because the address of the in-
> struction to be branched to is
> odd.

UNCONDITIONAL BRANCH INSTRUCTIONS
WITH VARIATIONS

CLOSED SUBROUTINE

A closed subroutine may be defined as a subprogram that can be entered from any instruction in a main program and that will provide for automatic re-entry to the instruction following the exit point in the main program.

Closed subroutines are frequently desired in stored programs. As an example, it may be necessary to take the square root of different numbers at different points in the program. Whenever it is desired to take the square root of a number, the instructions to do so could be included in the program sequentially. However, this would mean that the same series of instructions would reappear whenever we wanted to calculate a square root. It is more desirable to include the series of instructions to calculate the square root once in the program, and to make use of this subroutine whenever required. To do this, three considerations must be met:

1. The address of the return point in the main program must be made available to the subroutine for re-entry to the main program.
2. The subroutine must know where the argument(s) is/are located and the main program must know where the result is stored.

3. Provisions must be made for transfer out of the sequence of the main program to the subroutine.

The following three Branch instructions are specifically designed for programming the closed subroutine.

Instruction: Branch and Transmit
Operation Code: 27
Symbolic Name: BT
Description:

This instruction always performs three functions: (1) the address of the next instruction in sequence is automatically saved by being stored in a special register, (2) the Q field data is serially transmitted to the core storage position whose address is 1 less than the P address. Transmission of data continues to successively lower numbered core positions until terminated by the flag in the high-order position of the Q field data, and (3) the program branches to the instruction at the P address (the P address must be even).

The field data at the Q address remains unchanged.

As previously discussed, the primary use of the Branch and Transmit instruction is to facilitate the programming of a closed subroutine. This one instruction saves the return address, locates the argument, and branches to the subroutine.

A Branch Back instruction, to be discussed shortly, is used as the last instruction in the subroutine and provides a branch to the instruction address that was saved in a special register by the action of the Branch and Transmit instruction.

Execution Time in Microseconds: $200 + 40D_q$

Example: 27   15000   12035

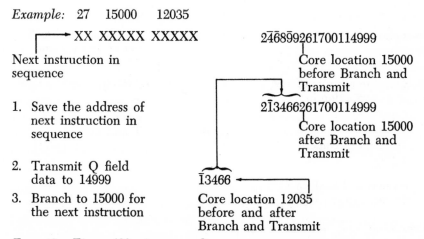

XX XXXXX XXXXX

Next instruction in
sequence

1. Save the address of
   next instruction in
   sequence

2. Transmit Q field
   data to 14999

3. Branch to 15000 for
   the next instruction

2$\overline{4}$68$\overline{9}$9261700114999

Core location 15000
before Branch and
Transmit

2$\overline{1}$34662̲61700114999

Core location 15000
after Branch and
Transmit

$\overline{1}$3466

Core location 12035
before and after
Branch and Transmit

Execution Time: 400 microseconds

Instruction: Branch and Transmit Immediate

Operation Code: 17

Symbolic Name: BTM

Description:

The Branch and Transmit Immediate instruction performs three functions (1) the address of the next instruction in sequence is automatically saved by being stored in a special register, (2) the field whose low-order position is the Q_{11} digit of the instruction is serially transmitted to the core storage location whose address is 1 less than the P address. Transmission of data continues to successively lower numbered core positions until terminated by the flag in the high-order position of the field being transmitted. Thus, part or all (depending on where the high-order flag is located) of the instruction itself is transmitted to the P address − 1, and (3) the program branches to the instruction at the P address (the P address must be even).

The primary use of the Branch and Transmit Immediate instruction is to facilitate programming a closed subroutine. The field whose low-order position is the Q_{11} digit of the instruction may be the address of the argument, in which case it is this address that is transmitted to the P address − 1. The Q_{11} position of the instruction may be the units position of the argument, in which case the argument is transmitted to the P address − 1. In either case the requirement that the argument be in a location known to the subroutine is satisfied.

Execution Time in Microseconds: $200 + 40D_q$

Example: 17   10000   12035

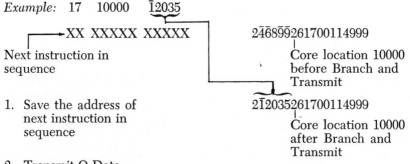

XX XXXXX XXXXX

Next instruction in
sequence

246899261700114999

Core location 10000
before Branch and
Transmit

1. Save the address of
   next instruction in
   sequence

212035261700114999

Core location 10000
after Branch and
Transmit

2. Transmit Q Data
   to 09999

3. Branch to 10000 for
   the next instruction

Execution Time: 400 microseconds

Instruction: Branch Back
Operation Code: 42
Symbolic Name: BB
Description:

Branch unconditionally to the instruction at the address saved by (1) the execution of the last Branch and Transmit, or Branch and Transmit Immediate, instruction, or (2) a previous depression of the Save key on the console (the Save key function is described in Appendix VI). The Save key function has priority over the Branch and Transmit and Branch and Transmit Immediate instructions. The P and Q portions of the instruction are not utilized.

If the main program exits to a closed subroutine with a Branch and Transmit or Branch and Transmit Immediate instruction, the Branch Back instruction can be used as the last instruction in the subroutine to return to the main program.

Execution Time in Microseconds: 200 (constant)

CONDITIONAL BRANCH INSTRUCTIONS

Instruction: Branch on Digit
Operation Code: 43
Symbolic Name: BD
Description:

The program will branch to the instruction at the P address if the core storage location specified by the Q address does not contain a zero. If the core position contains a zero, the next instruction in sequence is executed. The 1, 2, 4, and 8 core planes of the core storage position specified by the Q address are tested. If *any one* of these bits is present, the program will branch. Thus a ‡ (C-2-8) will also cause the program to branch. Since the P operand of the Branch on Digit instruction is the address of an instruction, it must reference an even-numbered core position.

Execution Time in Microseconds: 240 if a branch occurs
                                   200 if a branch does not occur

Example: 43 15000 10312

0 ←────────────────┐
                   │
Core location 10312

The program will not branch
but will execute the next
instruction in sequence

Execution Time: 200 microseconds

Example: 43 12012 19013

‡ ←────────────────┐
                   │
Core location 19013

The program will branch
to the instruction at
core position 12012

Execution Time: 240 microseconds

Example: 43 12060 04000

$\bar{0}$ ←────────────────┐
                           │
Core location 04000

The program will not branch
but will execute the next
instruction in sequence

Execution Time: 200 microseconds

Example: 43 06000 13068

7 ←────────────────┐
                   │
Core location 13068

The program will branch
to core location 06000

Execution Time: 240 microseconds

Example: The following program will
branch to location 16488 if
any nonzero digit is dis-
covered between positions
19000 – 19003 inclusive

LOCATION	INSTRUCTION
00500	43 16488 19000
00512	43 16488 19001
00524	43 16488 19002
00536	43 16488 19003

Instruction: Branch no Flag

Operation Code: 44

Symbolic Name: BNF

Description:

The program will branch to the instruction at the P address if the core storage location specified by the Q address does not contain a flag. If a flag is present, the next instruction in sequence is executed. Since the P address of the Branch no Flag instruction is the address of an instruction, it must reference an even-numbered core position.

This instruction may be used to test the sign of a data field or to find the length of a data field by testing for the field-defining flag.

Execution Time in Microseconds: 240 if a branch occurs
200 if the branch does not occur

Example: 44 15000 12013

The program will branch
to the instruction at
core position 15000.

6 ◄────────────────┐
Core location 12013

Execution Time: 240 microseconds

Example: 44 12068 19012

The program will not branch
but will execute the next
instruction in sequence.

5̄ ◄────────────────┐
Core location 19012

Execution Time: 200 microseconds

Example: 44 15000 00612

The program will branch
to the instruction at
core position 15000.

‡ ◄────────────────┐
Core location 00612

Execution Time: 240 microseconds

Instruction: Branch no Record Mark

Operation Code: 45

Symbolic Name: BNR

Description:

The program will branch to the instruction at the P address if the core storage location specified by the Q address does not contain a record mark. If a record mark is present, the next instruction in sequence is executed. Since the P address of the Branch no Record Mark instruction is the address of an instruction, it must reference an even-numbered core position.

Execution Time in Microseconds: 240 if a branch occurs
200 if the branch does not occur

Example: 45 07000 13268

$\bar{0}$ ⟵⎤

Core location 13268

The program will branch
to the instruction
at location 07000.

Execution Time: 240 microseconds

Example: 45 09024 15012

‡ ⟵⎤

Core location 15012

The program will not branch
but will execute the next
instruction in sequence.

Execution Time: 200 microseconds

Instruction: Branch on Indicator

Operation Code: 46

Symbolic Name: BI

Description:

The program will branch to the instruction at the P address if the indicator or program switch specified by the Q_8 and Q_9 positions of the instruction is on. The Q_7, Q_{10}, and Q_{11} positions of the instruction are not utilized. The 2-digit indicator codes used in the Q_8 and Q_9 positions of the instruction are as follows:

01—Program switch 1
02—Program switch 2
03—Program switch 3
04—Program switch 4
06—Read Check indicator
07—Write Check indicator
09—Last Card indicator
11—High/Positive indicator
12—Equal/Zero indicator
13—High/Positive or Equal/Zero indicator
14—Overflow indicator
15—Exponent Overflow indicator
16—Memory Buffer Register (MBR)—
   Even Check indicator
17—Memory Buffer Register (MBR)—
   Odd Check indicator
19—Any Data Check indicator

Indicator codes 01 through 04 refer to the four program switches located on the console. These switches are manually set to either an on or an off position.

The Read Check (06), Write Check (07), MBR-Even Check (16), and MBR-Odd Check (17) indicators reflect the results of parity checking during input-output operations and memory read-in and read-out cycles. If a parity error is discovered, the appropriate indicator is turned on.

The Any Data Check (19) indicator is turned on if any one, or more, of the Read Check, Write Check, MBR-Even Check, or MBR-Odd Check indicators is on.

The High/Positive (11), Equal/Zero (12), and Overflow (14) indicators are turned on or off during arithmetic operations (see Chapter 5). The Exponent Overflow indicator (15) is discussed in the appendix on floating point hardware. The High/Positive or Equal/Zero indicator (13) is turned on if *either* the High/Positive *or* the Equal/Zero indicator is turned on.

Except for the Any Data Check indicator, the High/Positive indicator, the Equal/Zero indicator, and the High/Positive-Equal/Zero indicator, all indicators are turned off if they are interrogated by their respective Branch Indicator instruction. The status of the console switches remain unchanged since they are manually controlled.

Execution Time in Microseconds: 200 if the branch occurs
                                   160 if the branch does not occur

Example: Branch to the address specified
by the configuration of the
program switches as follows:

PROGRAM SWITCHES		BRANCH TO
1 off	4 off	14000
1 off	4 on	15000
1 on	4 off	16000
1 on	4 on	17000

LOCATION	INSTRUCTION	
00500	46 00536 00100	Branch if 1 on
00512	46 15000 00400	1 off and 4 on
00524	49 14000 00000	1 off and 4 off
00536	46 17000 00400	1 on and 4 on
00548	49 16000 00000	1 on and 4 off

Instruction: Branch no Indicator

Operation Code: 47

Symbolic Name: BNI

Description:

The Branch no Indicator instruction is the same as the Branch Indicator instruction except that the branch to the P address occurs if the
indicator specified by the Q_8 and Q_9 positions of the instruction is off.

At first glance it may seem a duplication of effort to have two Branch
instructions which test the same indicators for opposite conditions. However, with a little thought it becomes evident that being able to test
directly for either condition will both simplify programming and save
program steps.

Execution Time in Microseconds: 200 if the branch occurs
160 if the branch does not occur

Example: If program switch 1 is off,
branch to location 04688 for
the next instruction. If it
is on, continue sequential
instruction execution.
Solution using Branch Indicator
instruction:

00500 46 00524 00100
00512 49 04688 00000
00524

Solution using Branch no Indicator
instruction:

00500 47 04688 00100
00512

One program step is saved
using the Branch no
Indicator instruction.

Example: If the data fields at locations
17156 and 12123 are not equal,
branch to location 00500 for
the next instruction.

$$24\ 17156\ 12123$$
$$47\ 00500\ 01200$$

Problems

Give the results to the following problems as actual numbers or in an algebraic symbolic notation. For example, if the first problem summed the numbers from one to 1000, the answer could be expressed as $\sum\limits_{i=1}^{1000} i$

1. When the following program halts, what will the field whose units position is core location 13000 contain?

$$00500\quad 16\ 13000\ \overline{0}0000$$
$$00512\quad 11\ 13000\ 0000\overline{1}$$
$$00524\quad 47\ 00512\ 01400$$
$$00536\quad 48\ 00000\ 00000$$

2. When the following program halts, what will the field whose units position is core location 13966 contain?

$$14168\quad 16\ 13966\ \overline{0}0000$$
$$14180\quad 16\ 06745\ 000\overline{0}0$$
$$14192\quad 11\ 13966\ 0000\overline{2}$$
$$14204\quad 11\ 06745\ 0000\overline{1}$$
$$14216\quad 14\ 06745\ 00\overline{1}00$$
$$14228\quad 47\ 14192\ 01200$$
$$14240\quad 48\ 00000\ 00000$$

3. When the following program halts, what will the field whose units position is core location 07000 contain?

$$00700\quad 16\ 07000\ \overline{0}0000$$
$$00712\quad 16\ 07081\ 000\overline{0}0$$
$$00724\quad 11\ 07081\ 0000\overline{1}$$
$$00736\quad 14\ 07081\ 00\overline{1}00$$
$$00748\quad 46\ 00784\ 01200$$
$$00760\quad 11\ 07000\ 000\overline{0}2$$
$$00772\quad 49\ 00724\ 00000$$
$$00784\quad 48\ 00000\ 00000$$

4. When the following program halts, what will the field whose units position is core location 17800 contain?

$$
\begin{array}{lll}
00800 & 16\ 00835 & \bar{0}0001 \\
00812 & 16\ 17800 & \bar{0}0000 \\
00824 & 11\ 17800 & 00000 \\
00836 & 11\ 00835 & 000\bar{0}1 \\
00848 & 14\ 00835 & \bar{0}0101 \\
00860 & 47\ 00824 & 01200 \\
00872 & 48\ 00000 & 00000 \\
\end{array}
$$

5. When the following program halts, what will the fields whose units positions are core locations 19000 and 17199 contain?

$$
\begin{array}{lll}
00464 & 16\ 17199 & \bar{0}0000 \\
00476 & 16\ 19\bar{0}00 & 00000 \\
00488 & 16\ 00511 & 0\bar{0}001 \\
00500 & 11\ 17199 & 00000 \\
00512 & 23\ 00511 & 00511 \\
00524 & 21\ 19000 & 00099 \\
00536 & 11\ 00511 & 000\bar{0}1 \\
00548 & 14\ 00511 & 0\bar{0}200 \\
00560 & 47\ 00500 & 01200 \\
00572 & 48\ 00000 & 00000 \\
\end{array}
$$

6. When the following program halts, what will the fields whose units positions are core locations 14000 and 18000 contain?

$$
\begin{array}{lll}
02178 & 16\ 14000 & 000\bar{0}3 \\
02190 & 16\ 18000 & \bar{0}0000 \\
02202 & 11\ 18000 & 00\bar{0}01 \\
02214 & 11\ 02213 & 000\bar{0}1 \\
02226 & 14\ 02213 & 00\bar{1}01 \\
02238 & 47\ 02202 & 01200 \\
02250 & 12\ 14000 & 000\bar{0}1 \\
02262 & 46\ 02298 & 01200 \\
02274 & 16\ 02213 & 000\bar{0}1 \\
02286 & 49\ 02202 & 00000 \\
02298 & 48\ 00000 & 00000 \\
\end{array}
$$

7. The following problem is solving a quadratic equation of the form $AX^2 + BX + C = 0$ by a trial and error method. An integer solution is assumed. What is the equation (what are values of A, B, and C)?

$$
\begin{array}{llll}
07988 & 16 & 18500 & \overline{0}0001 \\
08000 & 23 & 18500 & 18500 \\
08012 & 26 & 19000 & 00099 \\
08024 & 13 & 19000 & 000\overline{1}3 \\
08036 & 26 & 19000 & 00099 \\
08048 & 13 & 18500 & 000\overline{0}9 \\
08060 & 21 & 19000 & 00099 \\
08072 & 14 & 19000 & 00\overline{5}04 \\
08084 & 46 & 08120 & 01200 \\
08096 & 11 & 18500 & 000\overline{0}1 \\
08108 & 49 & 08000 & 00000 \\
08120 & 48 & 00000 & 00000 \\
\end{array}
$$

8. When the following program halts, what will the field whose units position is core location 15000 contain?

$$
\begin{array}{llll}
00588 & 16 & 15\overline{0}00 & 00000 \\
00600 & 13 & 00611 & 00\overline{0}01 \\
00612 & 21 & 15000 & 00099 \\
00624 & 11 & 00611 & 000\overline{0}2 \\
00636 & 47 & 00600 & 01400 \\
00648 & 48 & 00000 & 00000 \\
\end{array}
$$

Chapter 8

The Input-Output Instructions

To be a useful tool, the digital computer must be able to communicate with man. It must have the ability to receive information and data, and, after processing this data at microsecond speeds, it must be able to communicate the results back to man.

The 1620 has the following input-output devices to perform this communication: the typewriter, the card reader, the paper tape reader, the card punch and the paper tape punch. Only one input-output device may be selected at any time. The Q_8 and Q_9 positions of all the input-output instructions which will be discussed in this chapter specify the input-output[1] device through a 2-digit code as follows:

CODE	I/O DEVICE
01	Typewriter
02	Paper Tape Punch
03	Paper Tape Reader
04	Card Punch
05	Card Reader

Instruction: Read Numerically
Operation Code: 36
Symbolic Name: RN
Description:

Numerical information from the input device specified by the Q_8 and Q_9 positions of the Read Numerically instruction is transmitted serially to the core storage location specified by the P address and through successively higher core locations until terminated by one of the following conditions:

[1] The industry accepted abbreviation for input-output is generally I/O.

1. Sensing of the end-of-line character (written for demonstration purposes as E/L) when the input is from the paper tape reader. At that time, a record mark is generated automatically by the 1620 and is placed in core following the last character read from tape.
2. Depression of the Release key on the console when input is from the typewriter. In this case a record mark is *not* generated automatically by the computer. If it is desired to place a record mark in core storage when entering information from the typewriter, the Record Mark key on the typewriter must be depressed.
3. Reading into core storage the 80th character from the card input buffer storage. Here again a record mark is *not* generated automatically by the computer. If it is desired to place a record mark in core storage from the card reader, the record mark character (0-2-8) must be punched in a card. If a record mark is present in a card, it does *not* terminate the reading of data from the card input buffer. A full 80 columns of a card are always read regardless of their contents (excepting parity errors which could cause check stop conditions).

Each numerical character from the input device along with its flag (if any), is stored in a single core storage location. Check bits, if needed, are generated internally to observe parity.

The Q_7, Q_{10}, and Q_{11} positions of the Read Numerically instruction are not utilized.

Read Numerically is an example of destructive read-in: the old information is replaced by the new data for the total area of input.

The execution time of this instruction depends upon the speed of the input device selected and the number of characters that are read from that device.

Example: 36 10012 00300

3121206̄945‡1672E/L
Paper tape input

3121206̄945‡1672‡
Core location 10012
after instruction execution

Instruction: Read Alphamerically
Operation Code: 37
Symbolic Name: RA
Description:

Alphameric information from the input device specified by the Q_8 and Q_9 positions of the Read Alphamerically instruction is transmitted serially to the core storage location specified by the P address and through successively higher core locations until terminated by one of the following conditions:

1. Sensing of the end-of-line character when the input is from the paper tape reader. At that time, an alphameric record mark character (a numeric zero digit followed by a single record mark character) is generated automatically by the computer and is placed in core storage following the last character read from tape.

2. Depression of the Release key on the console when the input is from the console typewriter. An alphameric record mark character is *not* generated automatically by the computer. If it is desired to place an alphameric record mark in core storage when entering information from the typewriter, the Record Mark key on the typewriter must be depressed.

3. Reading into core storage the 80th character from the card *input* buffer storage. A record mark is *not* generated automatically in core storage. If it is desired to read a record mark into core storage from the card reader, the record mark character (0-2-8) must be punched in a card. The full 80 columns of a card are always read regardless of their contents (excepting parity errors which could cause check stop conditions).

The P address of the Read Alphamerically instruction must specify an odd-numbered core location (the P_6 digit must be odd); otherwise, the input information is not placed in core storage correctly and parity errors may occur during reading. This is due to the fact that when information is read alphamerically, it is automatically converted to the 2-digit alphameric code. The odd-numbered location must contain the right-hand (numerical) digit of the 2-digit alphameric code read from the input device. The zone digit is generated and placed in the adjacent even-numbered core position automatically.

Information from the input device may be a random mixture of numeric, alphabetic, and special characters. Each character from the input device is stored in core storage as two digits (the alphameric code discussed in Chapter 2). Flags are not transmitted into core storage on characters read by the input device; **flags already in the core storage area when the information is read in remain unchanged.**

The Q_7, Q_{10}, and Q_{11} positions of the Read Alphamerically instruction are not utilized. The execution time depends on the input device selected and the number of characters transmitted.

Example: 37 15001 00300

3ABC271984F+/J‡E/L
Paper tape input

┌─► 7341424372777179787446102151O‡0‡
└── Core location 15000
    after instruction execution

Note:

It is permissible to read alphameric information in the numeric mode but the characters *do not* enter the 1620 alphamerically. Table 8.1 demonstrates the translation effect of alphameric information read numerically.

Table 8-1*

CHARACTER	CORE REPRESENTATION
A, B, . . . , I	1, 2, . . . , 9
J, K, . . . , R	$\bar{1}, \bar{2}, . . . , \bar{9}$
S, T, . . . , Z	2, 3, . . . , 9
/	1
.	821
,	821
@	C84
)	C84
(	C84
=	821
★	F84
—	F
+	C

* The period (.), comma (,), and equal sign (=) will behave as a record mark in the Transmit Record instruction.

Instruction: Write Numerically

Operation Code: 38

Symbolic Name: WN

Description:

Numerical information from core storage, beginning with the character at the core storage location specified by the P address and continuing through successively higher core addresses, is transmitted serially to the output device specified by the Q_8 and Q_9 positions of the Write Numerically instruction.

Transmission of data continues until terminated by one of the following conditions:

1. Sensing of a record mark character in core storage if the output device is the typewriter or the paper tape punch. If the output device is the paper tape punch, sensing a record mark character in core storage causes an end-of-line character to be punched in the tape. If the output device is the typewriter, sensing a record mark character in core storage terminates transmission but is not written on the typewriter.
2. Depressing the Release key on the console.
3. Writing of the 80th position in the card output buffer storage.

Each numerical character in core storage, along with its flag (if any), is written on the output device. The characters in core storage remain unchanged. No alphamerical or special character represented in core storage as two numerical characters can be written on the output device as a single character by this instruction.

If no record mark is encountered in core storage when the typewriter or paper tape punch is used as the output medium, and the highest numbered core storage address is written, the next position transmitted is 00000 and transmission continues. If the numerical blank character appears in memory (C-8-4), it will be printed as "@" on the typewriter, punched as C-8-4 on paper tape, or will leave a blank column on the card.

For typewriter and paper tape output, the P address of this instruction may not reference a record mark. The Q_7, Q_{10}, and Q_{11} positions of the Write Numerically instruction are not utilized.

The execution time of this instruction depends upon the speed of the device selected and the number of characters written.

Example: 38 12000 00100

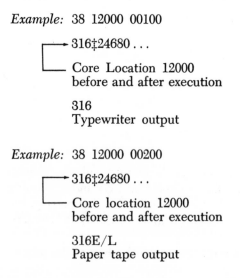

316‡24680 . . .

Core Location 12000
before and after execution

316
Typewriter output

Example: 38 12000 00200

316‡24680 . . .

Core location 12000
before and after execution

316E/L
Paper tape output

Example: 38 12000 00400

┌──►316‡24680...
└── Core location 12000
      before and after execution

316‡24680... (80 characters)

Card output

Instruction: Write Alphamerically

Operation Code: 39

Symbolic Name: WA

Description:

Alphameric information from core storage, beginning with the character at the core storage location specified by the P address and continuing through successively higher core addresses, is transmitted serially to the output device specified by the Q_8 and Q_9 positions of the Write Alphamerically instruction.

Transmission continues until terminated by one of the following conditions:

1. Sensing of an alphameric record mark in core storage if the output device is the typewriter or the paper tape punch. If the output device is the paper tape punch, sensing an alphameric record mark in core storage causes an end-of-line character to be punched in the tape. If the output device is the typewriter, sensing an alphameric record mark in core storage terminates transmission but is not written on the typewriter.
2. Depression of the Release key on the console.
3. Writing of the 80th position in the card output buffer.

Each alphameric character in core storage consists of two numeric digits and is written on the output device as a single alphameric character. The characters in core storage remain unchanged. No flags are written on the output device.

The P address of the Write Alphamerically instruction must be odd (P_6 must be an odd digit), otherwise the information in core storage, expressed in alphameric (double-digit) code, is not correctly converted to the single character output representation. The Q_7, Q_{10}, and Q_{11} positions of the instruction are not utilized. For typewriter and paper tape output, the P address of this instruction may not reference an alphameric record mark.

The execution time is dependent upon the speed of the output device and the number of characters written.

Example: 39 09001 00100

┌─→ 48415954565549430041554153686249620‡ . . .
└── Core location 09000
before and after execution
HARMONIC ANALYSIS
Typewriter output

Example: 39 15791 00200

┌─→ 49556345596541530055560300770‡ . . .
└── Core location 15790
before and after execution
INTERVAL NO. 7E/L
Paper tape output

Instruction: Dump Numerically
Operation Code: 35
Symbolic Name: DN
Description:

Numerical information from core storage, beginning with the character at the core storage location specified by the P address and continuing through successively higher core addresses, is transmitted serially to the output device specified by the Q_8 and Q_9 positions of the Dump Numerically instruction. Transmission is terminated after the character from the highest numbered core storage address *of that module* has been written. This is the character at core position 19999, 39999 or 59999 depending on the module that the P address specified. If it is desired to stop transmission before the character in the highest numbered core storage position is transmitted, the Release key on the console may be depressed.

Each numerical character, with its flag (if any), as well as any single record mark character, is written on the output device. The character in core storage remains unchanged. If the output device is the paper tape punch, an end-of-line character is punched in the tape immediately following the last character dumped by the instruction. This end-of-line character will be punched into the paper tape only if the instruction has been completely executed and will not be punched if the Release key has been depressed before the highest character in the storage module has been punched.

The Q_7, Q_{10}, and Q_{11} digits of this instruction are not utilized. The execution time of this instruction depends upon the speed of the output device selected and the number of characters written on that device.

Example: 35 15000 00100

```
    ┌──▶ 36482‡00‡198 . . .
    └───Core location 15000 before
        and after execution
```

36482‡00‡198 . . .

Typewriter output

Problems

State in as few sentences as possible the function of each of the following programs.

1.	00500	36 10000	00300
	00512	38 10000	00200
	00524	49 00500	00000
2.	00500	37 10001	00500
	00512	39 10001	00400
	00524	49 00500	00000
3.	00620	37 10001	00500
	00632	31 10160	00678
	00644	46 00680	00100
	00656	39 10001	00400
	00668	49 00620	0000‡
	00680	39 10001	00200
	00692	49 00620	00000
4.	00000	35 00000	00400
	00012	16 00022	00000
5.	00500	16 19999	00000
	00512	36 10000	00500
	00524	11 19999	00001
	00536	47 00512	00900
	00548	15 00000	0000‡
	00560	38 19995	00100

Chapter 9

Miscellaneous Instructions

The five instructions discussed in this chapter complete the basic[1] repertoire of 1620 instructions. The functions that they perform are not closely related, so they are grouped under the general name of miscellaneous instructions.

The reader should not let the term miscellaneous connote insignificance. The Set Flag, Clear Flag, Halt, No Operation, and Control instructions, if used carefully and thoughtfully, can greatly facilitate and sophisticate programming.

Instruction: Set Flag

Operation Code: 32

Symbolic Name: SF

Description:

A flag is placed at the core location specified by the P address, and a check bit is either added or removed to adjust for parity checking. If a flag is present, the instruction has no effect. The Q portion of the instruction is not utilized. The digit at the P address is not altered by the instruction.

The primary use of the Set Flag instruction is to define the high-order position of data fields. Of course, the data may be flagged when it is prepared for input, but this is not always practical or desirable.

Execution Time in Microseconds: 200 (constant)

[1] See Appendixes I, II, IV for additional 1620 instructions.

Example: 32 10000 00000

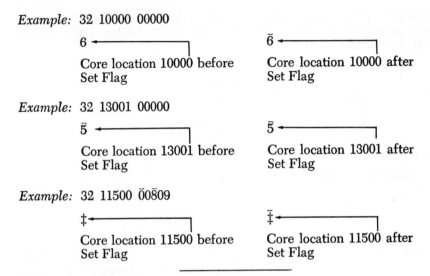

6 ←————————————┐
Core location 10000 before
Set Flag

6̄ ←————————————┐
Core location 10000 after
Set Flag

Example: 32 13001 00000

5̄ ←————————————┐
Core location 13001 before
Set Flag

5̄ ←————————————┐
Core location 13001 after
Set Flag

Example: 32 11500 0̄0̄8̄09

‡ ←————————————┐
Core location 11500 before
Set Flag

‡̄ ←————————————┐
Core location 11500 after
Set Flag

Instruction: Clear Flag

Operation Code: 33

Symbolic Name: CF

Description:

The flag in the core location specified by the P address is removed, and a check bit is either added or removed to adjust for parity checking. If no flag is present, the instruction has no effect. The Q portion of the instruction is not utilized. The digit at the P address is not altered by the instruction.

The Clear Flag instruction may be used when it is desired to make a negative field positive. The flag in the units position of the field is simply removed with the instruction. If flags are not wanted as a part of output, the Clear Flag instruction can be used to remove them.

Execution Time in Microseconds: 200 (constant)

Example: 33 05421 00000

6̈ ←————————————┐
Core location 05421 before
Clear Flag

6 ←————————————┐
Core location 05421 after
Clear Flag

Example: 33 12000 68291

2 ←————————————┐
Core location 12000 before
Clear Flag

2 ←————————————┐
Core location 12000 after
Clear Flag

Example: The following program reverses the sign of a data field stored in locations 01690 − 01699, and then branches to location 06000 for the next instruction.

LOCATION	INSTRUCTION
00500	44 00536 01699
00512	33 01699 00000
00524	49 06000 00000
00536	32 01699 00000
00548	49 06000 00000

Instruction: Halt

Operation Code: 48

Symbolic Name: H

Description:

Program execution is halted and the computer stops in the manual mode. Depression of the Start key on the console will cause the computer to continue program execution beginning with the next instruction in sequence. The P and Q portions of the instruction are not utilized.

After a Halt instruction has been executed, the address of the Q_{11} position of the instruction is displayed on the console in the Memory Address Register indicator lights. Thus, it is possible to distinguish between several different Halt instructions in the same program.

The Halt instruction has many important uses. It may be employed to interrupt program execution for operator intervention. The operator may take advantage of the halt to load a tape, set program switches, investigate the contents of certain portions of core storage, and so forth. It is also very helpful in debugging and for error indication purposes. Different error conditions encountered in a problem may be programmed to branch to different Halt instructions. By noting the address of the Q_{11} position of the Halt instruction in the Memory Address Register lights, we can tell which error condition stopped program execution. The following program serves to demonstrate this principle. A record mark is assumed in core location 15001.

00500	14 13000 5̄0000	Compare with 5̄0000
00512	46 00584 01300	Branch if number ≥ 50000
00524	22 15000 13000	Subtract
00536	47 00572 01300	Branch if result negative
00548	38 14996 00100	Type out result
00560	48 00000 98640	Halt—program completed
00572	48 00000 00̄000	Halt—negative result
00584	48 00000 00080	Halt—number ≥ 50000

The above program contains three Halt instructions. Two of the Halt instructions signal error conditions; the third indicates the successful completion of the program. The error conditions exist if the data field at core location 13000 is greater than or equal to 50000, or if the result of the subtract operation is negative. When the program executes a Halt instruction, the address in the memory address register lights indicates which Halt instruction terminated program execution. Then, from a listing of the program it can be determined which condition caused the program to halt. If the address displayed is 00571, the program was successfully completed. If the displayed address is 00583, the program halted because the result of the subtract operation was negative. If the data field at location 13000 was greater than 50000, the program would have halted and the displayed address would be 00595.

Judiciously placed Halt instructions are a great aid in program debugging. Groups of instructions may be checked out by interspersing Halt statements throughout the program. If the program should "hang up," the troublesome portion can be isolated as being between the last executed Halt instruction and the next Halt instruction in sequence.

Execution Time in Microseconds: 160 (constant)

Instruction: No Operation
Operation Code: 41
Symbolic Name: NOP [2]
Description:

Perform no operation and advance to the next instruction in sequence. The P and Q portions of the No Operation instruction are not utilized.

The No Operation instruction has two major functions. The No Operation instructions when judiciously placed throughout a program allow for the insertion of additional instructions at a later time without any of the program having to be relocated. If only one instruction is to be inserted, it may be located in the core positions used by the No Operation instruction. If it is desired to insert more than one instruction, the No Operation instruction may be replaced by a Branch instruction, which will branch the program to an unused part of memory where the additional instructions will be added.

A second use of the No Operation instruction is to eliminate a Halt or any other instruction without relocating the rest of the program. The operation code of the instruction to be eliminated is replaced by the operation code of the No Operation instruction (41). This may be done from the console or as a part of the program itself.

Execution Time in Microseconds: 160 (constant)

[2] Pronounced no-op.

Example: In the following program it is desired to branch to a sub-routine located at 09012 only after the first card is read. The instruction to branch to the subroutine is in location 00414. Since the same read instruction will be used to read in all the cards it is necessary to alter the Branch instruction so that it is operative only after the first card is read. This is accomplished by having a Transmit Digit Immediate instruction in the subroutine which changes the operation code of the Branch instruction (49) to the operation code of the No Operation instruction (41). Now, as all subsequent cards are read, a branch to the subroutine will not occur.

00402	36	13000	00500	Read a card
00414	49	09012	00000	Branch to subroutine
00426	11	13010	00$\overline{1}$00	Main program continues
.	.	.	.	
.	.	.	.	
.	.	.	.	
01626	49	00402	00000	Go to read another card
09012	11	06900	000$\overline{1}$0	Subroutine begins here
.	.	.	.	
.	.	.	.	
.	.	.	.	
09612	15	00415	00001	Modify Branch instructions to NOP
09624	49	00426	00000	Return to main program

Instruction: Control

Operation Code: 34

Symbolic Name: K

Description:

This instruction is used to control the functions of spacing, tabulating, and returning the carriage on the typewriter. The Q_8 and Q_9 positions of this instruction always contain an 01, specifying the typewriter, since this is the only unit that can be controlled by this instruction. The Q_{11} position specifies the control function desired with a 1-digit code. The codes are as follows:

CODE	FUNCTION
1	Space
2	Return Carriage
8	Tabulate

The entire P operand and the Q_7 and Q_{10} portions of the Control instruction are not utilized.

Execution Time in Microseconds: This is dependent upon the control function and the position of the typewriter carriage at the time of instruction execution.

Example: 34 00000 00108

The typewriter is tabulated

Example: 34 99999 90102

The carriage is returned

Example: 34 ‡‡900 00101

The typewriter is spaced one position horizontally. This instruction is equivalent to depressing the space bar on the typewriter.

Chapter 10

Introduction to a Symbolic Programming System

We are now at a stage of development where absolute machine language coding is cumbersome. One must have a complete table of operation codes and necessary Q address modifiers at hand in order to write a program. In addition, one must keep track of where program steps lie in memory, and extensive charts must be kept as road maps for the internal data arrangement. The housekeeping necessitated by absolute coding is cumbersome and the flow of logic is difficult to trace. Lastly, and of greatest importance, errors are easily made and difficult to locate. If computers are as "intelligent" as is commonly supposed, why not allow the computer to do its own housekeeping?

Throughout the chapters on machine operations, a symbolic name was associated with every machine code: 21-A, 34-K, 13-MM, and so forth. How difficult would it be for a programmer to construct a program to read an instruction whose operation code was symbolic, replace this with machine language coding, punch the translated instruction, and repeat this sequence until all instructions were translated?

On the surface, this may sound like a frightening task. However, it is not exceedingly difficult; the basic logic is described in the diagram shown in Figure 10.1. The logic employed is simply one of exhaustion: check the alphabetic representation of the OP code against all allowable representations. It must match one of them or it is in error.

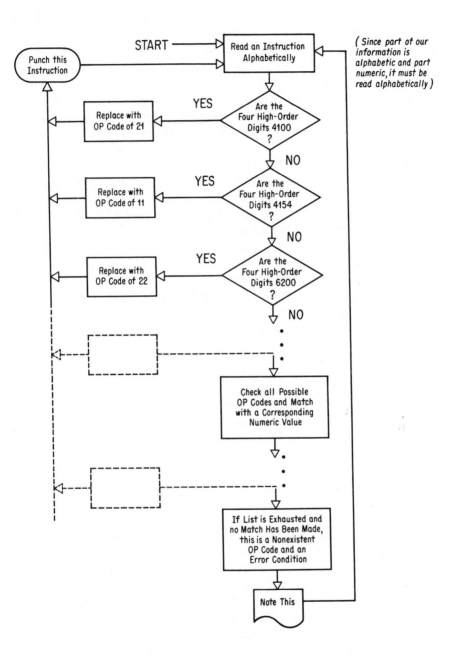

Fig. 10.1. Flow Chart of an OP Code Translator.

If the input to such a program were A_ 12345 02378 (the underscore "_" is used to indicate a blank character), the output would be 21 12345 02378. The program translated the alphabetic representation of "A_" into the machine OP code of "21." ("A_" is "4100" in alphabetic double-digit representation.) The blank is necessary for it is possible to have a 2-letter OP code: AM, BD, and so forth. Note also that this logic scheme would not allow for 3-letter OP codes: TDM, BNF, and so forth. In that case it would be necessary to check the six high-order digits instead of the present four. BNR would appear as 425559, and so forth.

Upon close inspection of the logic diagram of Figure 10.1, one begins to see all sorts of exceptions that would cause this particular program to be totally unusable. However, all of these can be overcome by more extensive programming until the desired goal of total OP code translation is obtained. In this way, one would not have to remember the numeric representation of operation codes but could choose the corresponding mnemonic form which is more easily retained.

This then is the basic philosophy of a symbolic system: substituting alphabetic information for numerics and forcing the computer, under control of a special program, to do the housekeeping.

The performance of this sort of translation implies three elements:

1. An error-catching processor that handles symbolic input and produces absolute output.
2. A program written in the language acceptable to the processor. This is called the "source program."
3. An accurate worker that will understand the processor's directions and perform the translation of a source program which it does not understand to one which it will understand. (The choice of future tense is quite important.) The worker is the computer and the translated source program is termed the "object program."

Consider an instruction such as 34 00000 00102 which, upon execution, would cause a carriage return on the typewriter. Why not keep this instruction stored in core and generate it whenever a symbolic operation code such as RCTY (Return Carriage on the TYpewriter) is encountered? Also, by the same logic, TBTY (TaBulate the TYpewriter) would always generate 34 00000 00108 and SPTY (SPace the TYpewriter) would yield 34 00000 00101.

Of course, the commands K 00000 00102, K 00000 00108, and K 00000 00101 would also generate the identical instructions but RCTY, TBTY, and SPTY are more easily remembered.

This philosophy may also be extended to I/0 commands that use a specific Q address modifier to state which unit is to be employed during the I/0 operation.

RNTY 12345 (Read Numerically from the TYpewriter) would cause a Read Numerically (36) command to be generated and also a modifier of 01 in positions Q_8 and Q_9 with all other Q digits 0. Then, the processor would "slip" the P address of 12345 between the OP code and the Q portion of the instruction to obtain 36 12345 00100. RNPT 12345 (Read Numerically from Paper Tape) would generate 36 12345 00300 in a similar fashion.

Notice that certain portions of instructions are predetermined by the nature of the instruction. An instruction such as RNPT 10000 followed by RNPT 12000 would cause two instructions to be generated which differ only in the P address:

$$36 \quad 10000 \quad 00300$$
$$36 \quad 12000 \quad 00300$$

Branching instructions also follow this logic. A symbolic instruction to generate a branch on an equal condition might be written as BI XXXXX 01200. This generates the machine instruction 46 XXXXX 01200. But since the E/Z indicator (12) is as unique as BI, we can alternatively choose the unique mnemonic BE or BZ. Either of these would generate 46 XXXXX 01200. Thus, BNH (Branch Not High) would generate 47 XXXXX 01100 as would BNP (Branch Not Positive). Continuing in this fashion, we can generate a complete set of unique mnemonics which comprise our translator's dictionary of acceptable operation codes. These symbolic operations are listed in table 10.1 and form the basic material for a working symbolic processor.

Table 10.1

Operation	Unique Mnemonic	Portion of Instruction Generated
Arithmetics		
Add	A	21 ----- -----
Add Immediate	AM	11 ----- -----
Subtract	S	22 ----- -----
Subtract Immediate	SM	12 ----- -----
Multiply	M	23 ----- -----
Multiply Immediate	MM	13 ----- -----
Load Dividend°	LD	28 ----- -----
Load Dividend Immediate°	LDM	18 ----- -----
Divide°	D	29 ----- -----
Divide Immediate°	DM	19 ----- -----
Compare	C	24 ----- -----
Compare Immediate	CM	14 ----- -----
Floating Add°	FADD	01 ----- -----
Floating Subtract°	FSUB	02 ----- -----
Floating Multiply°	FMUL	03 ----- -----
Floating Divide°	FDIV	09 ----- -----

Table 10.1 *(continued)*

OPERATION	UNIQUE MNEMONIC	PORTION OF INSTRUCTION GENERATED				
Internal Data Transmission						
Transmit Digit	TD	25	- - - - -		- - - - -	
Transmit Digit Immediate	TDM	15	- - - - -		- - - - -	
Transmit Field	TF	26	- - - - -		- - - - -	
Transmit Field Immediate	TFM	16	- - - - -		- - - - -	
Transmit Record	TR	31	- - - - -		- - - - -	
Move Flag°	MF	71	- - - - -		- - - - -	
Transfer Numeric Strip°	TNS	72	- - - - -		- - - - -	
Transfer Numeric Fill°	TNF	73	- - - - -		- - - - -	
Floating Transmit Field° (Transmit Floating Field)	TFL	06	- - - - -		- - - - -	
Floating Shift Right°	FSR	08	- - - - -		- - - - -	
Floating Shift Left°	FSL	05	- - - - -		- - - - -	
Branching Instructions						
Branch	B	49	- - - - -		- - - - -	
Branch No Flag	BNF	44	- - - - -		- - - - -	
Branch No Record Mark	BNR	45	- - - - -		- - - - -	
Branch on Digit	BD	43	- - - - -		- - - - -	
Branch and Transmit	BT	27	- - - - -		- - - - -	
Branch and Transmit Immediate	BTM	17	- - - - -		- - - - -	
Floating Branch and Transmit° (Branch and Transmit Floating)	BTFL	07	- - - - -		- - - - -	
Branch Back	BB	42	- - - - -		- - - - -	
Branch Indicator	BI	46	- - - - -		- - - - -	
Branch Console Switch 1 On	BC1	46	- - - - -	- 01 - -	
Branch Console Switch 2 On	BC2	46	- - - - -	- 02 - -	
Branch Console Switch 3 On	BC3	46	- - - - -	- 03 - -	
Branch Console Switch 4 On	BC4	46	- - - - -	- 04 - -	
Branch Last Card	BLC	46	- - - - -	- 09 - -	
Branch High	BH	46	- - - - -	- 11 - -	
Branch Positive	BP	46	- - - - -	- 11 - -	
Branch Equal	BE	46	- - - - -	- 12 - -	
Branch Zero	BZ	46	- - - - -	- 12 - -	
Branch Not Low	BNL	46	- - - - -	- 13 - -	
Branch Not Negative	BNN	46	- - - - -	- 13 - -	
Branch Overflow	BV	46	- - - - -	- 14 - -	
Branch Exponent Overflow°	BXV	46	- - - - -	- 15 - -	
Branch No Indicator	BNI	47	- - - - -		- - - - -	
Branch Console Switch 1 Not On	BNC1	47	- - - - -	- 01 - -	
Branch Console Switch 2 Not On	BNC2	47	- - - - -	- 02 - -	
Branch Console Switch 3 Not On	BNC3	47	- - - - -	- 03 - -	
Branch Console Switch 4 Not On	BNC4	47	- - - - -	- 04 - -	
Branch Not Last Card	BNLC	47	- - - - -	- 09 - -	
Branch Not High	BNH	47	- - - - -	- 11 - -	
Branch Not Positive	BNP	47	- - - - -	- 11 - -	
Branch Not Equal	BNE	47	- - - - -	- 12 - -	
Branch Not Zero	BNZ	47	- - - - -	- 12 - -	
Branch Low	BL	47	- - - - -	- 13 - -	
Branch Negative	BN	47	- - - - -	- 13 - -	
Branch No Overflow	BNV	47	- - - - -	- 14 - -	
Branch No Exponent Overflow°	BNXV	47	- - - - -	- 15 - -	

Table 10.1 *(continued)*

Operation	Unique Mnemonic	Portion of Instruction Generated		
Input-Output				
Read Numerically	RN	36	- - - - -	- - - - -
Read Numerically from Typewriter	RNTY	36	- - - - -	-01- -
Read Numerically from Paper Tape Reader	RNPT	36	- - - - -	-03- -
Read Numerically from Card Reader	RNCD	36	- - - - -	-05- -
Write Numerically	WN	38	- - - - -	- - - - -
Write Numerically onto Typewriter	WNTY	38	- - - - -	-01- -
Write Numerically onto Paper Tape Punch	WNPT	38	- - - - -	-02- -
Write Numerically onto Card Punch	WNCD	38	- - - - -	-04- -
Dump Numerically	DN	35	- - - - -	- - - - -
Dump Numerically onto Typewriter	DNTY	35	- - - - -	-01- -
Dump Numerically onto Paper Tape Punch	DNPT	35	- - - - -	-02- -
Dump Numerically onto Card Punch	DNCD	35	- - - - -	-04- -
Read Alphamerically	RA	37	- - - - -	- - - - -
Read Alphamerically from Typewriter	RATY	37	- - - - -	-01- -
Read Alphamerically from Paper Tape Reader	RAPT	37	- - - - -	-03- -
Read Alphamerically from Card Reader	RACD	37	- - - - -	-05- -
Write Alphamerically	WA	39	- - - - -	- - - - -
Write Alphamerically onto Typewriter	WATY	39	- - - - -	-01- -
Write Alphamerically onto Paper Tape Punch	WAPT	39	- - - - -	-02- -
Write Alphamerically onto Card Punch	WACD	39	- - - - -	-04- -
Miscellaneous				
Control	K	34	- - - - -	- - - - -
Return Carriage on Typewriter	RCTY	34	- - - - -	-01-2
Tabulate Typewriter	TBTY	34	- - - - -	-01-8
Space Typewriter	SPTY	34	- - - - -	-01-1
Set Flag	SF	32	- - - - -	- - - - -
Clear Flag	CF	33	- - - - -	- - - - -
Halt	H	48	- - - - -	- - - - -
No Operation	NOP	41	- - - - -	- - - - -

* Items marked by an asterisk have not yet been discussed.

With such a translator, a card-to-card duplication program might look like this:

Location	Instruction	
00500	RNCD	10000
00512	WNCD	10000
00524	B	00500

A card-to-tape duplication program could be written as follows:

Location	Instruction		
00500	TDM	10080	0000‡
00512	RNCD	10000	
00524	WNPT	10000	
00536	B	00512	

A card-to-tape or card-to-card duplication program under control of console switch 1 would be as follows:

Location	Instruction		
00500	BC1	00560	
00512	TDM	10080	0000‡
00524	RNCD	10000	
00536	WNPT	10000	
00548	B	00524	
00560	RNCD	10000	
00572	WNCD	10000	
00584	B	00560	

Here is an alternate and shorter program for the same problem:

Location	Instruction		
00500	TDM	10080	0000‡
00512	RNCD	10000	
00524	BC1	00560	
00536	WNPT	10000	
00548	B	00512	
00560	WNCD	10000	
00572	B	00512	

However, even this type of programming is somewhat cumbersome. There is still too much detail in that absolute addresses are necessary and we must constantly keep track of instruction locations. After all, it might be necessary to reference an instruction through a branching operation.

The concept of a dictionary of machine operations alone is necessary but not sufficient. This dictionary is machine oriented and does not change from problem to problem. We would like to introduce the concept of a second dictionary, whose word makeup would be dictated by the programmer. Of course, the processor needs information about the symbols that will lie in this new dictionary.

Consider the first program given above (card-to-card duplication):

LOCATION	INSTRUCTION
00500	RNCD 10000
00512	WNCD 10000
00524	B 00500

If we give this same program to a symbolic processor and precede it with sentences of explanatory nature, it could appear as follows:

Information Sentence 1: This program begins at location 00500.

Information Sentence 2: The symbolic word "Input" is synonymous with core location 10000.

Information Sentence 3: There is no more information of explanatory nature. The source program follows.

```
RNCD   INPUT
WNCD   INPUT
B         00500
```

If we add another sentence of explanatory nature, we can symbolize the entire program:

Information Sentence 1: This program begins at location 00500.

Information Sentence 2: The symbolic word "Input" is synonymous with core location 10000.

Information Sentence 3: The symbolic word "Begin" is synonymous with core location 00500.

Information Sentence 4: There is no more information of explanatory nature. The source program follows.

```
RNCD   INPUT
WNCD   INPUT
B         BEGIN
```

Our information sentences cause the second dictionary to be built up. The first word in this new dictionary can be called the "origin counter" and it has its initial value given by the first information sentence. In our case it is 00500. For each instruction proper, this origin counter is incremented by 12. In this fashion, reference to our origin counter always yields the location of the instruction presently being processed.

Directly below our first entry in the new dictionary, we now place the symbol "Input" and, contiguous to it, a 5-digit field, 10000. Any reference to the symbolic name "Input" would generate the associated absolute location. The third word in our dictionary, "Begin," has the address 00500 placed contiguous to it. Similarly, any reference to the symbol "Begin" causes a substitution of the address 00500.

Some thoughts that come to mind are the following: why was position 10000 chosen as our input area and why did our program begin at location 00500? Why were the names "Input" and "Begin" chosen rather than "Data" and "Start" perhaps? The only valid answers to these questions are (1) personal whim and (2) mnemonic content. The program might have been written as follows:

Information Sentence 1: This program begins at location 12346.

Information Sentence 2: The symbolic word "Zxpflq" is synonymous with core location 00825.

Information Sentence 3: The symbolic word "Pfwxyn" is synonymous with core location 12346.

Information Sentence 4: There is no more information of explanatory nature. The Source program follows:

```
RNCD   ZXPFLQ
WNCD   ZXPFLQ
B      PFWXYN
```

The resultant object program would be:

LOCATION	INSTRUCTION
12346	36 00825 00500
12358	38 00825 00400
12370	49 12346 00000

The disadvantage of this program is the impossibly bad choice of symbolic names. The word "ZXPFLQ" conjures up very little connotation of an input area of core memory. Nonetheless, the program is perfectly translatable by the processor. Its dictionary is unique and there are no contradictions in the command structure of the source program.

However, we have not even begun to exercise the true abilities of our machine dictionary concept. Consider the following program:

Information Sentence 1: Begin this program at the first available location after the addition and multiplication tables.

Information Sentence 2: A symbol "Input" will be used. It is 80 positions long.

Information Sentence 3: A symbol "Begin" will be used. It is synonymous with the location chosen for the first instruction of the source program.

Information Sentence 4: There is no more information of explanatory nature. The source program follows.

```
RNCD   INPUT
WNCD   INPUT
B      BEGIN
```

The generated program would be as follows:

LOCATION	INSTRUCTION
00480	36 00400 00500
00492	38 00400 00400
00504	49 00480 00000

The first information sentence stated that our origin counter was to begin at 00400. (The addition and multiplication tables occupy positions 00100–00399.) The next piece of information in the source program caused the word "Input" to be placed in the dictionary, associated the origin counter address with the symbol, and incremented the origin counter by the length of the defined symbol, 80 positions. The third sentence placed the symbol "Begin" in the dictionary and the origin counter address of 00480 was placed contiguous to it as the fourth information sentence was encountered.

Carrying this logic a little further, we can decide to build a rule of the following nature into the processor:

If an instruction bears a symbolic name, the origin counter, at that point, will be chosen as the synonymous core location to be associated with that name.

Thus, our source program looks like this:

Information Sentence 1: Begin this program at the first available location after the addition and multiplication tables.

Information Sentence 2: A symbol Input will be used. It is 80 positions long.

Information Sentence 3: There is no more information of explanatory nature. The source program follows.

```
RNCD    INPUT; THE NAME OF THIS
                STATEMENT IS "BEGIN."
WNCD    INPUT
B       BEGIN
```

The resultant object program generated is as follows:

LOCATION	INSTRUCTION
00480	36 00400 00500
00492	38 00400 00400
00504	49 00480 00000

If it were necessary to write all of these cumbersome directions, it might not be worth the trouble. After all, the computer does not need such an aggregation of verbs and nouns to tell it what to do. It merely desires the facts in as concise a form as possible. Let us rewrite again:

```
ORIGIN:400
INPUT:SYMBOL:80
BEGIN:RNCD:INPUT
      WNCD:INPUT
   B     :BEGIN
END OF PROGRAM
```

Now this is more like it. Just the facts without the frills have told the processor where to start, where to stop and also that the symbols "Input" and "Begin" have been defined.

Everything becomes grist for the processor's mill. But since *we* must be able to differentiate between concepts, let us call instructions to the processor *declaratives*. All else are machine *instructions* in symbolic form desirous of translation.

In our last example, only one instruction (RNCD:Input) has an identifying name (Begin). This "label" went into the dictionary and the instruction received no special treatment beyond that. Of course, the processor is quite fair; it treats all input in an equal fashion *up to a point*. At first glance, it had no idea that the statement "Origin: 400" was a declarative and not a symbolic instruction. It took a good deal of complex logic and detailed investigation by the processor to determine that this input statement belongs to the declarative category. The second statement (Input:Symbol:80) is also recognized to be declarative in nature. Certain clues, the presence of the word "Symbol" for instance, cause this statement to be treated in a different fashion than "Origin: 400."

A processor, then, is a program that has the ability to read information and classify it into two categories:

1. Directions to itself, of which there are a wide variety.
2. Symbolic instructions that are to be translated according to the general rules of the processor and the specific instructions of this translation.

The process of translation is termed *assembling* a program. The translator is called an *Assembly System*. The assembly system for the 1620 is called the *Symbolic Programming System* and bears the shortened title "SPS."

Once an individual has learned the rules of writing in SPS language, program construction, which is challenging to begin with, can be quite enjoyable. These rules make difficult taskmasters, however. The assembly system cannot be told approximately what to do. It must be given exact, noncontradictory, properly ordered, carefully chosen statements. The next chapter gives the rules for the 1620 symbolic system. Although they are unique for this particular system, the concept of symbolic programming extends to almost all digital computers. Some systems, unique to other computers, bear rather amusing acronyms: SOAP (Symbolic Optimal Assembly Program), SAP (Symbolic Assembly System), and SOS (Share Operating System).

The construction of such a system often occupies many man-years. The 1620's SPS took approximately four man-years to complete.

Chapter 11

The Symbolic
Programming System

In the previous chapter, a pseudo-symbolic system was introduced to give the student an initial glance at a processor that manipulates symbols. We now come to a comprehensive analysis of the actual system with its myriad rules.

All information relevant to coding and subsequent assembly is entered on an SPS coding sheet as seen in Figure 11.1. The information required to process a program falls into two main categories:

1. *Instructions*—Source statements in the symbolic language that specify the job to be done by the object program. These entries will be translated into the object program.

2. *Declaratives*—The actual equivalents of Information Sentences discussed in the previous chapter. There are three categories of declaratives:

   (a) Area Definitions—These statements assign core storage for input, output, and working areas. Area definition statements are *never* executed in the *object* program.

   (b) Constant Definitions—These statements allow one to define constants needed in the execution of the object program. The constants become part of the object program, but the statements themselves are not executed at the object level.

   (c) Processor control operations—These statements allow programmer control over portions of the assembly. As in the case of area and constant definitions, these statements are never executed in the object program.

USE OF THE CODING SHEET

The identifying information at the top of the coding sheet ("Program," "Programmed By," and "Date") is not part of the source program and

IBM

1620 Symbolic Programming System
Coding Sheet

Program ——————

Programmed by ——————

Date ——————

Page No. [ ] of ——

LINE	LABEL	OPERATION	OPERANDS & REMARKS
0,1,0			
0,2,0			
0,3,0			
0,4,0			
0,5,0			
0,6,0			
0,7,0			
0,8,0			
0,9,0			
1,0,0			
1,1,0			
1,2,0			
1,3,0			
1,4,0			
1,5,0			
1,6,0			
1,7,0			
1,8,0			
1,9,0			
2,0,0			

Fig. 11.1 Sample of a 1620 SPS Coding Sheet.

is not punched in the source tape or card deck.[1] It is used to prevent mix-up of programs while the coding is in the source document.

PAGE NUMBER

The 2-character page number will be punched as the first characters of each source statement. Although there are no "columns" in a paper tape, we will be able to identify position if we call the first punching location "column 1." The page number (00–99) is punched in columns 1 and 2 of the card and tape systems. Their function is to sequence the coding sheets and also to allow for sorting cards in the event that they are out of order. (Card dropping is a hazard of the profession.) The processor does not check for sequential or multiple page numbering. This is the programmer's responsibility.

LINE NUMBER

The 3-character line number is punched contiguous to the page number in columns 3–5 of both card and tape systems. Its function is to sequence the statements on each coding sheet.

The first 20 lines are prenumbered 010–200. The six unnumbered lines at the bottom of the page are provided for the entry of statements inadvertently omitted and/or for sheet extension. If a statement is omitted and added at a later time, its line number should fall between those statements where the correction is to be inserted. It will be noted that provision has been made for up to nine such insertions. If more are required, it is possible to give a multiplicity of statements the same line number. However, this partially defeats the purpose of having the line number. Insertions of the type discussed must be placed in their proper sequence when a source program is being assembled since assembly is a serial process and sequence of line numbers is not checked. Thus, a statement out of order will be assembled out of order.

LABEL

The 6-character label is a symbolic name chosen by the programmer and is punched in columns 6–11 in both card and tape systems. It is not necessary to utilize all six positions of the label field. A label is usually associated with an area being defined or an instruction referred to elsewhere in the program. All labels are assigned addresses in storage during

---

[1] The physical preparation of tape and/or cards is referred to throughout this and subsequent chapters as *punching*. There is a variety of devices used for preparation of source program information.

the assembly. A reference to a label in the program is a reference to the *address* of the area or instruction which bears that label. Although any statement may be labeled, unnecessary labels delay the process of assembly. Consequently, only those items specifically referred to elsewhere in the program should be labeled. Instructions and declaratives that are unlabeled should contain blanks in columns 6–11.

LABEL RULES

1. A label may contain from 1 to 6 alphanumeric characters at least one of which must be alphabetic or one of the special characters:

> Equal sign (=)
> Period (.)
> Solidus (/)
> Commercial at (@)

2. Unused portions of a label are left blank.
3. Blanks are not permitted *within* a label.
4. All labels begin in column 6.

The number of labels permitted in the symbol table is a function of the core available and the size of the labels employed. In a 20,000-core-position 1620, approximately 170 6-character labels are permitted.

It is wise to choose labels that have high mnemonic values. Labels that have obvious meanings provide easily remembered references for the programmer and also assist others who may assume responsibility for the program. The following demonstrates a few valid labels:

DATA	A21456	TEMP1
INPUT	Z12345	TEMP2
OUTPUT	PPPPP	CON
X23BFG	GGGG	12A
GO	INAREA	A=B
START	DATAIN	X@C1
BEGIN	SYMBOL	9.23/X

OPERATION

The 4-digit operation field contains the mnemonic representation of (1) machine language operation codes, (2) declaratives, and (3) macro-instructions (to be discussed in Chapter 13). Punching in the operation field is in columns 12–15 of both card and tape systems.

A complete list of mnemonic machine language operation codes may be found in Table 10.1. Actual 1620 machine codes in their numeric form are also permitted but, in this case, checking by the processor is not performed to determine if the numeric OP code is valid.

OPERANDS AND REMARKS FOR INSTRUCTIONS

If the input to the processor is an instruction rather than a declarative, the operands and remarks section may contain, *at most,* 4 items separated by commas. The entire statement must be terminated by an E/L character in the paper tape system. This restriction is not applicable in the card system, but the presence of the record mark (0–2–8) as the last element of a statement will not affect the processing. Missing operands are noted by using commas in their place.

Three of the four permitted items are operands and the fourth item, if present, is a comment which has no effect on the assembly. Such remarks, if present, are printed during a listing of the assembled program. The purpose of these comments is to enable one to identify the effect of certain instructions. It is quite easy to forget why one put this or that instruction in the program in the first place. Such comments and remarks can be quite useful if one returns to a program after a prolonged period of inactivity. The first three items are referred to respectively as the P, Q, and Flag operands.

1. *P Operand*—This portion may be either a symbolic, absolute, or asterisk address [2] and will assemble as the P portion of the object level instruction.
2. *Q Operand*—This portion may be either a symbolic, absolute, or asterisk address and will assemble as the Q portion of the object level instruction.
3. *Flag Operand*—This item is always numeric and is used to set flags in the assembled instruction.

Any instruction may have 0, 1, 2, 3, or 4 items in the "operands and remarks" portion of the coding sheet. These are punched in columns 16–75 in both the card and tape systems. In the card system, columns 76–80 are not utilized and may contain identifying information if it is so desired.

OPERANDS AND REMARKS FOR DECLARATIVES

The number of items in a declarative field is variable depending upon the declarative chosen. Each declarative will be discussed separately. Punching of declarative operands and remarks occupies columns 16–75, as do punching of instruction operands and remarks.

DISCUSSION OF OPERANDS

P AND Q OPERANDS

The operands that will be assembled as the P and Q portion of an

_____

[2] See pages 105 and 106 for a discussion of symbolic, absolute, and asterisk addresses.

instruction are of three types: actual (synonymously termed absolute), symbolic, and asterisk.

ACTUAL

An actual address consists of five or fewer digits and is the actual 1620 core storage address of a piece of data or an instruction. High-order zeros of an actual address may be eliminated. See Figure 11.2 for an example of instructions where both P and Q addresses are absolute.

LINE	LABEL	OPERATION	OPERANDS & REMARKS			
0 1 0		A	1,2,3,4,5, ,1,7,5,6,2,			
0 2 0						
0 3 0		M	5,3,2, ,0,1,2,1,7			
0 4 0						
0 5 0		T,F,	1,5,0,0,0, ,9,9			
0 6 0						
0 7 0		H,				
0 8 0						
0 9 0		T,D,M	1,9,9,9,9, ,5			
1 0 0						

Fig. 11.2.   Sample of Absolute Addressing.

Figure 11.2—Commentary

Assume the location counter is at position 10000 when we encounter these source statements. If this is the case, the following five instructions will be generated:

$$
\begin{array}{lll}
(10000) & 21 & 12345 & 17562 \\
(10012) & 23 & 00532 & 01217 \\
(10024) & 26 & 15000 & 00099 \\
(10036) & 48 & 00000 & 00000 \\
(10048) & 15 & 19999 & 00005
\end{array}
$$

The above program has no purpose other than demonstration of actual address assignment.

Note that the processor fills in high-order positions of P and Q addresses with zeros if less than 5 digits should be present. Some programmers enjoy the uniformity of always utilizing 5-digit fields whether or not they are required.

SYMBOLIC

The symbolic address is a name or label assigned by the programmer to a piece of data or an instruction. Such a symbolic address is valid if and only if it appears somewhere in the source program in the Label field. Either one or both of the P and Q operands may be symbolic. See Figure 11.3 for an example of symbolic addresses.

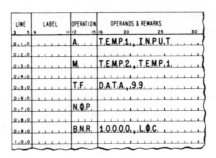

Fig. 11.3. Symbolic Addressing.

Figure 11.3—Commentary

Assume the following core locations for all elements used in symbolic form:

$$
\begin{array}{ll}
\text{TEMP1} & (404) \\
\text{TEMP2} & (410) \\
\text{DATA} & (420) \\
\text{INPUT} & (455) \\
\text{LOC} & (512)
\end{array}
$$

Also, assume that the location counter stands at 800 when these instructions are encountered by the processor. The following instructions are generated:

$$
\begin{array}{lll}
(00800) & 21 \ 00404 \ 00455 \\
(00812) & 23 \ 00410 \ 00404 \\
(00824) & 26 \ 00420 \ 00099 \\
(00836) & 41 \ 00000 \ 00000 \\
(00848) & 45 \ 10000 \ 00512
\end{array}
$$

Note that an instruction may have mixed symbolic and actual P and/or Q operands. This is exhibited by the "TF DATA,99" and "BNR 10000,LOC" instructions. It is customary to differentiate the alphabetic "O" from the numeric zero. Note that the letter "Ø" is slashed and the number zero is not.

Of course, this example assumes that at some point in the program all symbols employed were properly defined by appearing in a label field of an instruction or declarative.

ASTERISK

The character, asterisk (★), when used as an operand in the P and/or Q portions of an instruction, makes reference to the present value of the location counter. (The location counter is the true correspondent to the origin counter discussed in the previous chapter.) This is equivalent to the address of the 0_0 (high-order—left-hand) position of the instruction which contains the asterisk. See Figure 11.4 for an example of asterisk addresses. **The asterisk rule is somewhat different in the case of a declarative. Be sure to note it.**

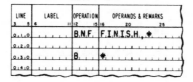

Fig. 11.4.   Asterisk Addressing.

Figure 11.4–Commentary

Assume that location "Finish" is synonymous with core location 15000 and that the location counter stands at 900 when these instructions are encountered by the assembly system. The following instructions are therefore generated:

$$(00900) \quad 44 \ 15000 \ 00900$$
$$(00912) \quad 49 \ 00912 \ 00000$$

The latter instruction is a classic example of how *not* to use a computer. A never-ending branch has been developed with no way out.

FLAG OPERANDS

A flag is placed in those positions of the assembled instruction specified by the flag operand. In the event that an instruction is of the Immediate type, a flag is automatically placed over the Q_7 digit of the assembled instruction. However, the presence of the flag operand takes precedence. Thus, a flag operand of 8 causes a flag to be set in Q_8 and not in Q_7.

If more than one flag is desired in an assembled instruction, the flag operand must indicate all positions to be flagged. Thus, if a flag is desired in Q_7 and Q_{11}, the flag operand reads "711." The order of elements in the flag operand is quite critical here. If one wishes a flag at position O_0 and O_1, the flag operand is written as "01" and not as "10." This latter configuration would cause a flag to be placed at position Q_{10}. If one desires every digit of an assembled instruction to be flagged, the flag operand would read "01234567891011."

There is one exception to the rule governing the use of an Immediate instruction without a flag operand: the instruction Transmit Digit Immediate will assemble with no flag placed on the assembled instruction unless specifically told otherwise through the use of the flag operand. See Figure 11.5 for examples of the flag operand in use.

Any instruction may have a flag operand but its use is most effective in the Immediate type.

The Symbolic Programming System

LINE	LABEL	OPERATION	OPERANDS & REMARKS
0.1.0		A.M.	D.A.T.A.,,1.2.0.5.7.
0.2.0			
0.3.0		A.M.	D.A.T.A.,,1.2.0.5.7.,,7
0.4.0			
0.5.0		A.M.	D.A.T.A.,,1.2.0.5.7.,,1.0.
0.6.0			
0.7.0		S.M.	I.N.F.O.,,1.0.0.,,9.
0.8.0			
0.9.0		T.D.M.	D.A.T.A.,,2.
1.0.0			
1.1.0		T.D.M.	D.A.T.A.,,2.,,1.1
1.2.0			
1.3.0		T.F.M.	C.O.U.N.T.,,1.5.7.,,8.
1.4.0			
1.5.0		B.	T.H.E.R.E.,,,2.
1.6.0			
1.7.0		N.O.P.	,,,0.1.2.3.4.5.6.7.8.9.1.0.1.1.
1.8.0			
1.9.0		H.	,,,,P.R.O.G.R.A.M. I.S. C.O.M.P.L.E.T.E.
2.0.0			

Fig. 11.5. Samples of Instructions with Flag Operands.

Figure 11.5—Commentary

Assume the following core locations for all elements used in symbolic form:

DATA   (12027)
INFO   (17956)
COUNT   (406)
THERE   (2000)

The location counter stands at 512 when these instructions are encountered by the processor. The following instructions are generated:

11 12027 $\bar{1}$2057
11 12027 $\bar{1}$2057
11 12027 120$\bar{5}$7
12 17956 00$\bar{1}$00
15 12027 00002
15 12027 0000$\bar{2}$
16 00406 0$\bar{0}$157
49 $\bar{0}$2000 00000
$\bar{4}\bar{1}$ $\overline{00000}$ $\overline{00000}$
48 00000 00000

Note the three commas of the last instruction to denote the three missing operands before the remarks operand which is present. Also observe that the presence of the remark did not affect the assembly or generate any coding.

ADDRESS ARITHMETIC

Any P and/or Q address, symbolic, asterisk, or actual, may be incremented (+), decremented (−), or multiplied (⋆) by a numeric constant or a symbol representing a numeric quantity.[3] By utilizing a variety of address arithmetic, any P and/or Q address may assume any variation of the following form:

$$A \overset{\star}{\pm} B \overset{\star}{\pm} C \overset{\star}{\pm} D \overset{\star}{\pm} \ldots$$

where A, B, C, and D are numeric, asterisk, or symbolic, and multiplication is of prime order.

Symbolic instructions of the form:

```
RNCD     INPUT−79
B        START+24
TF       LOC⋆16,DATA+5⋆L−CONST
AM       ⋆+23,5,10
```

are permissible.

Figure 11.6 contains extensive examples of address arithmetic.

Symbols Used In Operands	Equivalent
ALPHA	1000
START	4000
L	12
ORIGIN	600
OUTPUT	15000

P or Q Operands	Equivalent After Assembly
START + 40,	04040
ALPHA - 30,	00970
START + 2 * L,	04024
START * 3,	12000
ALPHA * 5 + 40,	05040
4 * 13 + OUTPUT,	15052
START + 4 * L - 1,	04047
ALPHA * L,	12000
500 + 20 * 3 - 11,	00549
OUTPUT - L * ALPHA + ORIGIN	03600

Fig. 11.6.   Samples of Address Arithmetic.

[3] Note this alternate function of the asterisk symbol. In all, there are four separate and distinct uses for asterisk of which two have been discussed: (1) an instruction operand and (2) a symbol implying multiplication.

DECLARATIVES—CARD AND TAPE SYSTEM

Declaratives, as defined previously, are instructions to the processor for control of a specific assembly. The variety of declaratives may be initially confusing but the student is not expected to learn them all simultaneously. As each declarative is introduced, a variety of examples will be given. Close study of these should give an excellent understanding of their function.

The use of the asterisk (★) in a declarative operand has a slightly different meaning than it has when used as an instruction operand (see page 106). It is with this third use of the asterisk symbol that the discussion of declaratives begins.

ASTERISK RULE FOR DECLARATIVE OPERANDS

The character asterisk (★), when used as an operand of a declarative, makes reference to the low-order digit of the last field whose address was assigned by the processor. This last field may have been the result of a declarative statement or an instruction.

DORG (DEFINE ORIGIN)

The code DORG is used to initiate address assignment in that it initializes the orgin counter to a specified address. It is the true equivalent of Information Sentence 1 of Chapter 10. The rules of the DORG follow.

1. The operation code DORG appears in columns 12–15 of the operation field.
2. The address at which assignment is to begin is specified as the first operand. This operand may be actual, symbolic, or asterisk. If symbolic, the symbol must have been previously encountered in the source program.[4]
3. A DORG may be used at any point in the source program.
4. The first instruction or declarative entry after a DORG will begin its location in core at the address specified by the DORG's operand. Subsequent entries will be assigned subsequent addresses.
5. If no DORG is encountered as the first statement of a source program, the processor begins the assembly at location 00402.
6. The lowest location that should be chosen for a DORG is 00402.
7. The maximum number of operands that may be used with a DORG is two. The second operand, if present, is a comment and does not affect the processing.

See Figure 11.7 for examples of the DORG statement properly written.

---

[4] Any declarative operand that is permitted an actual, symbolic, or asterisk address is also permitted address arithmetic in that operand.

LINE	LABEL	OPERATION	OPERANDS & REMARKS						
3 5	6	11 12 15	16 20 25	30	35	40	45	50	
0,1,0		D,O,R,G	1,5,0,0,0,						
0,2,0									
0,3,0		D,O,R,G	1,0,5,2,8,						
0,4,0									
0,5,0		D,O,R,G	4,1,7,						
0,6,0									
0,7,0		D,O,R,G	S,Y,M,B,O,L,+,2,2,						
0,8,0									
0,9,0		D,O,R,G	D,A,T,A,-,5,2,7,						
1,0,0									
1,1,0		D,O,R,G	*,-,3,						
1,2,0									
1,3,0		D,O,R,G	4,0,2,.,N,O D,O,R,G S,H,O,U,L,D B,E,G,I,N B,E,L,O,W 4,0,2,						
1,4,0									

Fig. 11.7. Examples of the DORG Declarative.

DEND (DEFINE END)

The code DEND is used to inform the processor that it has processed all of the source statements. The last statement of a source program must be DEND. The rules of the DEND follow.

1. The operation code DEND appears in columns 12–15 of the operation field.
2. The address at which the object program is to begin execution may be stated as the first operand. The object program will then contain an automatic Branch to this instruction after loading and halting. This automatic Branch is obtained by depressing the Start key. The address specified as the first operand may be symbolic, actual, or asterisk. If symbolic, the symbol must have been previously encountered in the source program.
3. A DEND may not be labeled.
4. The maximum number of operands with a DEND is two. The second operand, if present, is a comment and does not affect the processing.

See Figure 11.8 for examples of the DEND statement properly written.

LINE	LABEL	OPERATION	OPERANDS & REMARKS				
3 5	6	11 12 15	16 20 25	30	35	40	
0,1,0		D,E,N,D					
0,2,0							
0,3,0		D,E,N,D	B,E,G,I,N,				
0,4,0							
0,5,0		D,E,N,D	S,T,A,R,T,+,2,4,				
0,6,0							
0,7,0		D,E,N,D	4,0,2,.,B,E,G,I,N P,R,O,G,R,A,M A,T 4,0,2,				
0,8,0							

Fig. 11.8. Examples of the DEND Declarative.

DS (DEFINE SYMBOL)

The code DS may be used to define a contiguous area of core storage that will contain numeric data. An alternate function is to generate synonymity between symbols or between symbols and addresses. The rules of the DS follow.

1. The operation code DS appears in columns 12–13 of the operation field.
2. The label by which this field may be referenced appears in columns 6–11. The label refers to the units (low-order) position of the field.[5]
3. The length of the field appears as the first operand. The length operand may be actual, symbolic, or asterisk. If symbolic, the symbol must have been previously encountered in the source program.
4. If a second operand is present, the processor assumes a synonymous relationship between the label and this second operand. This operand allows the programmer to assign the address of a symbol. The presence of the synonymity operand *does not* affect the sequence of of addresses assigned by the processor. The location counter remains unchanged regardless of the size of the first operand. The synonymity operand may be actual, symbolic, or asterisk. If symbolic, it must have been previously encountered in the source program.
5. The maximum number of operands in a DS is three. The third operand, if present, is a comment and does not affect the processing.
6. Omission of the label in a DS reserves storage which will not be referred to symbolically.

See Figure 11.9 for examples of the DS statement properly written.

To demonstrate the variety of uses for the DS statement, a sample program will be repeated with variations in the programming. Commentary will be presented with each example. Both the source program and object program are displayed. Only the first example will be shown

LINE	LABEL	OPERATION	OPERANDS & REMARKS					
0.1.0	L.A.B.E.L.	D.S.	1.0					
0.2.0								
0.3.0	K.O.N.	D.S.	1.5.					
0.4.0								
0.5.0	T.E.M.P.1.	D.S.	,L.A.B.E.L.-.7.					
0.6.0								
0.7.0	M.A.T.R.I.X	D.S.	1.0.,.,T.H.I.S. .I.S. .T.H.E. .F.I.R.S.T. .E.L.E.M.E.N.T..					
0.8.0								
0.9.0		D.S.	4.9.0.,.,R.O.O.M. .F.O.R. .4.9. .M.O.R.E. .E.L.E.M.E.N.T.S.					
1.0.0								
1.1.0	A.R.E.A.	D.S.	,.1.5.0.0.0.,.C.O.M.M.E.N.T.S. .A.N.D. .R.E.M.A.R.K.S.					
1.2.0								

Fig. 11.9. Examples of the DS Declarative.

[5] A label does not refer to an entire field. It refers to a single core position.

on a coding sheet while all others demonstrate the actual 1620 type-writer output listing: source statements on the left, assembled statements on the right.

The details of assembling a program will be discussed at a later point. It is sufficient to say that the processor must read the source program twice.

The first pass of the source program builds up a dictionary of labels, assigns storage locations, and yields certain error messages. During the second pass, the source data is re-entered and the following takes place:

1. Operation codes are changed from symbolic to actual.
2. Operands are processed by dictionary look-up and address arithmetic is performed where necessary.
3. The assembled instructions (object program) are punched on cards or tape.

In addition, a variety of error messages may appear during either pass designating certain error conditions.

The object program for both card and tape systems contains loading instructions which appear at the beginning of the tape or card deck and the arithmetic tables which appear at the end.

Thus, a single tape or card deck, consisting of loader, object program, constants, arithmetic tables, and so forth, is provided by the processor. An optional listing of the source program versus the assembled program may also be obtained. It is this listing that is given for each demonstration program.

Problem

Generate a program to reproduce a deck of punched, 80-column cards. The program is to run until the card reader is empty, at which point the program will stop for lack of cards. The cards contain no alphabetic information and all 80 columns are punched with numeric data. There are no blank columns in the cards.

LINE	LABEL	OPERATION	OPERANDS & REMARKS
0,1,0		D,Ø,R,G	4,0,2,
0,2,0	I,N,P,U,T,	D,S,	8,0,
0,3,0	B,E,G,I,N,	R,N,C,D	I,N,P,U,T,-,7,9
0,4,0		W,N,C,D	I,N,P,U,T,-,7,9,
0,5,0		B,	B,E,G,I,N,
0,6,0		D,E,N,D	
0,7,0			

Example 1A

01010	DORG	402	00402		
01020INPUT	DS	80	00481	00080	
01030BEGIN	RNCD	INPUT-79	00482	36 00402	00500
01040	WNCD	INPUT-79	00494	38 00402	00400
01050	B	BEGIN	00506	49 00482	00000
01060	DEND		00000		

Example 1B

Example 1—Commentary

A total of 80 positions is needed for an input area. Consequently the symbol "Input" is designed to be 80 positions long. Since I/0 commands reference the high-order position of data, the I/0 P-operand references not "Input" (the address of the low order position) but "Input-79" (the address of the high-order position. This disconcerting bit of arithmetic may be justified by asking yourself how many numbers lie between 0 and 5, *inclusive*. The answer is, of course, 6. Similarly, there are 80 positions between Input and Input-79:

$$INPUT - [INPUT - 79] + 1.$$

The processor, having been told to begin its assembly at location 00402 by the DORG statement, generates an address of 00481 for the units position of the symbol "Input." The processor assigns addresses as it encounters information. Hence, the instruction labeled "Begin" starts at 00482. Synonymous with location 00482 is the label name "Begin." When this label is used as an operand, as in the case of "B Begin," the corresponding core location is substituted.

The DEND statement completes processing of both passes. The listing shown above is the output of the second pass of the source program.

01010	DORG	402	00402		
01020BEGIN	RNCD	INPUT-79	00402	36 00438	00500
01030	WNCD	INPUT-79	00414	38 00438	00400
01040	B	BEGIN	00426	49 00402	00000
01050INPUT	DS	80	00517	00080	
01060	DEND		00000		

Example 2

Example 2—Commentary

This example differs only slightly from Example 1. In this case the definition of "Input" was made after the symbolic instructions. The object program thus produced will accomplish the same task but the addresses, of course, are entirely changed. This is because the location counter came across the statements in a different order.

01010	DORG 10000	10000			
01020GPXPL	RNCD BPFZQX-79	10000	36	10036	00500
01030	WNCD BPFZQX-79	10012	38	10036	00400
01040	B GPXPL	10024	49	10000	00000
01050BPFZQX	DS 80	10115	00080		
01060	DEND	00000			

Example 3

Example 3—Commentary

In this case the DORG instruction specifies 10000.

This problem is given to demonstrate the fact that the choice of symbolic names does not affect the processing. It does make the logic more difficult to follow.

01010	DORG 403	00403			
01020GO	RNCD DATA-79	00404	36	00440	00500
01030	WNCD DATA-79	00416	38	00440	00400
01040	B GO	00428	49	00404	00000
01050DATA	DS 80	00519	00080		
01060	DEND	00000			

Example 4

Example 4—Commentary

Notice that the DORG requested an initial address of 403. The processor will not allow instructions to begin at odd locations. Thus, the location counter was incremented by 1 before processing the instruction labeled "Go."

01010	DORG 500	00500			
01020START	RNCD INPUT-79	00500	36	00512	00500
01030INPUT	DS 80	00591	00080		
01040	WNCD INPUT-79	00592	38	00512	00400
01050	B START	00604	49	00500	00000
01060	DEND	00000			

Example 5

Example 5—Commentary

The processor has no way to determine that a major programming rule has been violated in this problem.

After assembly, an attempt to run this program will result in the reading of just one card. This is due to the fact that the 1620 will attempt execution of the instruction in location 512 after execution of the instruction in 500. Unfortunately, there is no instruction in location 512.

The problem was introduced by defining the symbol between two instructions which should be contiguous at the object level. This is not an error in the processor since this type of programming is often desirable. In this case, however, all we have is an unworkable program.

01010	DORG 402		00402			
01020BEGIN	RNCD	INPUT-79	ER 5			
			00402	36	00000	00500
01030	WNCD	INPUT-79	ER 5			
			00414	38	00000	00400
01040	B	BEGIN	00426	49	00402	00000
01050	DEND		00000			

Example 6

Example 6—Commentary

This program demonstrates what will occur should you forget to define a symbol after having used it as a P and/or Q operand. The ER 5 message states that an undefined symbol is present in the symbolic instruction to which it is attached. The resultant instruction has 00000 in that operand which contained the undefined symbol. A complete list of error conditions will be discussed at the conclusion of this chapter.

01010	DORG 402		00402			
01020	RNCD	INPUT-79	00402	36	00438	00500
01030	WNCD	INPUT-79	00414	38	00438	00400
01040	B	*-24	00426	49	00402	00000
010501NPUT	DS	80	00517	00080		
01060	DEND		00000			

Example 7

Example 7—Commentary

The first instruction of the program has no label. However, we must refer to it in order to be able to branch to it. Consequently, the asterisk form of address is employed. Each instruction is 12 digits long, which makes the P operand of the Branch instruction "★−24" since we wish to reference the second instruction before the Branch.

01010	DORG 520		00520			
01020FIRST	RNCD	INPUT	00520	36	00556	00500
01030	WNCD	INPUT	00532	38	00556	00400
01040	B	FIRST	00544	49	00520	00000
010501NPUT	DS	1	00556	00001		
01060	DS	79	00635	00079		
01070	DEND		00000			

Example 8

Example 8—Commentary

In this example, the Input declarative was changed. This necessitates a change in the I/0 statement. However, since all of core is at our disposal after position 556, is the unlabeled "DS 79" necessary?

01010	DORG	520	00520			
01020	FIRST	RNCD	INPUT	00520	36 00556	00500
01030		WNCD	INPUT	00532	38 00556	00400
01040		B	FIRST	00544	49 00520	00000
01050	INPUT	DS	1	00556	00001	
01070		DEND		00000		

Example 9

Example 9—Commentary

The question posed in Example 8 is answered here: the definition of 79 core positions contiguous to "Input" is not necessary in this case.

Can the same technique be employed if "Input" is defined as a 1-digit symbol before the instruction labeled "First"?

01010	DORG	402	00402			
01020	GO	RNCD	INPUT	00402	36 15000	00500
01030		WNCD	INPUT	00414	38 15000	00400
01040		B	GO	00426	49 00402	00000
01050	INPUT	DS	,15000	15000	00000	
01060		DEND	GO	00402		

Example 10

Example 10—Commentary

Notice that "Input" has been made synonymous with position 15000 of core storage. In truth, there is no need for this concept in this particular program, but it is presented to demonstrate how a symbol can be located in any desired location.

Note also the presence of an operand with the declarative DEND.

01010	DORG	402	00402			
01020	INPUT	DS	80	00481	00080	
01030	OUTPUT	DS	, INPUT-79	00402	00000	
01040	START	RNCD	INPUT-79	00482	36 00402	00500
01050		WNCD	OUTPUT	00494	38 00402	00400
01060		B	START	00506	49 00482	00000
01070		DEND	START	00482		

Example 11

Example 11—Commentary

Here is an example of synonymity between symbols. We may refer to "Input-79" or "Output" and achieve the same assembled address. The definition of the symbol "Input" must appear before definition of "Output" because of rule 4 of DS statements. However, may the definition of "Output" appear anywhere after the definition of "Input"?

01010		DORG	402	00402		
01020	INPUT	DS	80	00481	00080	
01030	GO	RNCD	INPUT-79	00482	36 00402	00500
01040	OUTPUT	DS	,INPUT-79	00402	00000	
01050		WNCD	OUTPUT	00494	38 00402	00400
01060		B	GO	00506	49 00482	00000
01070		DEND		00000		

Example 12

Example 12—Commentary

Since "Output" reserves no storage, does not affect the location counter, and is used to define a synonymous name for core position "Input-79," it may be placed anywhere after the definition of the symbol "Input" without adverse effects. This answers the question posed in Example 11. See Example 5 for a violation of this concept.

Example 13 demonstrates the following problem:

Problem

Generate a program to duplicate card-to-card or card-to-tape. If switch 1 is on, the second alternative is to be chosen. A record mark is available at location 400 if needed. All card data is numeric and all 80 columns of the card are punched.

01010		DORG	402	00402		
01020		TD	INPUT+80,400	00402	25 00578	00400
01030		BC1	*+48	00414	46 00462	00100
01040		RNCD	INPUT	00426	36 00498	00500
01050		WNCD	INPUT	00438	38 00498	00400
01060		B	*-24	00450	49 00426	00000
01070		RNCD	INPUT	00462	36 00498	00500
01080		WNPT	INPUT	00474	38 00498	00200
01090		B	*-24	00486	49 00462	00000
01100	INPUT	DS	1	00498	00001	
01110		DEND	402	00402		

Example 13

Example 13—Commentary

Through the proper use of asterisk operands, we can limit the number of labels to as few as possible. But since the assembly system is available for the purpose of allowing symbol manipulation, this type of programming is not desirable for a program of any substantial size.

The first instruction of the program places a record mark at the necessary location if tape output is the case. If card output is desired, we have wasted an instruction but have not damaged the intent of the program.

Examples 14 and 15 demonstrate two varieties of the same program. The first is quite straightforward. The second is shorter but not as easily followed. This latter problem demonstrates the first example of a concept unique to digital computers: instruction modification.

Both examples are presented without comment for your study.

Switch 1 On: Card-to-card duplication
Switch 2 On: Card-to-tape duplication
Switch 3 On: Tape-to-tape duplication
Switch 4 On: Tape-to-card duplication

Allow for the possibility of operator negligence concerning switch settings. A record mark is available in location 400 if needed. Card records are 80 numeric characters. Tape records are 81 numeric characters, the last of which is an E/L character.

01010	DORG	402		00402		
01020GO	BC1	C2C		00402	46 00570	00100
01030	BC2	C2T		00414	46 00522	00200
01040	BC3	T2T		00426	46 00486	00300
01050	BNC4	ERROR		00438	47 00606	00400
01060T2C	RNPT	INPUT		00450	36 00618	00300
01070	WNCD	INPUT		00462	38 00618	00400
01080	B	T2C		00474	49 00450	00000
01090T2T	RNPT	INPUT		00486	36 00618	00300
01100	WNPT	INPUT		00498	38 00618	00200
01110	B	T2T		00510	49 00486	00000
01120C2T	TD	INPUT+80, 400		00522	25 00698	00400
01130	RNCD	INPUT		00534	36 00618	00500
01140	WNPT	INPUT		00546	38 00618	00200
01150	B	C2T+12		00558	49 00534	00000
01160C2C	RNCD	INPUT		00570	36 00618	00500
01170	WNCD	INPUT		00582	38 00618	00400
01180	B	C2C		00594	49 00570	00000
01190ERROR	H			00606	48 00000	00000
01200INPUT	DS	1		00618	00001	
02010	DEND	GO		00402		

Example 14

01010		DORG 402		00402		
01020 INPUT	DS	1		00402 00001		
01030	DS	80		00482 00080		
01040 GO	BC1	C2C		00484 46	00628	00100
01050	BC2	C2T		00496 46	00592	00200
01060	BC3	T2T		00508 46	00568	00300
01070	BNC4	ERROR,,,ALWAYS PREPARE FOR		00520 47	00652	00400
01080 GENUSE	RNPT	INPUT,,,THE UNEXPECTED. IT		00532 36	00402	00300
01090 A	WNCD	INPUT,,,IS POSSIBLE TO FOR-		00544 38	00402	00400
01100	B	GENUSE,,,GET SWITCH SETTINGS.		00556 49	00532	00000
01120 T2T	TDM	A+9,2		00568 15	00553	00002
01130	B	GENUSE		00580 49	00532	00000
01140 C2T	TDM	GENUSE+9,5		00592 15	00541	00005
01150	TD	INPUT+80,400		00604 25	00482	00400
01160	B	T2T		00616 49	00568	00000
01170 C2C	TDM	GENUSE+9,5		00628 15	00541	00005
01180	B	GENUSE		00640 49	00532	00000
01190 ERROR	H			00652 48	00000	00000
01200	DEND	GO		00484		

Example 15

Example 16 demonstrates a solution to the following problem. Can you write another?

Problem

A 5 Chars.	E/L	B 2 Chars.	E/L	C 3 Chars.	E/L	D 7 Chars.	E/L

Data Representation on Paper Tape

A is of the form XXX.XX
B is of the form .XX
C is of the form XX.X
D is of the form XXXX.XXX

All data is positive and flagged in the high order position of the field. Calculate $(A + B)(C + D)$ to one decimal place of accuracy. The answer is to be typed.

01005	DORG 2178	02178		
01010GO	RNPT INPUTA-5	02178	36 02310	00300
01020	RNPT INPUTB-2	02190	36 02316	00300
01030	A INPUTA-1,INPUTB-1	02202	21 02314	02317
01040	RNPT INPUTC-3	02214	36 02319	00300
01050	RNPT INPUTD-7	02226	36 02323	00300
01060	A INPUTD-3,INPUTC-1	02238	21 02327	02321
01065	M INPUTD-1,INPUTA-1	02250	23 02329	02314
01070	TF INPUTD-1,95	02262	23 02329	00095
01080	RCTY	02274	34 00000	00102
01090	WNTY INPUTD-8	02286	38 02322	00100
01100	H	02298	48 00000	00000
01110INPUTA	DS 6	02315	00006	
01120INPUTB	DS 3	02318	00003	
01130INPUTC	DS 4	02322	00004	
01140INPUTD	DS 8	02330	00008	
01150	DEND GO	02178		

Example 16

Example 16—Commentary

All areas of input are one core position larger than is needed. This is to allow for the entry of the E/L characters into core. Note the double usage made of the record mark which entered with the D data as an E/L character.

Example 17 demonstrates a solution to the following problem. Can you write a second, a third, etc?

Problem

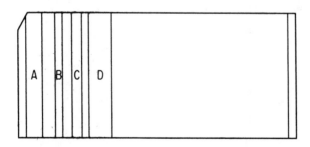

A occupies columns 1–5 of the card and is of the form XXX.XX
B occupies columns 10–11 of the card and is of the form .XX
C occupies columns 15–17 of the card and is of the form XX.X
D occupies columns 20–26 of the card and is of the form XXXX.XXX
All data is positive and flagged in the high-order position of the field. Calculate $(A + B)(C + D)$ to one decimal place of accuracy. The answer is to be typed.

01010	DORG	402	00402			
01020GO	RNCD	INPUT	00402	36	00498	00500
01030	A	A,B	00414	21	00502	00508
01040	A	D-2,C	00426	21	00521	00514
01060	M	A,D	00438	23	00502	00523
01070	TD	96,400	00450	25	00096	00400
01080	RCTY		00462	34	00000	00102
01090	WNTY	88	00474	38	00088	00100
01100	H		00486	48	00000	00000
01110INPUT	DS	1	00498	00001		
01120A	DS	,INPUT+4	00502	00000		
01130B	DS	,INPUT+10	00508	00000		
01140C	DS	,INPUT+16	00514	00000		
01150D	DS	,INPUT+25	00523	00000		
01160	DEND	GO	00402			

Example 17

Example 17—Commentary

There were no record marks left over from data input since card reading is not terminated in the same fashion as is tape. Hence, it was necessary to borrow the record mark at location 400.

DC (DEFINE CONSTANT)

The code DC may be used to define a numeric constant that will be used in the computation procedure of the object program. The rules of the DC follow.

1. The operation code DC appears in columns 12–13 of the operation field.
2. The label by which this constant may be referenced appears in columns 6–11. The label refers to the units (low-order) position of the constant.
3. The length of the constant appears as the first operand. The length operand may be actual, symbolic, or asterisk. If symbolic, the symbol must have been previously encountered in the source program.
4. The second operand is the constant being defined and is always numeric.
5. Omission of the first and/or second operands is invalid.
6. If a third operand is present, the processor assumes a synonymous relationship between the label and this third operand. This operand allows the programmer to assign the address of a constant. The presence of the synonymity operand does *not* affect sequence of addresses assigned by the processor. The location counter remains unchanged regardless of the size of the first operand which, unlike the DS size operand, must always be present. The synonymity operand may be actual, symbolic, or asterisk. If symbolic, it must have been previously encountered in the source program.

7. The processor will place a flag over the left-hand (high-order) digit of the constant.

8. Negative constants are preceded by a minus sign (−) which is not counted as part of the length operand. The presence of the minus sign causes a flag to be placed in the units position of the constant.

9. A record mark may appear only in the units position of the constant field and is written as "@." This is interpreted by the processor as "‡."

10. Negative constants containing a record mark (@) will have a flag placed over the digit preceding the record mark.

11. Constants may not exceed 50 characters.

12. Should the length operand be greater than the number of digits specified in the constant, the constant will be right justified with high-order zeros inserted.

13. A length operand less than the number of digits in the specified constant is invalid.

14. The maximum number of operands with a DC is four. The fourth operand, if present, is a comment and does not affect the processing.

See Figure 11.10 for examples of the DC statement properly written.

LINE	LABEL	OPERATION	OPERANDS & REMARKS
0,1,0	X	D.C.	5,,1,2,3,4,5,
0,2,0			
0,3,0	C,O,N	D,C,	2,,1,5,
0,4,0			
0,5,0	N,U,M,B,	D,C,	4,,2,,S,Y,M,B,O,L,,−,1,0,
0,6,0			
0,7,0	R,E,C,R,D,	D.C.	1,,@,‡,
0,8,0			
0,9,0	O,U,T,P,U,T	D,C,	1,1,,,@
1,0,0			
1,1,0	K,O,N,4,3,	D.C.	J,,1,7,,L,O,C,
1,2,0			
1,3,0	T,E,M,P,	D,C,	1,5,,0,,,,C,O,M,M,E,N,T,
1,4,0			
1,5,0	R,E,C,M,R,K	D,C,	5,,1,2,@,4,5,,,,T,H,I,S, S,T,A,T,E,M,E,N,T, I,S, I,N,V,A,L,I,D,,
1,6,0			
1,7,0	K,O,N,	D,C,	2,,1,5,7,,,,T,H,I,S, S,T,A,T,E,M,E,N,T, I,S, I,N,V,A,L,I,D,,
1,8,0			

Fig. 11.10. Examples of the DC Declarative.

Examples 18, 19, and 20 are given to demonstrate proper use of the DC statement. These three examples are different solutions to the same problem.

Problem

Given cards of the following form

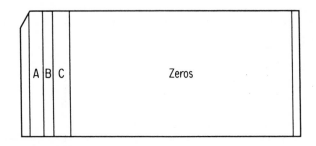

with A, B and C integers such that

1. $0 \leq A \leq 9998$ in columns 1–4
2. $0 \leq B \leq 992$ in columns 5–7
3. $0 \leq C \leq 99984$ in columns 8–12

For each input card, generate a single output card with integers X, Y, and Z such that

1. $X = A + 1$ punched in columns 1–4
2. $Y = B + 7$ punched in columns 5–7
3. $Z = C + 15$ punched in columns 8–12

With the remainder of the card zeros.

Repeat until all cards are exhausted.
All input data is flagged in the high-order position of the field.

01010	DORG	402	00402		
01020GO	RNCD	INPUT	00402	36 00474	00500
01030	A	A,KON1	00414	21 00477	00557
01040	A	B,KON2	00426	21 00480	00560
01050	A	C,KON3	00438	21 00485	00565
01060	WNCD	INPUT	00450	38 00474	00400
01070	B	GO	00462	49 00402	00000
01080INPUT	DS	1	00474	00001	
01090	DS	79	00553	00079	
01100A	DS	,INPUT+3	00477	00000	
01110B	DS	,INPUT+6	00480	00000	
01120C	DS	,INPUT+11	00485	00000	
01130KON1	DC	4,1	00557	00004	0001
01140KON2	DC	3,7	00560	00003	007
01150KON3	DC	5,15	00565	00005	00015
01160	DEND	GO	00402		

Example 18

Example 18—Commentary

The constants needed for proper operation of the program are defined as Kon1, Kon2, and Kon3, respectively. Other than the introduction of the new declaratives, this program presents no new ideas.

01010	DORG	402		00402			
01020GO	RNCD	INPUT		00402	36	00474	00500
01030	A	INPUT+3,CON1		00414	21	00477	00555
01040	A	INPUT+6,CON2		00426	21	00480	00557
01050	A	INPUT+11,CON3		00438	21	00485	00559
01060	WNCD	INPUT		00450	38	00474	00400
01070	B·	GO		00462	49	00402	00000
01080INPUT	DS	1		00474	00001		
01090	DS	79		00553	00079		
01100CON1	DC	2,1		00555	00002	01	
01110CON2	DC	2,7		00557	00002	07	
01120CON3	DC	2,15		00559	00002	15	
01130	DEND	GO		00402			

Example 19

Example 19—Commentary

This program is identical with the previous one with the single exception of size of constants defined. Are more than 2-digit constants really necessary?

01010	DORG	402		00402			
01020GO	RNCD	INPUT		00402	36	00474	00500
01030	AM	INPUT+3,1,10		00414	11	00477	00001
01040	AM	INPUT+6,7,10		00426	11	00480	00007
01050	AM	INPUT+11,15,10		00438	11	00485	00015
01060	WNCD	INPUT		00450	38	00474	00400
01070	B	GO		00462	49	00402	00000
01080INPUT	DS	1		00474	00001		
01090	DEND	GO		00402			

Example 20

Example 20—Commentary

The problem is executed in this program by using the Immediate commands instead of defining constants. In any computer program, *space is money!*

Examples 21, 22, 23, 24, and 25 present five variations on the same problem. They are presented without comment for your study.[6]

[6] In Examples 24 and 25 what is the purpose of the declarative DORG ★—3 which is so liberally sprinkled throughout the program?

```
01010          DORG 402                              00402
01020 GO       RNCD INPUT                            00402 36 00642 00500
01030          SF   INPUT                            00414 32 00642 00000
01040          C    INPUT+6,CON                      00426 24 00648 00727
01050          BH   TAPOUT                           00438 46 00582 01100
01060          BNF  CRDOUT,INPUT+6                   00450 44 00534 00648
01070          TF   OUTPUT-1,INPUT+6                 00462 26 00734 00648
01080          CF   OUTPUT-7                         00474 33 00728 00000
01090          RCTY                                  00486 34 00000 00102
01100          WNTY OUTPUT-7                         00498 38 00728 00100
01120          BNLC GO                               00510 47 00402 00900
01130          H                                     00522 48 00000 00000
01140 CRDOUT   CF   INPUT                            00534 33 00642 00000
01145          WNCD INPUT                            00546 38 00642 00400
01150          BNLC GO                               00558 47 00402 00900
01160          H                                     00570 48 00000 00000
01170 TAPOUT   TF   OUTPUT-1,INPUT+6                 00582 26 00734 00648
01180          CF   OUTPUT-7                         00594 33 00728 00000
01190          WNPT OUTPUT-7                         00606 38 00728 00200
01200          BNLC GO                               00618 47 00402 00900
02010          H                                     00630 48 00000 00000
02020 INPUT    DS   1                                00642 00001
02030          DS   79                               00721 00079
02040 CON      DC   6,500000                         00727 00006    500000
02050 OUTPUT   DC   8,@                              00735 00008    0000000‡
02060          DEND GO                               00402
```

Example 21

```
01010          DORG 402                              00402
01020 GO       RNCD INPUT                            00402 36 00626 00500
01030          SF   INPUT                            00414 32 00626 00000
01040          BNF  AHEAD,INPUT+6,,IS NUM. NEG.      00426 44 00510 00632
01050          TF   OUTPUT-1,INPUT+6                 00438 26 00624 00632
01060          CF   OUTPUT-7                         00450 33 00618 00000
01070          RCTY                                  00462 34 00000 00102
01080          WNTY OUTPUT-7                         00474 38 00618 00100
01090 TEST     BNLC GO                               00486 47 00402 00900
01100          H                                     00498 48 00000 00000
01110 AHEAD    C    INPUT+6,CON                      00510 24 00632 00711
01120          BH   TAPE                             00522 46 00570 01100
01130          CF   INPUT                            00534 33 00626 00000
01140          WNCD INPUT                            00546 38 00626 00400
01150          B    TEST                             00558 49 00486 00000
01160 TAPE     TF   OUTPUT-1,INPUT+6                 00570 26 00624 00632
01170          CF   OUTPUT-7                         00582 33 00618 00000
01180          WNPT OUTPUT-7                         00594 38 00618 00200
01190          B    TEST                             00606 49 00486 00000
01200 OUTPUT   DC   8,@                              00625 00008    0000000‡
01210 INPUT    DS   1                                00626 00001
01220          DS   79                               00705 00079
01230 CON      DC   6,500000                         00711 00006    500000
01240          DEND GO                               00402
```

Example 22

01010	DORG	402	00402			
01020 GO	RNCD	INPUT-79	00402	36	00626	00500
01030	SF	INPUT-79	00414	32	00626	00000
01040	BNF	AHEAD,INPUT-73	00426	44	00510	00632
01050	TF	OUTPUT-1,INPUT-73	00438	26	00624	00632
01060	CF	OUTPUT-7	00450	33	00618	00000
01070	RCTY		00462	34	00000	00102
01080	WNTY	OUTPUT-7	00474	38	00618	00100
01090 TEST	BNLC	GO	00486	47	00402	00900
01100	H		00498	48	00000	00000
01120 AHEAD	C	INPUT-73,.CON	00510	24	00632	00711
01130	BH	TAPE	00522	46	00570	01100
01150	CF	INPUT-79	00534	33	00626	00000
01152	WNCD	INPUT-79	00546	38	00626	00400
01160	B	TEST	00558	49	00486	00000
01170 TAPE	TF	OUTPUT-1,INPUT-73	00570	26	00624	00632
01180	CF	OUTPUT-7	00582	33	00618	00000
01190	WNPT	OUTPUT-7	00594	38	00618	00200
01200	B	TEST	00606	49	00486	00000
01210 OUTPUT	DC	8,@	00625	00008	0000000‡	
01212 INPUT	DS	80	00705	00080		
01230 CON	DC	6,500000	00711	00006	500000	
01240	DEND	GO	00402			

Example 23

01010	DORG	402	00402			
01020 GO	RNCD	INPUT	00402	36	00586	00500
01030	SF	INPUT	00414	32	00586	00000
01040	TF	OUTPUT,X	00426	26	00508	00592
01050	CF	HIGH	00438	33	00502	00000
01060	BNF	AHEAD,X	00450	44	00510	00592
01070 DATA1	RCTY		00462	34	00000	00102
01080	WNTY	HIGH	00474	38	00502	00100
01090 TEST	BNLC	GO	00486	47	00402	00900
01100 DATA2	H		00498	48	00000	00000
01110 AHEAD	C	X,CON	00510	24	00592	00469
01120	BH	TAPE	00522	46	00566	01100
01130	CF	INPUT	00534	33	00586	00000
01140	WNCD	INPUT	00546	38	00586	00400
01150	B	TEST	00558	49	00486	00000
01160	DORG	*-3	00566			
01170 TAPE	WNPT	HIGH	00566	38	00502	00200
01180	B	TEST	00578	49	00486	00000
01190	DORG	*-3	00586			
01200 OUTPUT	DS	,DATA2+10	00508	00000		
02010	DC	1,@,OUTPUT+1	00509	00001	‡	
02020 HIGH	DS	,OUTPUT-6	00502	00000		
02030 CON	DC	6,500000,DATA1+7	00469	00006	500000	
02040 INPUT	DS	1	00586	00001		
02041 X	DS	,INPUT+6	00592	00000		
02050	DEND	GO	00402			

Example 24

01010	DORG	402	00402			
01020INPUT	DS	1	00402	00001		
01030	DS	79	00481	00079		
01040X	DS	,INPUT+6	00408	00000		
01050GO	RNCD	INPUT	00482	36	00402	00500
01060	SF	INPUT	00494	32	00402	00000
01070	BNF	AHEAD,X	00506	44	00590	00408
01080	TF	OUTPUT,X	00518	26	00588	00408
01090	CF	HIGH	00530	33	00582	00000
01100DATA1	RCTY		00542	34	00000	00102
01120	WNTY	HIGH	00554	38	00582	00100
01130TEST	BNLC	GO	00566	47	00482	00900
01140DATA2	H		00578	48	00000	00000
01150AHEAD	C	X,CON	00590	24	00408	00549
01160	BH	TAPE	00602	46	00646	01100
01170	CF	INPUT	00614	33	00402	00000
01180	WNCD	INPUT	00626	38	00402	00400
01190	B	TEST	00638	49	00566	00000
01200	DORG	*-3	00646			
01210TAPE	TF	OUTPUT,X	00646	26	00588	00408
02010	CF	HIGH	00658	33	00582	00000
02020	WNPT	HIGH	00670	38	00582	00200
02030	B	TEST	00682	49	00566	00000
02040	DORG	*-3	00690			
02050OUTPUT	DS	,DATA2+10	00588	00000		
02060	DC	1,@,DATA2+11	00589	00001	‡	
02070HIGH	DS	,OUTPUT-6	00582	00000		
02080CON	DC	6,500000,DATA1+7	00549	00006	500000	
02090	DEND	GO	00482			

Example 25

Problem

Many cards are in the read hopper of the 1622. Each card is punched in columns 1–7 with a 7-digit number, X, such that:

$$-9999999 \leq X \leq 9999999$$

No data is flagged in the high-order position. However, negative data does have a flag over the units position. Perform the following:

1. If $X > 500{,}000$, punch the number on tape.
2. If $0 \leq X \leq 500{,}000$, punch the number on a card in columns 1–7.
3. If $X < 0$, type the number.

The output number is to be *exactly* identical with the input number. Terminate the program after the last card has been processed.

The next examples, which demonstrate the use of the DC, are analogous to being told the answer and then asked to find the question. Four intricate programs are presented. What do they do?

The answers to the questions (in truth, the questions to the answers) are presented on pages 129 and 130. Arrive at your own conclusion as to their function before looking at the solutions. Do not let their small size fool you. There is a lot of labor being performed.

01010	DORG	402	00402			
01020A	TDM	19999,,2	00402	15	T9999	00000
01030	DC	1,@,*	00413	00001	‡	
01040	SM	A+6,1	00414	12	00408	Õ0001
01050	CM	A+6,LABEL+1	00426	14	00408	Õ0451
01060	BNE	A	00438	47	00402	01200
01070LABEL	H		00450	48	00000	00000
01080	DEND	A	00402			

Example 26

01010	DORG	402	00402			
01020	TF	19999,KON,2	00402	26	T9999	00461
01030	AM	*-6,10,1011	00414	11	00408	00010
01040	CM	*-18,9999,8	00426	14	00408	09999
01050	BNE	*-36	00438	47	00402	01200
01060	H		00450	48	00000	00000
01070KON	DC	10,-0,*	00461	00010	Õ00000000Õ	
01080	DEND	402	00402			

Example 27

01010	DORG	402	00402			
01020X100	TD	TEMP,KON-9,27	00402	25	00483	00464
01030	AM	X100+6,1,1011	00414	11	00408	0000T
01040	SM	X100+11,1,1011	00426	12	00413	0000T
01050	CM	X100+11,KON+1	00438	14	00413	00474
01060	BNE·	X100	00450	47	00402	01200
01070	H		00462	48	00000	00000
01080KON	DC	10,1234567890,*	00473	00010	T234567890	
01090TEMP	DS	10	00483	00010		
01100	DEND	X100	00402			

Example 28

01010	DORG	402	00402			
01020X100	TD	TEMP,KON-9,27	00402	25	00549	00530
01030	AM	X100+6,1,1011	00414	11	00408	0000T
01040	SM	X100+11,1,1011	00426	12	00413	0000T
01050	CM	X100+11,KON+1	00438	14	00413	00540
01060	BNE	X100	00450	47	00402	01200
01070	RCTY		00462	34	00000	00102
01080	WNTY	TEMP-9	00474	38	00540	00100
01090	TFM	X100+6,TEMP	00486	16	00408	00549
01100	TFM	X100+11,KON-9	00498	16	00413	00530
01110	TF	KON,TEMP	00510	26	00539	00549
01120	B	X100	00522	49	00402	00000
01130	DORG	*-3	00530			
01140KON	DC	10,-1234567890	00539	00010	T234567890	
01150TEMP	DS	10	00549	00010		
01160	DC	1,@	00550	00001	‡	
00170	DEND	X100	00402			

Example 29

Example 26 causes a record mark character to be placed in core from positions 19999 to 452 inclusive. When this is accomplished, the program halts.

Example 27 causes the 10-digit field $\overline{0}000000000$ to be placed at 19999, 19989, 19979, ..., 10019, 10009. When this is accomplished, the program halts.

Example 28 obtains a mirror image of the field $\overline{1}234567890$. The number thus produced is $098765432\overline{1}$ and is not a field due to the lack of the high-order field-defining flag. When this is accomplished, the program halts.

Example 29 is a nonterminating program. There is nothing in the instruction set to cause the program to stop. A mirror image is made of the original field $\overline{1}23456789\overline{0}$ to obtain $\overline{0}98765432\overline{1}$. With this new field as an argument, the process repeats itself indefinitely. See Figure 11.11 for a portion of the output.

As a final comment for all four examples, modification of certain instruction addresses was necessary. Such modification assumed that the P field data (an instruction's P or Q operand) was flagged to allow for the necessary addition or subtraction. Consequently, the flag operand was used in locations where it seemed unnecessary. For example, note the first instruction of Example 26: TDM 19999,,2.

$$\overline{0}98765432\overline{1}$$

$$\overline{1}23456789\overline{0}$$

$$\overline{0}98765432\overline{1}$$

$$\overline{1}23456789\overline{0}$$

$$\overline{0}98765432\overline{1}$$

$$\overline{1}23456789\overline{0}$$

$$\overline{0}98765432\overline{1}$$

$$\overline{1}23456789\overline{0}$$

$$\overline{0}98765432\overline{1}$$

$$\overline{1}23456789\overline{0}$$

$$\overline{0}98765432\overline{1}$$

$$\overline{1}23456789\overline{0}$$

$$\overline{0}98765432\overline{1}$$

$$\overline{1}23456789\overline{0}$$

$$\overline{0}98765432\overline{1}$$

Fig. 11.11. Object Program Typewriter Output of Example 29.

DSS (DEFINE SPECIAL SYMBOL)

The code DSS is identical with the declarative DS, except for the fact that the label refers to the high-order position of the field as opposed to the units position in the case of the DS.

Except for the above statement and the fact that DSS occupies columns 12–14 of the operation field, all rules of the DSS are identical with those of the DS.

DSC (DEFINE SPECIAL CONSTANT)

The code DSC is identical with the declarative DC, with the following two exceptions:

1. The label refers to the high-order position of the constant.
2. The constant will be processed without a high-order field-defining flag.

Except for the above statements, and the fact that DSC occupies columns 12–14 of the operation field, all rules of the DSC are identical with those of the DC.

DAS (DEFINE ALPHAMERIC SYMBOL)

The code DAS may be used to define a field that will contain alphameric information. These fields are generally used as I/O areas. The rules of the DAS follow.

1. The operation code DAS appears in columns 12–14 of the operation field.
2. The length of the field appears as the first operand and this will be doubled by the processor. This accommodates the alphameric coding of data which is in double-digit representation internally. The length operand may be actual, symbolic, or asterisk. If symbolic, the symbol must have been previously encountered in the source program.
3. The label by which this field may be referenced appears in columns 6–11. This label refers to the *high-order-plus-one* position of the field. Thus, the high-order position of the field is Label-1. The low-order position of the field is Label$+2{\star}$L-2, where L is the length operand.
4. The processor assigns an *even* address to the high-order digit of the field, and the label, referring to the adjacent position, thereby references an odd core location. This satisfies the I/O rule concerning alphabetic information.

5. If a second operand is present, the processor assumes a synonymous relationship between the label and this second operand. This operand allows the programmer to assign the address of a symbol. The label still refers to the high-order-plus-one position in this case but the core location is not necessarily odd. Thus, when assigning a synonymity operand for a DAS, one must be certain that the operand references an odd core location. The presence of the synonymity operand does not affect the sequence of addresses assigned by the processor. The location counter remains unchanged regardless of the size of the first operand. The synonymity operand may be actual, symbolic, or asterisk. If symbolic, it must have been previously encountered in the source program.
6. The maximum number of operands in a DAS is three. The third operand, if present, is a comment and does not affect the processing.
7. Omission of the label in a DAS reserves storage which will not be referred to symbolically.

See Figure 11.12 for examples of the DAS statement properly written.

LINE (3–5)	LABEL (6–11)	OPERATION (12–15)	OPERANDS & REMARKS (16–50)
010	DATA	DAS	25
020			
030	ALFAIN	DAS	80
040			
050	LØC	DAS	,INPUT+12
060			
070	CARD	DAS	80,,JUST LØNG ENØUGH FØR ØNE CARD
080			

Fig. 11.12. Examples of the DAS Declarative.

The card-to-card, card-to-tape, and so forth, duplication programs given as examples of the DS statement had two major faults which were not discussed at the time. First, blank card columns read numerically produce zeros internally. Thus, reading a blank card and punching the input information produces a card with 80 zeros. Second, if the input information contained mixed alphabetic-numeric characters, the reproduction was not necessarily valid.

Since the DAS is discussed after the DS, it was better to define the statement of the problem in such a fashion as to utilize the DS only (no blanks, numerics only, and so forth).

Now that the materials are handy to cope with the situation, all-purpose card-to-card duplication programs are presented for your study as well as proper use of the DAS. These programs are a slight extension of the reproduction programs that were demonstrated previously.

01010	DORG 402	00402
01020GO	RACD INPUT	00402 37 00439 00500
01030	WACD INPUT	00414 39 00439 00400
01040	B GO	00426 49 00402 00000
01050INPUT	DAS 80	00439 00080X2
01060	DEND GO	00402

Example 30

01010	DORG 402	00402
01020GO	RACD INPUT	00402 37 00435 00500
01030	WACD INPUT	00414 39 00435 00400
01040	B GO	00426 49 00402 00000
01050	DORG *-3	00434
01060INPUT	DAS 1	00435 00001X2
01070	DEND GO	00402

Example 31

Example 32 demonstrates proper low-order addressing of an alphameric field.

Problem

Construct a card-to-card duplicator program such that the input and output areas are distinct. (Transfer the input data to another area before writing.)

01010	DORG 402	00402
01020GO	RACD INPUT	00402 37 00473 00500
01030	SF INPUT-1	00414 32 00472 00000
01040	TF OUTPUT+2*80-2,INPUT+2*80-2	00426 26 00791 00631
01050	CF OUTPUT-1	00438 33 00632 00000
01060	WACD OUTPUT	00450 39 00633 00400
01070	B GO	00462 49 00402 00000
01080	DORG *-2,WHY *-2 INSTEAD OF *-3	00471
01090INPUT	DAS 80	00473 00080X2
01100OUTPUT	DAS 1	00633 00001X2
01110	DEND GO	00402

Example 32

Example 33 is essentially the same problem demonstrated in Example 32, with a single exception. This exception demonstrates the use of the last card indicator with counting.

Problem

Reproduce N cards with distinct input and output areas. After all cards have been duplicated, type N. $(1 \le N \le 9999)$

01010	DORG	402		00402			
01020START	TFM	COUNT..8		00402	16	00508	00000
01030GO	RACD	INPUT		00414	37	00511	00500
01040	TF	OUTPUT+158,INPUT+158		00426	26	00829	00669
01050	WACD	OUTPUT		00438	39	00671	00400
01060	AM	COUNT,1,10		00450	11	00508	00001
01070	BNLC	GO		00462	47	00414	00900
01080	RCTY			00474	34	00000	00102
01090	WNTY	COUNT−3		00486	38	00505	00100
01100	H			00498	48	00000	00000
01120INPUT	DAS	80		00511	00080X2		
01130OUTPUT	DAS	1		00671	00001X2		
01140COUNT	DS	,INPUT−3		00508	00000		
01150	DC	1,@,INPUT−2		00509	00001		±
01155	DC	2,0,INPUT		00511	00002		00
01160	DEND	START		00402			

Example 33

Example 33—Commentary

On first observation it would seem that the TF instruction will fail. At no point have we set a flag on the high-order digit of our Input area. However, the saving grace is the last DC statement of the program. Why?

DAC (DEFINE ALPHAMERIC CONSTANT)

The code DAC may be used to define a constant consisting of alphameric data. These constants are generally used for computer-operator-programmer communication or for column headings on the printed page of answers. The rules for the DAC follow.

1. The operation code DAC appears in columns 12–14 of the operation field.
2. The length of the constant appears as the first operand and this will be doubled by the processor. This accommodates the alphameric coding of data which is in double-digit representation internally. The length operand may be actual, symbolic, or asterisk. If symbolic, the symbol must have been previously encountered in the source program.
3. The label by which this constant may be referenced appears in columns 6–11. This label refers to the high-order-plus-one position of the constant. Thus, the high-order position of the field is Label−1. The low-order position of the field is Label+2*L−2, where L is the length operand.
4. The second operand is the alphameric constant desired.
5. Omission of the first and/or second operands is invalid.
6. If a third operand is present, the processor assumes a synonymous relationship between the label and this third operand. This operand allows the programmer to assign the address of a constant. The label still refers to the high-order-plus-one position in this case but

the core location is not necessarily odd. Thus, when a synonymity operand for a DAC is assigned, one must be certain that the operand references an odd core location. The presence of the synonymity operand does not affect the sequence of address assigned by the processor. The location counter remains unchanged regardless of the size of the first operand which, unlike the DAS size operand, must always be present. The synonymity operand may be actual, symbolic, or asterisk. If symbolic, it must have been previously encountered in the source program.

7. The processor will place a flag over the left-hand (high-order) digit of the constant.
8. A record mark may appear only in the units position of the constant field and is written as "@." This is interpreted as "0‡."
9. Constants may not exceed 50 alphameric characters *including* blanks and record mark.
10. A length operand less than or greater than the number of characters in the specified constant is invalid.
11. The maximum number of operands with a DAC is four. The fourth operand, if present, is a comment and does not affect the processing.

See Figure 11.13 for examples of the DAC statement properly written.

LINE	LABEL	OPERATION	OPERANDS & REMARKS
0110	CMNT	DAC	14,THE ANSWER IS@
0120			
0130	OUTPUT	DAC	16,ERROR CONDITION@
0140			
0150	STOP	DAC	5,STOP@,LOC-16
0160			
0170	RECMK	DAC	1,@,15003
0180			

Fig. 11.13. Examples of the DAC Declarative.

```
00100       DORG 402                          00402
01020CMNT1  DAC  16,NOW IS THE TIME@          00403 00016X2 NOW IS THE TIME‡
01030CMNT2  DAC  17,FOR ALL GOOD MEN@         00435 00017X2 FOR ALL GOOD MEN‡
01040CMNT3  DAC  19,TO COME TO THE AID@       00469 00019X2 TO COME TO THE AID‡
01050CMNT4  DAC  15,OF THEIR PARTY@           00507 00015X2 OF THEIR PARTY‡
01060GO     RCTY                              00536 34 00000 00102
01070       WATY CMNT1                        00548 39 00403 00100
01080       RCTY                              00560 34 00000 00102
01090       WATY CMNT2                        00572 39 00435 00100
01100       RCTY                              00584 34 00000 00102
01110       WATY CMNT3                        00596 39 00469 00100
01120       RCTY                              00608 34 00000 00102
01130       WATY CMNT4                        00620 39 00507 00100
01140       H                                 00632 48 00000 00000
01150       DEND GO                           00536
```

Example 34

Example 34 demonstrates a program the use of which is self-evident. See Figure 11.14 for the output of this program at object time. What is the purpose of the @ symbol at the end of each DAC statement?

```
NOW IS THE TIME
FOR ALL GOOD MEN
TO COME TO THE AID
OF THEIR PARTY
```

Fig. 11.14. Object Program Output of Example 34.

Example 35 demonstrates a more purposeful use of an operator message.

Problem

An 80-column card has two 2-digit numbers punched in columns 1–4. All data is flagged in its high-order position. Type a single message that states their relationship to one another (larger, smaller, equal). If the first element (A) is less than, equal to, or greater than the second element (B), state so in just such a fashion.

```
01010         DORG 402                      00402
01020BEGIN    RNCD INPUT                    00402 36 00664 00500
01030         C    INPUT+1,INPUT+3          00414 24 00665 00667
01040         BNE  A01080                   00426 47 00474 01200
01050         RCTY                          00438 34 00000 00102
01060         WATY CMNT1                    00450 39 00559 00100
01070         H                             00462 48 00000 00000
01080A01080   BH   A01110                   00474 46 00522 01100
01090         RCTY                          00486 34 00000 00102
01100         WATY CMNT2                    00498 39 00591 00100
01105         H                             00510 48 00000 00000
01110A01110   RCTY                          00522 34 00000 00102
01120         WATY CMNT3                    00534 39 00625 00100
01130         H                             00546 48 00000 00000
01140CMNT1    DAC  16,A IS EQUAL TO B@      00559 00016X2 A IS EQUAL TO B‡
01150CMNT2    DAC  17,A IS LESS THAN B@     00591 00017X2 A IS LESS THAN B‡
01160CMNT3    DAC  20,A IS GREATER THAN B@  00625 00020X2 A IS GREATER THAN B‡
01170INPUT    DS   1                        00664 00001
01180         DEND BEGIN                    00402
```

Example 35

Example 36 is a variation of Example 33. That is, it reproduces and counts cards. The output of this problem is a sentence that reads "THERE ARE XXXX CARDS." The number of cards does not exceed 9999.

The original source document is shown here. Notice how letters which could be confused with numbers are printed. The letter "O" has

LINE	LABEL	OPERATION	OPERANDS & REMARKS
0.1.0		DORG	40.2.
0.2.0	START.	TFM.	COUNT...8.
0.3.0	A01030	RACD	INPUT.
0.4.0		TF.	OUTPUT+158..INPUT+158.
0.5.0		WACD	OUTPUT.
0.6.0		AM.	COUNT..1..10.
0.7.0		BNLC	A01030.
0.8.0	A01080	CF.	COUNT,-3.
0.9.0		TD.	CMNT+20..COUNT,-3.
1.0.0		TD.	CMNT+22..COUNT,-2.
1.1.0		TD.	CMNT+24..COUNT,-1.
1.2.0		TD.	CMNT+26..COUNT.
1.3.0		RCTY	
1.4.0		WATY	CMNT.
1.5.0		H.	
1.6.0	COUNT.	DS.	..A01080.0+11.
1.7.0	CMNT.	DAC.	21..THERE..ARE.00.00..CARDS@.
1.8.0	INPUT.	DAS.	80.
1.9.0	OUTPUT	DAS.	80.
2.0.0		DC.	2..0..INPUT.
2.1.0		DEND	START.

Example 36

a slash through it "Ø" to avoid confusion with the number zero "0". The letter "I" is printed in the Roman form to avoid confusion with the number one (1).

Errors introduced while punching from the source document can be the most aggravating.

Two more declaratives for both the card and tape systems are available to the programmer. However, their use is not as instantaneously meaningful as was the use of the previous declaratives. Nonetheless, they are valuable declaratives even though the beginning programmer may not realize their potential value. At the point of sophistication where the coder requires these declaratives, their function will become quite meaningful. These declaratives are: Define Symbolic Address and Define Symbolic Block, and are of the area and constant definition category.

DSA (DEFINE SYMBOLIC ADDRESS)

It may be desirable, at some point in a program, to store a series of addresses as constants. The declarative that performs just such a function is DSA. The rules of the DSA follow.

1. The operation code DSA appears in columns 12–14 of the operation field.
2. Each entry in the operands field will cause its equivalent machine address to be stored as a 5-digit constant flagged in the high-order

position. The constants are stored contiguous to one another. These operands may be actual, symbolic, or asterisk. If symbolic, it is *not* necessary for the symbol to have been previously encountered in the source program.

3. The label field of this statement *must* contain the symbol by which this table of constants may be referenced. The label refers to the units position of the *first* operand. Subsequent operands are referred to symbolically as Label+5, Label+10, etc.

4. Neither a remarks nor synonymity operand is permitted with the DSA.

5. The maximum number of operands permitted with a DSA is ten.

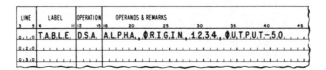

Fig. 11.15. Examples of the DSA Declarative.

See Figure 11.15 for examples of the DSA statement properly written.

In Figure 11.15, the symbols are equivalent to the addresses shown in Figure 11.6.

In the above statement, the 20-digit constant that is produced is:

$$\overline{0}100000600\overline{0}1234\overline{1}4950$$

If the first digit of the entire constant is located at 1200, then the address of Table is 01204 and the location counter will have been increased by 20.

DSB (DEFINE SYMBOLIC BLOCK)

The code DSB may be used to define an area of core storage for storage of numerical arrays. The rules of the DSB follow.

1. The operation code DSB appears in columns 12–14 of the operation field.

2. The first operand indicates the size of each element in the array.

3. The second operand indicates the number of elements in the array.

4. The label employed refers to the units position of the first element in the array.

5. If a third operand is present, the processor assumes a synonymous relationship between the label and this third operand. This operand allows the programmer to assign the address of the first element in the array. The presence of the synonymity operand does not affect the sequence of addresses assigned by the processor. The location counter remains unchanged regardless of the size of the first or second operands.

6. Any DSB operand may be actual, symbolic, or asterisk. If symbolic, the symbol must have been previously encountered in the source program.
7. The maximum number of operands in a DSB is four. The fourth operand, if present, is a comment and does not affect the processing.

See Figure 11.16 for examples of the DSB statement properly written.

LINE	LABEL	OPERATION	OPERANDS & REMARKS
0110	ARRAY	DSB	10,,15,
0120			
0130	DATA	DSB	2,,150,,,REMARKS,
0140			

Fig. 11.16. Examples of the DSB Declarative.

Figure 11.16—Commentary

The first DSB in Figure 11.16 reserves 150 positions of core. The ninth digit from the leftmost core position is synonymous with "Array."

The second example reserves 150 2-digit locations for a total of 300 positions. The first element in the array is called "Data."

Note: The use of the DSB may be circumvented by the use of two DS statements. See the following table.

DSB Usage	DS Usage
ARRAY DSB 10,15	ARRAY DS 10
	DS 140
DATA DSB 2,150	DATA DS 2
	DS 298

Three additional processor control operations are available for both the card and tape systems. As with DSB and DSA, a certain amount of programming sophistication is necessary before they can become useful.

These operations are: Transfer Control and Load, Transfer to Return Address, and Head.

TCD (TRANSFER CONTROL AND LOAD)

This code may be employed during the assembly process so that, during the loading of the object program, the loading operation may be temporarily interrupted. During this interruption, it is possible to execute the portion of the program that has just been read into core. At the conclusion of such execution, a return to the loader can be accomplished through the use of a TRA (to be discussed). A further segment of the object program can then be entered into memory, overlaying the portion just executed. In this fashion programs that are too large for existing core may be segmented by such a chaining technique.

As a TCD is encountered by the processor, the assembly system punches the arithmetic tables, a loader "interrupter," a Branch instruction, and another set of loading instructions. During the loading of this object program, the Branch instruction is preceded by the arithmetic tables and loader interrupter, but the new set of loading instructions does not enter core. These instructions will be called by the TRA command. The address of the Branch is specified by the operand of the TCD.

The rules of a TCD follow:

1. The code TCD appears in columns 12–14 of the operation field.
2. The first (and only) operand states the address of an unconditional branch to be generated by the processor. The address may be asterisk, symbolic, or actual. If symbolic, it must have been previously encountered in the source program.
3. A TCD may not be labeled.

Example 37 shows the use of TCD.

Problem

It is necessary to initialize an area of memory to 100 fields. Each field is 5 digits in length and is of the form: $\overline{0}0000$. The last field is to fall with its units position at 19999. At the conclusion of this initialization procedure, this program may be destroyed by entering the remainder of the program over it.

LINE	LABEL	OPERATION	OPERANDS & REMARKS
0,1,0	G0	TFM	COUNT,,100,,9,,INITIALIZATION BEGINS HERE
0,2,0		TFM	*+18,,19999,
0,3,0		TFM	,,0,
0,4,0		SM	*-6,,5,
0,5,0		SM	COUNT,,1,,10,
0,6,0	COUNT	DS	,*-2,
0,7,0		BNZ	*-36,
0,8,0		RELOADING INSTRUCTION LOCATED HERE,, SEE TRA DESCRIPTION,
0,9,0		TCD	G0
1,0,0		DORG	402
1,1,0	START		
1,2,0			
1,3,0			
1,4,0		REMAINDER OF PROGRAM WHICH OVERLAYS INITIALIZATION,
1,5,0			
1,6,0			
1,7,0			
1,8,0		DEND	START,
1,9,0			

Example 37

TRA (TRANSFER TO RETURN ADDRESS)

This code may be used to reinstate the loading procedure that was interrupted by the cards or tape records produced as a result of a TCD. Loading of the program will continue until another set of TCD produced records is encountered or until the records produced by the DEND interrupt the loading for final execution.

The rules of a TRA are:

1. The code TRA appears in columns 12–14 of the operation field.
2. The TRA produces two instructions to reinstate the loader. These are:

    RNCD (RNPT)   0
    B   0

3. Labeling the TRA is equivalent to labeling the first of the two produced instructions as mentioned in (2).
4. A TRA is without operands.

Example 38 shows the use of TRA.

Problem

It is necessary to initialize an input area to 80 fields. Each field is of the following form: 00. This 160-position area is to have a record mark following the highest addressed field: $\overline{0}0\overline{0}0\overline{0}0\ldots\overline{0}0\ddagger$
The record mark is to fall in position 15128.
At the conclusion of the initialization program, read in the main program and begin execution.

LINE	LABEL	OPERATION	OPERANDS & REMARKS
0,1,0		D,Ø,R,G	4,0,2,
0,2,0	G,Ø	T,F,M,	G,Ø,+,9,,,8,0,,,1,0,
0,3,0		T,D,M,	1,5,1,2,8,
0,4,0		D,C,	1,,,@,,,*,
0,5,0		T,F,M,	X,+,6,,,1,5,1,2,7,
0,6,0	X,	T,F,M,	,,0,,,1,0,
0,7,0		S,M,	G,Ø,+,9,,,1,,,1,0,
0,8,0		B,Z,	Ø,U,T,
0,9,0		A,M,	X,+,6,,,-,2,
1,0,0		B,	X,
1,1,0		D,Ø,R,G	*,-,3,
1,2,0	Ø,U,T,	T,R,A,	
1,3,0		T,C,D,	G,Ø,
1,4,0		D,Ø,R,G	4,0,2,
1,5,0	X,E,C,U,T,E		
1,6,0			
1,7,0			
1,8,0		D,E,N,D	X,E,C,U,T,E,
1,9,0			

Example 38

HEAD

Head cards (or tape records) may be employed whenever a conflict in label names is apt to occur.

As an example, consider a program written in five sections by five programmers. These sections appear as

Section 1	Programmer A
Section 2	Programmer B
Section 3	Programmer C
Section 4	Programmer D
Section 5	Programmer E

Unless careful attention is given to labeling before the programming begins, label conflicts can, and probably will, occur. That is, programmers B and D may use the label TEMP such that:

Section 2 – Programmer B
.

TEMP DS 12
.
.
.

Section 4 – Programmer D
.

TEMP DS ,LOC–11
.
.
.

These labels cause a conflict in that (1) there is a multiply-defined label condition existing, and (2) the labels reference entirely *different* areas.

To complicate the problem further, assume that programmer E of section 5 has used the label TEMP and that this label is to refer to the *same* area used by programmer D in section 4. On the surface, it appears that programmer B is in the minority and will have to change all references to label "TEMP" to, let us say, "TEMPX". However, it is conceivable that programmer A has used the label "TEMPX" and thus, the conflict compounds itself.

One obvious solution is to apportion certain labels to each programmer before the actual coding begins. However, this not only defeats the purpose of labeling, but is very restrictive and difficult to implement. The problem is resolvable, fortunately, by the proper use of Head cards.

If the sections were written as

HEAD A Section 1
HEAD B Section 2
HEAD C Section 3
HEAD D Section 4
HEAD E Section 5

all labels of 5 *or fewer* characters in each section would be said to be "headed" by the Head character which introduces that section.

In this fashion, the label "TEMP" of section 2 would be "TEMP" headed by B. This is *not* the same as the label "BTEMP." The "TEMP" of section 4 would be "TEMP" headed by D. This is *not* the same as the label "DTEMP." On the contrary, heading characters are considered to be on a different level from the label itself. Thus, all labels of section 1 are said to be headed by A, those of section 2 by B, of section 3 by C, of section 4 by D, and of section 5 by E. The term "all" in the previous statement refers only to labels of 5 or fewer characters. Six-character labels are immune from heading. This is a desirable feature which allows for cross referencing between sections of a program.

Suppose programmer E wished to branch to a location in section 1 and programmer A is aware of this. They need merely to agree on a standard 6-character label, which cannot be headed, and utilize it properly, namely:

In this way, the use of the 6-character label, and its property of being immune from heading, allows for cross referencing between sections.

Although the discussion thus far has used Head characters A, B, C, D, and E, there is no implication that the Head character must be a particular one. In fact, any character A–Z, 0–9, or blank may be employed as a valid heading symbol.

The concept of cross referencing between sections may be extended to include labels of 5 or fewer characters. The symbol $\alpha\$$ preceding any such label implies that the heading character to be used is α where α is any allowable Head character.

Thus, if section 1 is headed by A and has a label "Start," sections 2, 3, 4, or 5 may branch to that location as follows:

B   A$START

If section 3 is headed by C and has an area "LOC", and section 1 wishes to add the contents of X93 to the contents of LOC of section 3, this is written as:

A   C$LOC,X93

Suppose that section 5 wishes to add the contents of VKX2 of section 1 headed by A to the contents of 2.8Z of section 4 headed by D. This is done as:

A   D$2.8Z,A$VKX2

It is in this fashion that labels of fewer than six characters may be cross-referenced from section to section.

An unheaded section of a program is said to be *headed by blank*. In this fashion, reference to a label "KON" in an unheaded section, by a headed section, is done by referencing "$KON".

If a programmer wishes to discontinue the heading process at any time, a Head statement with a blank character must be used. If two programmers write three sections of a program, programmer A writing sections 1 and 3 and programmer B writing section 2, the routine might look as follows:

.

.

.

HEAD   X

.

.

.

HEAD

.

.

.

Of course, section 1 could have been preceded by a Head card with blank as the heading character, but this would be superfluous since all labels of section 1 are assumed to be headed by blank if no Head card is associated with the section.

If a symbol "A" in a section headed by X is to be identical with a symbol "A" in a section headed by Y, this can be accomplished through proper use of the Define Symbol declarative in one of the two sections. Thus, either

A   DS ,Y$A

will equate the two symbols if it appears in the section headed by X or

A   DS ,X$A

will equate the two symbols if it appears in the section headed by Y.

The rules of the Head statement follow.

1. The processor control operation Head appears in columns 12–15.
2. Any character A–Z, 0–9, or blank may be used as a valid heading character.
3. The heading character appears in column 16.
4. A Head statement may not be labeled.
5. Six-character labels are immune from heading.
6. Labels in an unheaded section of a program are said to be headed by blank.

DECLARATIVES—CARD SYSTEM ONLY

DNB (DEFINE NUMERIC BLANK)

This code may be used to define a contiguous area of numeric blanks (C–8–4). It is often desired to punch certain areas of a *card* with blanks. The rules of the DNB follow.

1. The code DNB appears in columns 12–14 of the operation field.
2. The first operand states the desired number of blanks.
3. The second operand, if employed, is the synonymity element.
4. The label refers to the low-order position of the blank field.
5. The third operand, if present, is a comment and does not affect the processing.
6. The first and second operands may be actual, symbolic, or asterisk. If symbolic, the symbol must have been encountered previously in the source program.
7. The maximum number of contiguous blanks that may be defined by a single DNB is 50.
8. In order to move a field of blanks by a TF command, any flagged digit should appear contiguous to the high-order position of the blank field.

LINE	LABEL	OPERATION	OPERANDS & REMARKS
0,1,0	B,L,A,N,K,S	D,N,B,	3,5,
0,2,0			
0,3,0	A,R,E,A,	D,N,B,	2,0,,1,5,0,0,0,
0,4,0			
0,5,0	L,Ø,C,	D,N,B,	1,0,,S,Y,M,B,Ø,L,
0,6,0			
0,7,0		D,N,B,	5,0,,,C,Ø,M,M,E,N,T,
0,8,0			

Fig. 11.17. Examples of the DNB Declarative.

9. The card punch unit is the *only* output device that will interpret C–8–4 coding as a blank. This coding produces the @ sign on the typewriter and paper tape punch.

See Figure 11.17 for examples of the DNB properly written.

DECLARATIVES—TAPE SYSTEM ONLY

SEND (SPECIAL END)

The code SEND is used to halt the assembly process temporarily to allow for the mounting of another tape, console switch alteration, etc. If the SEND statement is encountered in the card version of SPS, it is ignored. No object coding is generated by a SEND. The rules of the SEND follow.

1. The operation code SEND appears in columns 12–15 of the operation field.
2. A SEND may not be labeled.
3. A SEND may not have operands.
4. Depression of the Start key resumes the assembly if a SEND statement has been encountered.

GENERAL PROCESSOR INFORMATION

No statement in the source language may exceed 75 characters. In the SPS tape version, *every* source statement is terminated by an E/L character. A statement that bears an asterisk (★) in column 6 is interpreted as a comment and does not affect the processing. Extensive use of these comments which appear on the listing of the assembled statements and occupy no core assists in the debugging process.

As a review of the uses for the asterisk symbol, the four functions follow.

1. As an operand of an instruction.
2. As an operand of a declarative.
3. As a symbol implying multiplication.
4. As a symbol implying a comment statement.

ERROR DETECTION

Error messages arise from improper or careless programming and/or punching errors. The following 14 errors are detected by the assembly system and are reported in the form "ERn" where n is the error code.

1. ER1—A record mark is in the label or operation code field.
2. ER2—For address adjustment, a product greater than 10 digits has resulted from a multiplication.
3. ER3—An invalid operation code has been detected.
4. ER4—A dollar sign ($), which is being used as a Head indicator, is incorrectly positioned in an operand.
5. ER5—(a) The symbolic address contains more than six characters.
   (b) The actual address contains more than five characters.
   (c) An undefined symbolic address or an invalid special character is used in an operand.
6. ER6—A DSA statement has more than 10 operands.
7. ER7—A DSB statement has the second operand missing.
8. ER8—(a) A DC, DSC, DAC, or DNB has a length operand greater than 50.
   (b) A DC, DSC, or DAC has no constant specified.
   (c) A DC or DSC has a specified length less than the number of digits in the constant.
   (d) A DAC has a specified length not equal to the number of characters in the constant.
9. ER9—The table of labels is full.
10. ER10—A label has been defined more than once.
11. ER11—An assembled address is greater than 5 digits.
12. ER12—A Head statement contains an invalid special character as a heading character.
13. ER13—A Head statement contains more than one character.
14. ER14—An invalid special character is used in a label.

The procedure for handling errors will be discussed in Appendix VII, Console Operating Procedures.

Chapter 12

Floating Point Arithmetic

Scientific and engineering computations frequently involve lengthy and complex calculations in which it is necessary to perform arithmetic operations on numbers that may vary widely in magnitude. To obtain a meaningful answer, problems of this type usually require that as many significant digits as possible be retained during calculation and that the decimal point always be properly located. When such problems are applied to a computer, several factors must be taken into consideration, the most important of which is the decimal point location.

Generally speaking, a computer does not recognize the decimal point present in any quantity used during a calculation. Thus a product of 414154 will result regardless of whether the factors are 9.37 × 44.2, 93.7 × 0.442, or 937. × 4.42, and so forth. It is the programmer's responsibility to be cognizant of the decimal point location before and after the calculation and to arrange the program accordingly. For example, in an addition operation, the decimal point of all numbers in the operation must be lined up to obtain the correct sum. Therefore, the programmer must guarantee this arrangement by shifting the quantities as they are added.

Example:

$$XXX.XXXXX \longleftarrow A$$
$$.XXXXXXXX \longleftarrow B$$
$$X.XXXXXXX \longleftarrow C$$

where $A + B + C \leqq 999$

Program to calculate A + B + C

BNF	★+24,B
SF	B−3
A	A,B−3
BNF	★+24,C
SF	C−2
A	A,C−2

If the program were

A	A,B
A	A,C

the result would not be accurate (except by chance) since the decimal points are not properly aligned.

All of the digits in all of the data are not used in the first (correct) solution to the problem, but under the statement of the problem, there is little choice in the matter.

Another course might be to define an 11-digit field of zeros, symbolically called "Zeros," and produce the following program:

A	ZEROS−3,A
BNF	★+36,ZEROS−3
CF	ZEROS−3
SF	ZEROS−1
A	ZEROS−1,C
BNF	★+36,ZEROS−1
CF	ZEROS−1
SF	ZEROS
A	ZEROS,B

However, the only portion of the answer that has mathematical foundation is the portion "Zeros–10" through "Zeros–3" inclusive. The significant difference is that the first program ignored the possibility of carries whereas this program extends itself to propagate those carries into position "Zeros–3."

It is conceivable, though, that when numbers that vary greatly in magnitude are manipulated, the resulting quantity could exceed practical working limits.

The processing of numbers expressed in ordinary form (for example, 427.93456, 0.0009762, 5382., −623.147, 3.1415927, etc.) can be accomplished on a computer only with extensive analysis to determine the size and range of intermediate and final results. When programmed, this analysis and subsequent number scaling will frequently require a larger percentage of the total time needed to solve the problem than will the actual calculation. Furthermore, number scaling requires complete and accurate information regarding the bounds on the magnitude of all numbers that come into the computation (input, intermediate results, output). Since it is not always possible to predict the magnitude of all numbers in a given calculation, analysis and number scaling is sometimes impractical.

To alleviate this programming problem, a system must be employed in which information regarding the magnitude of all numbers accompanies the quantities in the calculation. That is, if all numbers are represented in some standard predetermined format which instructs the computer in an orderly and simple fashion as to the location of the decimal point, and if this representation is acceptable to a computer, then quantities that range from minute fractions having many decimal places to large whole numbers having many integer places may all be handled with ease.

The arithmetic system most commonly used, in which all numbers are expressed in a format having the above features, is called "floating point arithmetic." Specialized programs that handle floating point numbers are called "floating point subroutines." The notation used in floating point arithmetic is basically an adaptation of the scientific notation widely used today. In scientific work, very large or very small numbers are expressed as a number between .1 and .99..., times a power of 10. That is, the decimal point of all numbers is placed to the left of the high-order (leftmost) nonzero digit. Hence, all quantities may be thought of as a decimal fraction times a power of 10 (for example, 427.93456 as 0.42793456×10^3 and 0.0009762 as 0.9762×10^{-3}) where the fraction is called the "mantissa" and the power of 10, used to indicate the number of places the decimal point was shifted, is called the "characteristic." In addition to the advantages of uniformity inherent in scientific notation, the use of floating point numbers during processing eliminates the necessity of analyzing operations to determine the position of the decimal point in intermediate and final results since the decimal point is always immediately to the left of the high-order digit in the mantissa.

In the 1620 floating point arithmetic system, each quantity is expressed as an n digit number ($4 \le n \le 47$) consisting of a 2-digit characteristic and an (n–2)-digit fractional mantissa. This fraction, in absolute value, may extend between 0.100...00 and 0.999...99. This is shown in Figure 12.1.

$$\underbrace{\text{XXX}...\text{XXX}}_{m}\underbrace{\text{XX}}_{c}$$

Fig. 12.1. Form of a Floating Point Number.

In Figure 12.1, c represents the characteristic and m the mantissa, as explained below. The original number is $m \times 10^c$.

The mantissa (m), or fractional part of the number, consists of the leftmost (n–2) digits of the floating point number. The decimal point is always tacitly assumed to lie immediately to the left of the high-order mantissa digit. The sign of the original number is always associated with the mantissa and is designated by the presence (for negative) or absence (positive) of a flag in the units position of the mantissa. A mantissa is called "normal" or "normalized" when its high-order digit is nonzero. In 1620 floating point, the mantissa must always be normalized. The floating point subroutines always leave normalized floating point numbers as the result of a floating point operation, with one exception. The exception to the "normalized mantissa rule" is a floating point zero which is always expressed as 0.000...00 with a characteristic of −99.

The characteristic (c) represents the power of 10 used to specify the location of the decimal point in the original number. It stands for the number of places the decimal point was shifted in order to place it to the left of the high-order, nonzero digit. The direction of the shift is determined by the sign of the characteristic. Thus, if the sign of the characteristic is negative, the decimal point was shifted to the right the number of positions specified by the characteristic. If no sign is indicated—the absence of sign specifying a positive characteristic—the shift was to the left. Thus, the characteristic can assume a range of values from −99 to 99, inclusive,

$$-99 \le c \le 99.$$

Upon combining the ranges and the mantissa and characteristic, we see that floating point numbers may lie within the range

$$\pm 0.100...00 \times 10^{-99} \text{ to } \pm 0.999...99 \times 10^{99}.$$

In floating point form, both the characteristic and mantissa are always flagged over their respective high-order digits to indicate the end-of-field condition. Table 12.1 demonstrates the conversion of numbers in ordinary form to 1620 variable-size floating point notation.

Table 12.1

NUMBER	NORMALIZED	MANTISSA SIZE	FLOATING POINT FORM
123.45678	0.12345678×10^3	8 digits	$\overline{1}2345678\overline{0}3$
0.00765432	0.765432×10^{-2}	6 digits	$\overline{7}6543 2\overline{0}\overline{2}$
0.00765432	0.765432×10^{-2}	10 digits	$\overline{7}6543200 0\overline{0}\overline{2}$ °
-0.1234987623	$-0.1234987623 \times 10^0$	13 digits	$\overline{1}234987623 00\overline{0}\overline{0}\overline{0}$ °
-0.1234987623	$-0.1234987623 \times 10^0$	3 digits	$\overline{1}2\overline{3}\overline{0}\overline{0}$ ° °
-0.00001	-0.1×10^{-4}	2 digits	$\overline{1}0\overline{0}\overline{4}$ °
-0.00001	-0.1×10^{-4}	8 digits	$\overline{1}000000\overline{0}\overline{0}\overline{4}$ °
-0.0	-0.0×10^0	4 digits	$\overline{0}000\overline{9}\overline{9}$ °
0.0	0.0×10^0	4 digits	$\overline{0}000\overline{9}\overline{9}$ °

* Low-order zeros added to increase mantissa size to desired length.
** Mantissa truncated to reduce size to desired length.

GENERAL NOTES ON 1620 FLOATING POINT SUBROUTINES

In the 1620 floating point subroutines, an attempt to generate a characteristic of magnitude greater than 99 creates a condition called "characteristic overflow." An attempt to generate a characteristic less than -99 creates a condition called "characteristic underflow." Should either of these conditions be generated as a result of an arithmetic operation, the programmer will be provided with a choice of two options as follows:

OVERFLOW

    1. Program Halt
         or
    2. The floating point number

      $\overline{9}9 \ldots 99\overline{9}9$ is placed in the result field and the program continues.

		UNDERFLOW	
		Halt	Store Zeros in Result Field
O V E R F L O W	Halt	$\bar{0}$	0
O V E R F L O W	Store Nines in Result Field	$\bar{1}$	1

Fig. 12.2. Overflow-Underflow Schematic.

UNDERFLOW

1. Program Halt
   or
2. The floating point number

   $\bar{0}0\ldots00\bar{9}\bar{9}$ is placed in the result field and the program continues.

These options function independently of each other. Thus it is possible to halt on an underflow and place 9's in the result field on an overflow. The converse is also true. The detection of an overflow or underflow condition will cause the subroutine being executed to examine core position 00401 to determine the course of action. The programmer must make manual or programmed provisions for one of the four conditions in order to exercise his option.

GENERAL NOTES ON THE USE OF FLOATING POINT ARITHMETIC

During any floating point calculation the size of the two operands must be identical. Thus, it is not possible to "floating add" a 17-digit floating point number and an 8-digit floating point number.

Another form of floating point assumes a fixed word size of 10 digits consisting of a 2-digit characteristic and an 8-digit mantissa. The characteristic precedes the mantissa and a notation called "excess fifty" is employed. Excess fifty implies that the number 50 is added to the characteristic developed. Thus, the characteristic may assume values between 00 and 99 only. In this fashion, the number 25.3 (0.253×10^2) becomes $\bar{5}225300000$ in floating point form. Similarly, the number -0.0000001 (-0.1×10^{-6}) becomes $\bar{4}410000000\bar{0}$. This notation has been widely used in a great variety of decimal computers but does not lend itself well to variable-word-size floating point.

Problems

I: Convert the following numbers to floating point notation. The number in parentheses is the mantissa size desired.

1. 15.96(9)
2. $-50073.(12)$
3. 10128.965(4)
4. $-8.9(15)$
5. 0.127(5)
6. $-0.00001589(6)$
7. $-0.0(12)$
8. $-0.001248(4)$
9. 183.72(10)
10. 0.00000001(7)

II. Convert the following numbers to their fixed point representation. Use sufficient digits to fully express the number: 100000 is to be expressed as 0.1000 not as 0.1.

1. $\bar{5}38\bar{0}7$
2. $\bar{9}56121\bar{7}\bar{0}3$
3. $\bar{1}72152\bar{0}\bar{2}$
4. $\bar{8}102193\bar{1}\bar{2}$
5. $\bar{6}1\bar{0}0$
6. $\bar{7}522128\bar{1}1$
7. $\bar{1}111111\bar{1}\bar{1}\bar{1}$
8. $\bar{2}113419\bar{0}\bar{1}$
9. $\bar{6}116\bar{0}0$
10. $\bar{1}51719121\bar{8}\bar{1}\bar{0}$

Chapter 13

Macro-Instructions

Whenever the use of a subroutine is required by a main program, it must be suitably incorporated into that program. That is, the subroutine must be logically connected to the main program in such a way that the subroutine will be executed at the proper time and, at its completion, will return control to the main program to continue the execution of the problem.

One method by which this connection can be effected is to insert the subroutine directly into the larger program where needed. A subroutine incorporated in this fashion is called an "open subroutine" or "direct insert subroutine." In most cases, however, this method of connection is not entirely practical or desirable. For example, in a program that requires the evaluation of a square root at 15 different places, it would be superfluous to incorporate the same square root subroutine 15 times. The desirable solution is to store the subroutine once, out of the main line sequence of the program, and, when required, enter the subroutine by a branching operation. Provision must also be made to return control to the main program at the completion of the subroutine.

Subroutines connected in this fashion are called "closed" or "linked" subroutines. The instructions related to the entry and re-entry function constitute the linkage. In general, it is necessary for the linkage instructions to a closed subroutine to supply three items of information:

1. The address of the subroutine desired.
2. The return address after completion of the subroutine.
3. The address(es) of the argument(s) in question, or the actual argument(s) itself/themselves.

The instructions that provide this linkage may, of course, be written by the programmer. However, certain special *macro-instructions* may be employed by the programmer to cause automatic generation of these linkage instructions. A macro-instruction may be defined as a pseudo-instruction which, during assembly, generates more than one machine language instruction. For the 1620 Symbolic Programming System[1] there are 17 macro-instructions available. Each of these "macros," when used in a source program, will generate the instructions necessary to provide proper linkage to one of the 17 subroutines. The subroutines are of two categories: arithmetic and functional. Table 13.1 gives a list of all available macro-instructions.

Thus, by placing in the source program, at the point at which a particular subroutine is desired, the macro-instruction related to this subroutine, the programmer will cause the SPS processor to generate, during assembly, the linkage to the desired subroutine. In addition, the processor will arrange for the subroutine to be placed in core storage. Thus, when required during the execution of the object program, the subroutine will be transferred to and executed. The data and addresses required by the subroutine, and supplied by the macro-instruction, are incorporated into the linkage instructions where they are either (1) transmitted directly to the subroutine or (2) simply made available for use.

In this way, the subroutine obtains the information it requires to perform its given task and also obtains the information required to generate a return address to the main program. Control is returned to the main program at the completion of the subroutine by branching to the return address.

In the discussion of many of the macro-instructions, a reference is made to Appendix IV, "Floating Point Hardware," for a description of their operations. This is not to imply that macro-instructions are genuine machine commands but rather that their operation simulates the analogous machine code. With the realization that subroutine linkages are generated by use of these macro-instructions, the programmer may consider them as if they were actual machine commands.

---

[1] There are many versions of SPS, but the most commonly used is one which assumes a floating point word to always be 10 digits in length (8-digit mantissa and 2-digit characteristic). Another version allows for variability of the mantissa. It is the former version which is discussed in this chapter. Knowledge of this fixed-word-size system allows for immediate transition to the variable-mantissa system.

Table 13.1*

ARITHMETIC	FUNCTIONAL
Floating Add (FA)	Floating Square Root (FSQR)
Floating Subtract (FS)	Floating Sine (FSIN)—Radian argument
Floating Multiply (FM)	Floating Cosine (FCOS)—Radian argument
Floating Divide (FD)	Floating Arctangent (FATN)
Fixed Divide (DIV)	Floating Exponential (FEX)—Base e
	Floating Exponential (FEXT)—Base 10
	Floating Logarithm (FLN)—Base e
	Floating Logarithm (FLOG)—Base 10
	Floating Transmit Field (TFLS)
	Floating Branch and Transmit (BTFS)

* Two additional macro-instructions are also available, but their use is greatest with the variable mantissa version of SPS. These macros are Floating Shift Right (FSRS) and Floating Shift Left (FSLS). See Appendix IV "Floating Point Hardware," for a discussion of their function.

LINKAGE

A design for a subroutine linking scheme is generally a compromise between the maximum amount of information that can be obtained from the linkage and the minimum core required by the linkage. The primary linking instructions used by all macro-instructions in the 1620 symbolic system are as follows:

LINE	LABEL	OPERATION	OPERANDS & REMARKS
0,1,0		T,F,M	P,I,C,K+,K,,*,+,2,3,
0,2,0		B,	L,I,N,K,
0,3,0		D,O,R,G	*,-,4,
0,4,0		D,S,A,	A,,,B,,,C,
0,5,0			

where "Pick" is a subroutine used by all macros and "Link" is the location of a secondary linkage.

This secondary linkage generally takes the following form:

LINE	LABEL	OPERATION	OPERANDS & REMARKS
0,1,0		T,F,M	P,I,C,K+,C,,,S,U,B,
0,2,0		B,	P,I,C,K,+,J,
0,3,0			
0,4,0			

where "Sub" is the address of the desired subroutine and "K," "C," and "J" are constants supplied by the processor.

In this way the secondary linkage and the Pick subroutine act as intermediaries between the primary linkage and the actual subroutine desired. Pick is given the address of the *address* of the first argument by the primary linkage. Having this, Pick can then calculate the address of the address of the second argument, third, and so forth, and lastly the return address to the main program. The Pick routine is given the address of the main subroutine by the secondary linkage and the combination of these items allows Pick to operate as a successful "middle man."

All secondary linkages are located after the last instruction generated by the SPS source program, and the Pick subroutine follows the last of the secondary linkages. All subroutines follow Pick. Therefore, it is necessary to know the size of all these elements in order to be assured that the program will not overflow the available core storage. The schematic of the linkage system is presented in Figure 13.1.

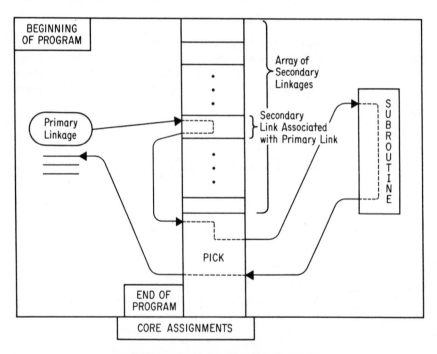

Fig. 13.1. Schematic of Linkage System.

ARITHMETIC MACRO-INSTRUCTIONS

FLOATING POINT

In each of the macro-instructions related to the four floating point subroutines, two addresses, represented by A and B, must be specified.

These addresses, which may be symbolic or actual, must reference the low-order characteristic digit of the floating point data to be added, subtracted, and so forth.

During the execution of the floating point arithmetic subroutines, the Overflow, H/P, and E/Z indicators will be used. The Overflow indicator is always reset at the beginning of each floating point arithmetic subroutine. Should its status prior to the execution of such a subroutine be desired, the indicator must be tested and its condition stored before the linkage instructions are executed.

After completion of the operation, the H/P and E/Z indicators will be set according to the mantissa of the result. All floating point subroutines (arithmetic and functional) require that the floating point quantities used contain flags over the high-order characteristic and mantissa digits. If any operation produces a zero result, the form assumed by the zero in floating point is $\overline{0}00000000\overline{9}\overline{9}$.

FLOATING ADD

1. Macro-instruction:

LINE	LABEL	OPERATION	OPERANDS & REMARKS
0,1,0		F,A,	A,, ,B,
0,2,0			
0,3,0			
0,4,0			

2. Operation: The operation of the macro "FA" is identical with that of the hardware command "FADD" described in Appendix IV.

FLOATING SUBTRACT

1. Macro-instruction:

LINE	LABEL	OPERATION	OPERANDS & REMARKS
0,1,0		F,S,	A,, ,B,
0,2,0			
0,3,0			
0,4,0			

2. Operation: The operation of the macro "FS" is identical with that of the hardware command "FSUB" described in Appendix IV.

FLOATING MULTIPLY

    1. Macro-instruction:

LINE	LABEL	OPERATION	OPERANDS & REMARKS
0010		F.M.	A, B
0020			
0030			
0040			

    2. Operation: The operation of the macro "FM" is identical with that of the hardware command "FMUL" described in Appendix IV.

FLOATING DIVIDE

    1. Macro-instruction:

LINE	LABEL	OPERATION	OPERANDS & REMARKS
0010		F.D.	A, B
0020			
0030			
0040			

    2. Operation: The operation of the macro "FD" is identical with that of the hardware command "FDIV" described in Appendix IV.

FIXED POINT

FIXED DIVIDE

    1. Macro-instruction:

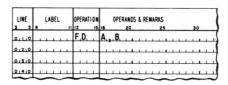

LINE	LABEL	OPERATION	OPERANDS & REMARKS
0010		D.I.V.	A, B, LD, D
0020			
0030			
0040			

    2. Operation: The macro operand "LD" is identical in operation to the hardware command "Load Dividend" discussed in Appendix II in the section on "Automatic Division." This operand may be symbolic or actual.

The macro operand "D" is identical in operation to the hardware command "Divide" discussed in Appendix II. This operand may be symbolic or actual.

The operands A and B specify the dividend and divisor respectively. A description of the macro "DIV" can be best obtained by referring to the sections explaining the hardware commands "Load Dividend" and "Divide" in Appendix II.

FUNCTIONAL MACRO-INSTRUCTIONS

At the conclusion of any functional subroutine, the status of the H/P, E/Z, and Overflow indicators will not necessarily reflect the result of the operation. These indicators will be in constant use during the execution of the subroutine and therefore their status at the conclusion of any subroutine should not be construed to be their status prior to the execution of the subroutine.

Several pairs of subroutines have been combined into single subroutines due to their mathematical similarity (sine-cosine; $\log_{10}$-$\log_e$; e^x-10^x). This is done to reduce the number of program steps that are common to both and, simultaneously, reduce storage requirements. The subroutines are distinguished from one another by their entry point and their correct use is obtained through the use of the macro pertaining to the particular subroutine desired.

As in the case of arithmetic macro-instructions, two addresses, symbolic or actual, are specified. These addresses reference the units position of the characteristics of the floating point numbers.

FLOATING SQUARE ROOT

1. Macro-instruction:

LINE	LABEL	OPERATION	OPERANDS & REMARKS		
0 1 0		F S Q R	A , B		
0 2 0					
0 3 0					
0 4 0					

2. Operation: The floating point data referenced by B will have its square root extracted and the resultant floating point number will be stored with its low-order characteristic digit at the core position referenced by A. The floating point number referenced by B is not altered.

FLOATING SINE AND COSINE

1. Macro-instruction:

LINE	LABEL	OPERATION	OPERANDS & REMARKS
0.1.0		F.S.I.N	A,,B
0.2.0		F.C.O.S	A,,B
0.3.0			
0.4.0			

2. Operation: The sine/cosine of the floating point data referenced by B (which must be in radian measurement) will be computed and the resultant floating point number will be stored with its low-order characteristic digit at the core position referenced by A. The floating point number referenced by B is not altered.

FLOATING ARCTANGENT

1. Macro-instruction:

LINE	LABEL	OPERATION	OPERANDS & REMARKS
0.1.0		F.A.T.N	A,,B
0.2.0			
0.3.0			
0.4.0			

2. Operation: The arctangent of the floating point data referenced by B will be computed and the floating point result, in radians, will be stored with its low-order characteristic digit at the core position referenced by A. The floating point number referenced by B is not altered.

FLOATING EXPONENTIAL

1. Macro-instruction:

LINE	LABEL	OPERATION	OPERANDS & REMARKS
0.1.0		F.E.X.	A,,B
0.2.0		F.E.X.T	A,,B
0.3.0			
0.4.0			

2. Operation: The antilogarithm of the floating point data referenced by B will be computed and the floating point result will be stored with its low-order characteristic digit at the core position referenced by A. The floating point number referenced by B is not altered. If the argument is negative, the subroutine operates with the absolute value of the argument and then computes the reciprocal value by division.

FLOATING LOGARITHM

1. Macro-instruction:

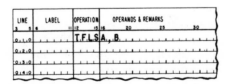

2. Operation: The logarithm of the floating point data referenced by B will be computed and the floating point result will be stored with its low-order characteristic digit at the core position referenced by A. The floating point number referenced by B is not altered.

FLOATING TRANSMIT FIELD (TRANSMIT FLOATING FIELD)

1. Macro-instruction:

2. Operation: The operation of the macro "TFLS" is identical with that of the hardware command "TFL" described in Appendix IV.

FLOATING BRANCH AND TRANSMIT
(BRANCH AND TRANSMIT FLOATING)

    1. Macro-instruction:

LINE	LABEL	OPERATION	OPERANDS & REMARKS
0,1,0		B,T,F,S	A,,,B,
0,2,0			
0,3,0			
0,4,0			

    2. Operation: The operation of the macro "BTFS" is identical with that of the hardware command "BTFL." This is described in Appendix IV.

RESTRICTIONS ON FUNCTIONAL ROUTINES

    1. FSQR—The argument must be positive. If the argument is less than zero, the subroutine executes a programmed halt. The operator may either (a) manually branch back to the main program or (b) depress the Start key and compute the square root of the absolute value of the argument.

    2. FSIN/FCOS—The subroutine will execute a programmed halt if the characteristic of the floating point argument is greater than 08. For all arguments with exponent less than or equal to 03, the maximum error produced will not exceed 10^{-8}. For arguments whose characteristic is greater than 03, the accuracy decreases as the characteristic increases.

    3. FATN—The Arctangent subroutine accepts any number in the floating point range.

    4. FEX—An argument that exceeds 227.95592 results in exponent overflow. An argument less than −227.95592 causes exponent underflow. Should such a condition arise, the subroutine examines core position 00401 to determine the course of action.

    5. FEXT—An argument that exceeds 98.900000 results in exponent overflow. An argument less than −98.900000 causes exponent underflow. The course of action is identical with that of exponent overflow/underflow for FEX.

    6. FLN/FLOG—The subroutine will execute a programmed halt if the argument is less than or equal to zero. A return to the main program can then be effected by the operator.

GENERAL MACRO-INSTRUCTION INFORMATION

In addition to creating linkage instructions to the subroutine desired, the use of a macro-instruction will cause the subroutine(s) required to be punched into the object program tape or card deck. The necessary subroutines will thus be loaded into core storage during the loading of the object program.

Incorporating the subroutines into the object program requires that all subroutines be available to the processor during assembly. Since their physical size precludes their being in core along with the processor, a separate tape or card deck containing all of the subroutines must be assembled in conjunction with the source program. The subroutine(s) required will be selected from the subroutine tape or deck, assigned core storage space, and punched into the object tape or deck.

Subroutines will be assigned to an area in core storage which immediately follows the Pick subroutine. Care must be exercised by the programmer to provide, between the last location assigned by the processor and 19999 (39999, 59999), sufficient space to accommodate the subroutines called for.

Each subroutine will be complete with the constants and working areas it requires for proper execution. These constants and working areas may be common to several subroutines and will be assembled into the object program only once. Sharing common storage and constants eliminates redundancy and minimizes storage requirements. It should be noted that four subroutines require the division operation. If a machine installation is without the automatic division feature, the division subroutine will be called in its place; core storage should be alloted for this. This decision is a function of which subroutine deck is utilized. The four subroutines are (1) Floating Divide, (2) Floating Arctangent, (3) Floating Exponential, and (4) Floating Logarithm.

A macro-instruction may be labeled in the source program. During assembly, a reference to this label will be a reference to the first instruction generated by this macro. The A address therefore is

$$LABEL+23$$

and the B address is

$$LABEL+28$$

where "Label" is the symbolic name given to the macro.

A macro-instruction may not contain a flag operand or a remarks operand.

SPECIFICATIONS OF THE PICK SUBROUTINE

The Pick subroutine is, common to all subroutines. During the execution of the object program, the Pick subroutine performs five major functions. These are:

1. The A and B operands are located in working areas.
2. A return address (to the main program) is calculated.
3. The subroutine is branched to.
4. The calculated result is stored in the proper location.
5. The return to the main program is effected.

In addition to the five functions described above, the Pick subroutine has the following three secondary functions:

1. All error messages are initiated by the Pick subroutine.
2. If the error condition is such that the processing may continue, the Pick subroutine returns to the subroutine in question.
3. Constants and working storage are provided by Pick.

The material in Table 13.2 gives the approximate core size for all subroutines that would be utilized on a 1620 without the automatic division feature. Following this, in Table 13.3, is the analogous chart for those subroutines that utilize the automatic division feature.

Table 13.2

Storage Requirements for Subroutines without Automatic Division

Subroutine	Fixed Mantissa	Variable Mantissa
PICK	872	1136
DIV	1047	1035
FA, FS (Combined)	543	
FM	239	1207*
FD	523	
FSQR	579	659
FCOS, FSIN	843	1098
FATN	1077	1487
FEXT, FEX	784	1258
FLOG, FLN	886	1209
FSRS	279	279
FSLS	372	372
TFLS	31	31
BTFS	79	79

* All four arithmetic floating point subroutines are combined in one set to save storage.

Table 13.3

Storage Requirements for Subroutines with Automatic Division

SUBROUTINE	FIXED MANTISSA	VARIABLE MANTISSA
PICK	872	1136
DIV*	187	199
FA, FS (Combined)	543	
FM	239	1163**
FD	335	
FSQR	579	659
FCOS, FSIN	843	1054
FATN	989	1379
FEXT, FEX	740	1118
FLOG, FLN	842	1145
FSRS	235	279
FSLS	279	372
TFLS	372	31
BTFS	79	79

* One may use the DIV macro-instruction with this deck. However, in this case the macro consists of hardware divide instructions. This is not the most efficient machine utilization technique, but it does allow one to assemble, on a machine with the division feature, those programs which were written utilizing the division macro. Also, no programming changes are necessary.
** All four arithmetic floating point subroutines are combined in one set so that storage may be utilized more economically.

NOISE

In operations associated with floating point arithmetic, a process termed "normalization" often takes place. Normalization is a left shifting operation which eliminates high-order zeros in the mantissa of a floating point number produced by a calculation. Thus, a product of two numbers

$$(\overline{1}10\overline{0}2) \times (\overline{1}10\overline{0}2)$$

produces the result

$$(\overline{1}21\overline{0}3)$$

and not

$$(\overline{0}12\overline{0}4)$$

Often, however, this left shift introduces zeros into the units position of a mantissa. Thus, a result before normalization might appear as

$$(\overline{0}0812 5\overline{0}6)$$

and after normalization as

$$(\overline{8}1250 0\overline{0}4)$$

A zero is chosen as the "fill" digit only because there is no knowledge of the digit that should be selected. When a digit other than zero is selected as the fill digit, the calculation is said to be performed in the "noisy" mode. The fill digit is termed the "noise" digit, or simply "noise."

In the normal execution of arithmetic, because the results are always truncated,[1] small, unavoidable errors are introduced in the results of the arithmetic operations. These errors may accumulate to the point where the final results are greatly affected. The noisy mode is used to detect the sensitivity of a computation to the growth of truncation errors. In the noisy mode, the results are modified slightly to determine the effect of such slight perturbations.

The 1620 linkage system allows the programmer to specify any noise digit he wishes. This can be any digit zero through nine. However, if a programmer runs a problem twice, once in the zero fill mode, and once in the nine fill mode, and no significant difference in his results are noted, it is probable that his results are good. If, on the other hand, a significant difference is noted between the two runs, the programmer should suspect that the computation is very sensitive to truncation error. Much numerical experimentation of these points remains to be done.

A noise digit *must always* be specified in any program which uses macros. This is done by preceding the DEND statement by the statement.

DAC 1,X

where "X" is the noise digit requested, 0 through 9.

Failure to specify a noise digit in the exact manner stated may cause a failure in the assembly process and also in the running of the object program.

This noise digit will be transferred to location PICK–1 by the subroutine processor and may be altered during the running of the object program by referencing

NOISE + 20★K

where "Noise" is the label of the statement

DAC 1,X

and "K" is the number of secondary linkages.

As an example, assume that the main body of the following sample program begins at location

ZEROFL + 12

and that five *separate* macro-instructions have been employed. If the programmer begins execution of the object program at location

---

[1] The terminology concerning error unfortunately is very vague. Truncation is generally understood to imply "cutting off" certain digits in order to carry a constant number of digits per data field. Thus, the product of two n-digit numbers produces a result of length $2n$, but only the first n digits are retained. It is not generally understood that a "round" may or may not take place before the truncation. The purpose of rounding is to improve the accuracy of the data field that is retained.

START

he will utilize zero fill or nine fill depending upon the setting of console
switch 1. If he chooses to begin his program at

ZEROFL+12

the fill digit will be 5.

LINE	LABEL	OPERATION	OPERANDS & REMARKS		
3 5	6	11 12 15	16 20 25 30		
0.1.0					
0.2.0					
0.3.0					
0.4.0	S,T,A,R,T	B,C,1,	Z,E,R,Ø,F,L		
0.5.0		T,D,M,	N,Ø,I,S,E,+,1,0,0,.,9		
0.6.0		B,	*+,2,4,		
0.7.0	Z,E,R,Ø,F,L	T,D,M,	N,O,I,S,E,+,1,0,0,.,0,		
0.8.0					
0.9.0					
1.0.0					
1.1.0	N,Ø,I,S,E	D,A,C,	1,.,5,		
1.2.0		D,E,N,D			
1.3.0					

Chapter 14

Introduction to Fortran

The past few years have seen vast technological advances made in computer design. Storage devices with access speeds measured in microseconds and even nanoseconds[1] have been developed; solid-state circuitry has greatly increased circuit reliability; highspeed magnetic tape units and disk files have been developed. The three advances listed here by no means exhaust the list; they serve as but a small sample from a large population. With these technological advances in computer design in mind, one might pose the question, have any advances been made in programming systems? Certainly this is a reasonable question.

We have studied in detail the Symbolic Programming System. It was noted that the symbolic system relieves the programmer of the tedious and error-breeding task of keeping track of numerical addresses; easy to remember mnemonics are substituted for numbers. This results in reducing programming time and thus reflects a monetary saving to the computer user. A large portion of the cost of solving a problem on a computer is programming time. It is not uncommon for a programmer to spend months programming an application and then have the computer execute the program and produce the results in a few minutes.

The reader will recall that each symbolic instruction produces one machine language instruction, except macro-instructions which generate more than one machine language instruction. Although the symbolic system eases the programming task, it is still necessary for the programmer

[1] One nanosecond is one one billionth of a second.

170

to write down the same number of program steps (macros excepted) to solve a problem as in machine language. Let us now imagine a processor so powerful that it can generate many machine language instructions for each source statement it receives. In this way we could issue a source statement such as $A = B + C + D + E$ and have the processor generate *all* the machine language instructions necessary to satisfy the requirements of the source statement. Such processors do exist. Fortran, Cobol, and Algol are all programming systems incorporating these powerful processors.

Fortran is the name that was given to a programming system developed primarily for use in the scientific and engineering areas. The purpose of the Fortran system is to simplify programming by allowing the programmer to state in a relatively simple language, closely resembling that of ordinary algebra, the steps of a procedure to be carried out for the solution of a problem, and to obtain automatically from the computer, under direction of the processor, an efficient machine language program for this procedure. The term "efficient" is very significant. It would not benefit us greatly in overall job time if programming time were decreased only to have the generated machine language program take four or five times as long to run as a hand-written machine language or SPS program. The 1620 Fortran system generates a highly efficient machine language program.

The following definitions of terminology are used in this and subsequent chapters:

1. Fortran language—A set of statements, similar to the expressions used in ordinary algebra. These statements are used by a programmer to define a problem.
2. Source statement—One Fortran language statement.
3. Source Program—A program written in the Fortran language. It is made up of a series of source statements.
4. Fortran Compiler (or Translator)—A machine language program which analyzes the source statements and converts them to machine language instructions.
5. Object Program—The totality of machine language instructions produced by the Fortran processor by operating on the statements of the source program.

The name "Fortran" comes from "*FOR*mula *TRAN*slation" and was chosen because many of the statements which this system accepts look like algebraic formulas. The Fortran system consists of two parts: the Fortran language and the Fortran compiler or translator. The programmer writes his instructions to the computer in the Fortran language. The Fortran processor is an extensive set of machine language instructions that direct the 1620 to translate the Fortran language statements into a machine language program. This process of translation is called "*com-pilation.*" Use of the Fortran system consists of the following steps:

1. Read the Fortran processor program into the 1620.
2. Each Fortran statement is read in and analyzed by the processor program, and the machine language instructions to satisfy the requirements of the source statement are punched.
3. Read in the subroutines and punch those required by the object program. Subroutines are prewritten programs that perform standard routines such as calculating the sine and cosine of an angle, raising a number to a power, or taking the natural logarithm of a number.
4. Read in the object program and the data.

The above steps are represented by Figure 14.1.

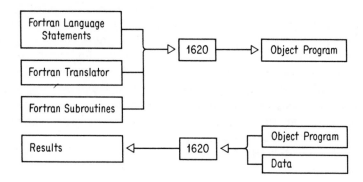

Fig. 14.1.   Steps in the Fortran System.

Virtually any numerical procedure may be expressed in the Fortran language. As an example of the power of the Fortran system let us write the Fortran statement to evaluate one of the roots of a quadratic equation given by the formula

$$X = \frac{-B+\sqrt{B^2-4AC}}{2A}$$

The Fortran statement expressing this formula is

$$X1 = (-B + SQRT(B**2-4.*A*C))/(2.*A)$$

This statement would cause the processor to generate the machine language instructions to evaluate the function to the right of the equal sign. The variable to the left of the equal sign would then be set equal to this value.

The Fortran system is available not only for the 1620, but also for many other computers. The Fortran language is very similar for each system and only minor changes to the source program need be made to run it on any computer. Each computer, however, has its own unique Fortran processor—this is to be expected since each computer has its own unique machine language codes.

These are a variety of Fortran systems for the 1620. The following chapter will discuss in detail one particular system, Basic Fortran.[2] However, with a knowledge of Basic Fortran, the more advanced Fortran systems can be easily learned.

[2] This system is also known as "Fortran with Format."

Chapter 15

Basic 1620 Fortran

Also Known as "Fortran with Format"

Fortran is an automatic coding system consisting of two major parts: the Fortran language and the Fortran compiler. The Fortran language is a set of statements, similar to the expressions used in ordinary algebra. These statements are used by the programmer to describe his problem. The Fortran compiler converts the Fortran language statements into machine language instructions which at a later time are executed by the computer to solve the problem.

Since Fortran is a programming language closely related to the language of ordinary algebra, it must provide a means for expressing certain elements basic to a mathematical language. These elements are: numeric constants, variable quantities, subscripted variables, operations, and expressions.

In the Fortran language, variables and constants may each be expressed in one of two modes: fixed point (restricted to integers) or floating point. Each floating point number is represented *internally* (in the core storage) in the floating point form (mantissa and characteristic) discussed in Chapter 12. However, basic Fortran does not permit a variable-length mantissa; the mantissa is of a fixed length—8 digits. Each fixed point number is represented *internally* by 4 decimal digits with a field-defining flag over the high-order digit. All quantities in the Fortran system are represented internally in either the fixed point mode or the floating point mode.

Obviously, the Fortran system must provide for two different types of arithmetic calculations: fixed point and floating point. Floating point calculations are performed through the use of floating point subroutines. Floating point calculations are carried out on two decimal numbers to an accuracy of 8 places. Fixed point calculations are also performed by subroutines. However, in the fixed point mode, calculations are carried out on integers only. No decimal portions of numbers are used.

The following illustrates floating point and fixed point arithmetic calculations:

Floating Point

ARITHMETIC STATEMENT	RESULT
$A = 6.2 + 3.171$	$A = 9.371$
$B = 9. \div 4.$	$B = 2.25$
$C = 1. - 3.2 + 1.6$	$C = -0.6$
$D = 25. \times 2.5$	$D = 62.5$
$E = 1. \div 3.$	$E = 0.33333333$
$F = (2.5 \div 2.) \times 6.21$	$F = 7.7625$

Fixed Point

ARITHMETIC STATEMENT	RESULT
$A = 5 \times 2$	$A = 10$
$B = 5 + 3 - 1$	$B = 7$
$C = 8 \div 2$	$C = 4$
$D = 9 \div 2$	$D = 4^*$
$E = (5 \div 2) \times (10 \div 3)$	$E = 6^{**}$

* The true answer is 4.5; however, the 0.5 is truncated.
** Truncation causes this to be calculated as 2×3.

CONSTANTS

Constants may appear as part of the source program or as input data. They may be written in one of two forms: fixed point or floating point. The type of arithmetic calculation to be performed on the constant determines in which form it should be written. If the constant is to be used in floating point calculations, it should be written in the floating point form; if it is to be involved in fixed point calculations only, it should be written in the fixed point form. If a constant is to be used in both fixed and floating point calculations, it must appear in both forms.

FIXED POINT

Fixed point constants are characterized by being from 1 to 4 decimal digits in length. (*Internally* fixed point constants are always 4 digits in length, the high-order zeros being automatically supplied if required.) The range, then, of a fixed point constant is from 0 to ±9999. The decimal point is always assumed to be to the right of the right-most digit; e.g., 375 means 375.0. However, the decimal point is *always omitted* in the representation of a fixed point constant. If a fixed point constant with more than 4 digits is written, only the 4 *low-order* digits are processed.

Fixed point constants may be positive or negative. If positive, they are written with or without a preceding plus sign. If negative, a minus sign *must* precede the constant.

General Form

One to four decimal digits without a decimal point. A preceding plus sign is optional. A minus sign is required if the constant is negative.

Examples

398
9
+6
06
−2832
0

FLOATING POINT

Floating point constants may be written in two forms: without exponents or with exponents.

WITHOUT EXPONENTS

Floating point constants without exponents are represented by any number of decimal digits, with a decimal point at the beginning, at the end, or between any two digits.

The decimal point must be written.

Floating point constants may be positive or negative. If positive, they are written with or without a preceding plus sign. If negative, a minus sign *must* precede the constant. Although any number of digits is permissible, only the 8 most significant digits are processed.

General Form

Any number of decimal digits with a decimal point. A preceding plus sign is optional. A minus sign is required if the constant is negative.

Examples

3.14176
+36000.
−82.5
.000065
−.00312
0.

WITH EXPONENTS

Floating point constants with exponents are represented by any number of decimal digits, with a decimal point at the beginning, at the end, or between any two digits. **The decimal point must be written.** This part of the number is called the *mantissa*. The mantissa (including decimal point) is followed by the letter "E," which is followed by a 1- or 2- digit exponent. The exponent is a fixed point constant that signifies the power of 10 by which the mantissa is to be multiplied. The exponent may be positive or negative. If positive, the exponent may be written with or without a preceding plus sign. If negative, a minus sign must precede the exponent.

General Form

Any number of decimal digits with a decimal point, followed by the letter "E" and a 1- or 2-digit exponent. Both the exponent and mantissa may be signed. A preceding plus sign is optional. A minus sign is required if the constant or exponent is negative.

Examples

$17.1E3$ (17.1×10^3)
$-16.0E+6$ (-16.0×10^6)
$+397.017E2$ (397.017×10^2)
$2.E32$ $(2. \times 10^{32})$
$-126.1E+10$ (-126.1×10^{10})
$-6.0E-3$ (-6.0×10^{-3})
$-132.6E+12$ (-132.6×10^{12})
$50.0E13$ (50.0×10^{13})

The following statements may prove helpful in writing or identifying fixed and/or floating point constants.

1. A fixed point constant *never* has a decimal point associated with it.
2. A floating point constant *always* has a decimal point associated with it.

Problem

Identify the following as either a permissible floating point constant or a permissible fixed point constant or neither.

1. 0	9. 6.28E+2
2. −916	10. −12E−12
3. 01234	11. 97.E12.
4. 9,123	12. 14.001E+99
5. 3.14161713	13. 21349
6. −88.9610002	14. 23.67.
7. −.00000000098765E−21	15. .86−8
8. 3E34	16. +92.12E−15

VARIABLES

Variables, like constants, may be fixed point or floating point depending on whether they are being used to represent an integral value or a decimal value. Names (for example, A, B, DELTA, X1) are assigned by the programmer to variables, and the variable names appear as part of the source program.

In order to distinguish between a floating point variable and a fixed point variable certain rules must be adhered to in assigning names to the variables.

FIXED POINT

Fixed Point variables are restricted to integral values and may take on only those values allowed fixed point constants. Fixed point variables are distinguished by the fact that the *first* character of the symbolic name chosen to represent the variable *must* be one of the following: I, J, K, L, M, or N. These symbolic names may be from one to five alphabetic or numerical characters in length. Special characters are not allowed as part of a variable name.

General Form

One to five alphabetic or numerical characters (no special characters) of which the first must be I, J, K, L, M, or N.

Examples

I
M2
JOBNO
L2345
N

FLOATING POINT

Floating point variables may take on only those values allowed floating point constants. The symbolic name chosen to represent the floating point variable is from one to five alphabetic or numerical characters in length. The first character must be *alphabetic* and other than I, J, K, L, M, or N. Special characters are not allowed as part of a variable name.

General Form

One to five alphabetic or numerical characters (no special characters) of which the first must be *alphabetic* but not I, J, K, L, M, or N.

Examples
DELTA
A
A614
Z3A2

Problem

Identify the following as either a permissible fixed point variable or a permissible floating point variable, or neither.

1.	B	6.	SAVING
2.	RATE2	7.	LOAD
3.	L	8.	A1/B
4.	M1234	9.	DELTA
5.	2L1	10.	A+3

CHOOSING VARIABLE NAMES

As in the symbolic programming system, it is advisable when possible to assign names with a high mnemonic content to variables. For example, if one wished to compute electric current from the formula $I = E \div R$, he might choose the names CURR, VOLT, and OHMS to represent the variables I, E, and R respectively. Of course, these names assume that the variables will take on floating point values. If fixed point arithmetic were being used, the names assigned might have been I, IVOLT, and IOHMS, respectively.

OPERATIONS

There are six basic operations associated with the Fortran language. Each operation is represented by a specific symbol as follows:

OPERATION	SYMBOL	EXAMPLE
Addition	+	A + B
Subtraction	−	A − B
Multiplication	★	A★B
Division	/	A/B
Exponentiation	★★	A★★B (A^B)
Equality	=	A = B

The equality operation (=) has a different meaning in the Fortran language than it does in an algebraic equation. This new meaning is discussed in the section on "Arithmetic Statements."

EXPRESSIONS

An expression in Fortran is a sequence of one or more constants and/or variables joined by any of the operation symbols (except the equality

symbol) to indicate a quantity or series of calculations to be performed.
The following are some simple Fortran expressions:

$$A + B - C$$
$$X\star\star2$$
$$IDELT/J2$$

Expressions are used in forming certain statements in the Fortran language. They must be formed according to a set of rules, which will be discussed later.

Parentheses are used in expressions to specify the order of operations just as they are used in ordinary algebra. In the expression $(A + 2.)\star B$ the addition would be performed first and the sum would be multiplied by B. In the expression $A\star\star(2. + Y)$ the floating point addition would be performed first and the variable A would then be raised to the $(2. + Y)$ power. If the parentheses had been omitted so that the expression was $A\star\star2. + Y$, it would have been calculated as $(A\star\star2.) + Y$.

If parentheses are not used to specify the order of operations, the hierarchy of operations is as follows:

1. Exponentiation   High
2. Multiplication and Division
3. Addition and Subtraction   Low

Thus the Fortran expression $A + B\star C\star\star D$ would be interpreted to mean $A + (B \times C^D)$ and $A + (B\star C)\star\star D$ would be interpreted to mean $A + (B \times C)^D$.

There are three exceptions to Fortran expression compatibility with the ordinary rules of mathematical notation. These are as follows:

1. In ordinary notation AB means A times B. However, in Fortran AB *never* means A times B, rather it is interpreted as a floating point variable with the symbolic name "AB." **The multiplication symbol cannot be omitted in Fortran.** The violation of this rule is one of the most common errors in Fortran programming.
2. In ordinary notation, expressions such as $A/B \cdot C$ and $A/B/C$ are considered to be ambiguous. In Fortran, however, such statements are acceptable and are interpreted as follows:

$A/B\star C$	means	$(A/B)\star C$
$A\star B/C$	means	$(A\star B)/C$
$A/B/C$	means	$(A/B)/C$

When expressions contain a string of operation symbols of equal rank in the hierarchy table, the order of operations is taken *from left to right*. As a further example:

W★AB★CD/X★E/D means ((((W★AB)★CD)/X)★E)/D

and

A + B − C + D − E means (((A + B)−C) + D) − E

3. In ordinary notation the expression $_AB^C$ is meaningful. However, the corresponding Fortran expression A★★B★★C *is not allowed* in the Fortran language. It should be written as A★★(B★★C) if $_AB^C$ is meant or as (A★★B)★★C if $(_AB)^C$ is meant.

Rules for Forming Expressions

1. *All* the variables and constants in an expression must be in the same mode. They must either be all floating point numbers or all fixed point numbers. Thus the following expressions are *not* allowable because they contain mixed-mode variables and/or constants.

A + 21★C

I★J + 2.

A + B − JDELT

The following expressions are allowable:

A + 21.★C

I★J + 2

IA + IB − JDELT

Exceptions. An exception to this rule is as follows: a floating point number may have a fixed point exponent. Thus the following Fortran expressions are valid:

A★★2

A + B★★(I + 2)

Exponentiation in Expressions. The following are valid forms which exponentiation may take in an expression:

A★★B

A★★I

where A and B are any floating point expressions and I is any fixed point expression. Exponentiation of the form I★★A and I★★J is not permitted. The following are examples of valid and invalid expressions.

EXPRESSION	VALIDITY
A★★(I + 2.)	Invalid (mixed mode within parentheses)
RAD★★2	Valid
3.1417★RAD★★2.	Valid
DIST★★I	Valid
A★★(B + 3.)	Valid
I★★(J + 3)	Invalid
MON★★2.	Invalid
3.1417★HEIGT★ALENG★R★★3	Valid

2. An operation symbol (excepting the equality symbol to be discussed shortly) must not precede a plus or a minus sign used to signify that a variable or constant is positive or negative. Use parentheses to enclose the sign and the variable or constant.

INVALID EXPRESSIONS	VALID EXPRESSIONS
A★−B	A★(−B)
A/+BDELT	A/(+BDELT)

Table 15.1 shows an algebraic statement and a correct and incorrect Fortran expression for it.

Table 15.1

ALGEBRAIC STATEMENT	INCORRECT FORTRAN EXPRESSION	CORRECT FORTRAN EXPRESSION
$A(-B)$	A★−B	A★(−B)
XY	XY	X★Y
A^{I+2}	A★★I + 2	A★★(I + 2)
$A^{E+2}B$	A★★(E + 2)★B	A★★(E + 2.)★B
AB/CD	A★B/C★D	(A★B)/(C★D)
		or A★B/(C★D)
		or A/C★B/D

Problem

Write Fortran expressions for the following algebraic statements.

1. $A - (B + C)$

2. $A(B + C)$

3. $\dfrac{A}{B} + N$

4. $AX^2 + BX + C$

5. $\dfrac{X + 37 + C}{19D}$

6. $\dfrac{(I^9 + 10)^3}{7 - (2N)}$

7. A^{X+2}

8. $\dfrac{10^{30}X}{-CB}$

9. $(B^2 - 4AC)^{1/2}$

10. Assuming the following Fortran statement to be valid, determine if it will produce the correct result

$$(B★★2 - 4.★A★C)★★(1/2)$$

FORTRAN STATEMENTS

There are five types of Fortran statements that are permitted in a source program. They are as follows:

1. Arithmetic statements
2. Control statements
3. Input-output statements
4. Specification statements
5. Comments

Arithmetic statements specify how variables should be calculated. Control statements enable the programmer to specify when the normally sequential execution of machine operations should be altered. Input-output statements provide for the entry of data and the output of results. Specification statements provide information to the processor as did SPS declaratives. Comment statements are not compiled. They are used for indentification purposes by the programmer.

ARITHMETIC STATEMENTS

An arithmetic statement in the Fortran language looks like a simple statement of equality in ordinary algebra (for example, $A = B$, $A = C + 2.\star B$). The left side (to the left of the equality symbol) of an arithmetic statement may be either a floating point variable or a fixed point variable. *Constants* and *expressions* involving an operation symbol are *not* allowed to the left of an equality symbol. The right side of all arithmetic statements are expressions.

The equality symbol takes on a unique meaning in the Fortran language. It literally means "to evaluate the expression on the right side and assign the result to the variable whose symbolic name is on the left side." Thus the statement $X = X + 1$. has a valid meaning in the Fortran language whereas in ordinary algebra the statement is meaningless.

General Form

a = b

where *a* is a variable (fixed or floating) and *b* is an expression (fixed or floating). By the above definition, statements of the form $A = I$ and $J = B$ are permissible where I and B are any *entirely* fixed or floating expressions (for example, $A = I + J2$; $J = B + C - 16$.).

Examples

A = B + 2.
AD = C$\star\star$2
PI = 3.14
DELT = I$\star$J
I = A + 1.
X = (− B + (B$\star\star$2 − 4.$\star$A$\star$C)$\star\star$.5)/(2.$\star$A)
L = B
C = K

If the expression to the right is in fixed point form and the variable on the left is in floating point form, the calculation is performed in fixed point arithmetic, put in floating point form, and stored in the location specified by the symbol on the left and vice versa.

Consider the quadratic equation $3X^2 + 1.7X - 31.92 = 0$. The algebraic representation for one of the two roots is

$$X = \frac{-B + \sqrt{B^2 - 4AC}}{2A}$$

A Fortran program that describes this calculation is as follows:

```
A = 3.
B = 1.7
C = -31.92
ROOT = (-B+(B**2 -4.*A*C)**.5)/(2.*A)
```

The first statement means: "Assign the value 3. to the variable A." The next two statements have a similar meaning. The fourth statement means: "Evaluate the expression on the right side and assign the result to the variable ROOT."

Of course, the program also could have been written as follows:

```
ROOT = (-1.7+(1.7**2-4.*3.*(-31.92))**.5)/(2.*3.)
```

STATEMENT NUMBERS

Fortran programs are sequential in nature. That is, the computer executes instructions in the object program in the order that they were compiled from the source statements. For example, if the fourth statement in the program above were to be moved up and made the first statement, the computer would evaluate ROOT before obtaining the desired values of A, B, and C. ROOT would therefore be evaluated using some arbitrary unknown values for these variables.

As in machine language and the symbolic programming system, it is not always desirable to execute program instructions sequentially. Some means, then, must be provided to assign a unique label or number to a statement so that it may be referenced when required. The Fortran language provides for this by allowing the programmer to assign statement numbers to those statements which will be referenced by another statement at some time in the program.

A statement number is in the form of any unsigned fixed point constant. Leading zeros are not required. It is advisable to number only those Fortran statements that will be referenced. Actually almost any Fortran statement may be assigned a statement number, but unnecessary and excessive numbering wastes core storage and delays the compilation process.

Statement numbers need not be sequentially assigned and the programmer may choose *any* fixed point number he wishes. However, no two statements may be assigned the same statement number. If it were desired to reference all the statements in the program to solve for one root of the quadratic equation, the program could be written as follows:

```
  96 A = 3.
   2 B = 1.7
1321 C = −31.92
  10 ROOT = (−B + (B★★2 −4.★A★C)★★.5)/(2.★A)
```

The Fortran programs illustrated thus far have been necessarily trivial since no methods of deviating from sequential instruction execution have been presented. Also, no input-output commands have been presented. The following two sections are devoted to (1) control statements which allow for deviation from sequential instruction execution and (2) input-output statements.

CONTROL STATEMENTS

Normally, Fortran statements are executed in the same sequence in which they occur in the source program. Control statements provide the means of deviating from this sequential instruction execution. As in SPS, two types of control statements are provided. One type provides for unconditional branching whereas the other type provides for branching only if some specific condition is met. Statement numbers provide the means for cross referencing Fortran statements.

Unconditional Go To Statement

General Form
GO TO n
where *n* is a statement number.

Examples
GO TO 6
GO TO 199

The unconditional Go To statement is used to specify, at some point in a program, that the next statement to be executed is not the one following as it normally would be. Instead, the statement bearing statement number *n* is executed next.

This statement is similar to the unconditional Branch instruction in SPS.

Example

Fortran Source Program:
```
    SUM = 0.
    X = 1.
12  SUM = SUM + X
    X = X + 1.
    GO TO 12
```

The above program will evaluate the sum of the numbers from 1 to infinity:

$$\left(\sum_{i=1}^{\infty} i \right)$$

The first two statements are called *initialization statements*. The statement SUM = 0. will assign the value zero to the variable SUM. This is done because the variable SUM will be used to develop a total; if the value of SUM is not zero to start with, an incorrect total will be developed. The statement X = 1. assigns an initial value of 1 to the variable X. The statement 12 SUM = SUM + X develops the sum of the numbers. The next statement causes the value of X to be increased by 1. The statement GO TO 12 causes statement 12 to be executed next. Thus a loop is developed and the last three statements of the program will be continually executed with the value of X being increased by 1 each time.

Actually, the above program will halt when the value in SUM exceeds the highest allowable floating point value ($\overline{9}999999999$). When this occurs, an overflow condition will be indicated.

Computed Go To Statement

General Form

GO TO (n_1, n_2, ..., n_m), i
where n_1, n_2, ..., n_m are statement numbers and i is an unsigned fixed point variable $(1 \leqslant i \leqslant m)$ *

Examples

GO TO (6, 7, 13, 2, 5), I
GO TO (199, 2), MKVD

The computed Go To statement is used to transfer control to one of several Fortran statements depending on the value of some fixed point variable. If, at the time of execution, the value of the fixed point variable i is j, then control is transferred to the statement with statement number n_j.

* $i > m$ is allowable but the object program will not run correctly except by chance.

Example
JDEL = 3
GO TO (196, 2, 47, 63, 1), JDEL

Commentary
The statement numbered 47 will be executed next

Example
Fortran Source Program:
```
      SUM = 0.
      TOTAL = 0.
      ADD = 0.
      I = 0
      X = 1.
    1 SUM = SUM + X**3
      X = X + 1.
      I = I + 1
      GO TO (1, 1, 1, 1, 1, 1, 1, 1. 9), I
    9 X = 2.
      I = 0
    3 TOTAL = TOTAL + X**2.
      X = X + 2.
      I = I + 1
      GO TO (3, 3, 3, 3, 3, 3, 3, 3, 4), I
    4 X = 3.
      I = 0
    5 ADD = ADD + X**3.
      X = X + 3.
      I = I + 1
      GO TO (5, 5, 5, 5, 5, 5, 5, 5, 6), I
    6 Complete program by writing out results
```

Commentary

$$SUM = \sum_{i=1}^{9} i^3$$

$$TOTAL = \sum_{i=1}^{9} (2i)^2$$

$$ADD = \sum_{i=1}^{9} (3i)^3$$

The statement with statement number 6 in the above program is not a legal Fortran statement but is merely inserted to express a completion condition since Input-output and Stop commands have not yet been discussed.

Example
Fortran Source Program:
```
      SUM = 0.
```

```
      ID = 1
      X = 1.
 15   SUM = SUM + (X★★5.2 + 2.★X + 6.)/3.
      GO TO (8, 8, 8, 8, 2),ID
  2   X = X + 2.
      GO TO 15
  8   X = X + 1.
      ID = ID + 1
      GO TO 15
```

Commentary

$$SUM = \sum_{i=1}^{5} (i^{5.2} + 2i + 6) \div 3 + \sum_{j=3}^{\infty} ((2j+1)^{5.2} + 2(2j+1) + 6) \div 3$$

The above program is presented solely to demonstrate the computed Go To statement. It is not a realistic program since no provisions have been made for ending the program.

Example

The following is an example of a never-ending multiple switching network.

```
 10   N = 1
  8   GO TO (1, 12, 31, 14, 10), N
  1   N = 2
      GO TO 8
 12   N = 3
      GO TO 8
 31   N = 4
      GO TO 8
 14   N = 5
      GO TO 8
```

If Statement

General Form

'IF (a) n_1, n_2, n_3
where a is any expression (fixed or floating) and n_1, n_2, and n_3 are statement numbers.

Examples

IF (A) 1, 2, 3
IF (I−2) 17, 9, 8
IF (A/B★C) 8, 9, 8

The expression a is evaluated. If the value of the expression is less than zero (negative), statement number n_1 is executed next. If the value of the expression is zero, statement number n_2 is executed next. If the value of the expression is greater than zero, statement number n_3 is executed next.

Suppose the variable XCORD has just been calculated in a Fortran program. If the value of XCORD is negative, an error routine at statement number 8 should be executed next. If the value of XCORD is zero, a special routine at statement number 2 should be executed next, and if the value of XCORD exceeds zero, statement number 102 is to be executed. The Fortran statements to accomplish this are as follows:

$$XCORD = B \star\star 2 - 4.\star A \star C$$
$$IF(XCORD)\ 8,\ 2,\ 102$$

The single Fortran statement shown below will accomplish the same branching conditions.

$$IF(B \star\star 2 - 4.\star A \star C)\ 8,\ 2,\ 102$$

The If statement is an excellent tool for use in programs where looping (repeating the same operations with different data) is desired. Example number 1 illustrates the use of the If statement in controlling the number of times a loop is to be executed.

Example 1

The following is a Fortran program to sum the numbers from 1 to 1000.

```
    SUM = 0.0
    A = 1.0
  3 SUM = A + SUM
    A = A + 1.
    IF(A − 1000.) 3, 3, 6
  6 Complete program by writing out results
```

Example 2

The following program will find the positive root of the following equation correct to two decimal places, $X^2 + 0.9X - 6.3 = 0$. The positive root lies between 1 and 10.

```
     I = 1
     X = 0.
   1 X = X + 1.
  15 ROOT = X★★2 + .9★X
     GO TO (3, 4, 18), I
   3 IF (ROOT −6.3)1, 7, 6
   6 I = 2
   4 IF (ROOT −6.3) 10, 7, 12
  12 X = X − .1
     GO TO 15
  10 I = 3
  18 IF (ROOT −6.3) 21, 7, 7
  21 X = X + .01
     GO TO 15
   7 End of program
```

IF SENSE SWITCH[1]

General Form

IF (SENSE SWITCH i) n_1, n_2
where n_1 and n_2 are statement numbers and i is 1, 2, 3, or 4.

Examples

IF (SENSE SWITCH 2) 10, 3
IF (SENSE SWITCH 4) 1, 119

The Sense switch corresponding to i is interrogated. If it is in the "on" position, the next statement to be executed is statement number n_1. If the program switch is "off," the next statement to be executed is statement number n_2. The four program switches are located on the 1620 console. The only method of setting or altering the settings of the switches is to position the switch *manually* to the "on" or "off" position.

INPUT-OUTPUT STATEMENTS

The Fortran language includes seven I/O statements to allow for the transfer of data between core storage and the input-output devices. The Input-output statements must specify three things: (1) What exactly is to be done. This may be to read a card, read paper tape, punch a card, and so forth. (2) How the data fields are arranged on the input medium or are to be arranged on the output medium. The arrangement of data is called "Format." (3) Which data fields are to be transmitted. The data is specified by the variable name chosen by the programmer.

The Fortran I/O statements specify items 1 and 3 in the above list. The Format (item 2) is specified by special Format statements which are referenced by the I/O statements. The I/O statements will be described first, then the Format statements will be discussed.

All I/O statements contain three things: (1) The instruction name that specifies what is to be done. (2) A statement number that references a Format statement which describes the arrangement of the data, and (3) A "list" that describes which data fields are to be transmitted.

SPECIFYING LISTS OF QUANTITIES

A list consists of one or more variable names separated by commas. The list specifies what quantities are to be transmitted between core storage and the I/O device. It may contain any number of variables (fixed and/or floating). The only limiting factor is the permissible

---

[1] "Sense switch" is synonomous with "program switch."

length of the Fortran statement, which in 1620 Fortran may not exceed 72 characters.

Examples of lists are as follows:

> DELTA, J, ONE
> A
> SIGMA, COUNT, IDENT, X, Y
> I, DELTA, 99 (This list is invalid because
> it contains a constant)

INPUT STATEMENTS

Read Statement

General Form

READ n, List
where n is the statement number of a Format statement, and *"list"* is as described above.

Examples

READ 2, A, DELTA, I
READ 106, A, B, C, D, E, F
READ 37, POUND, OHMS

The Read statement causes quantities to be read from a card in accordance with the specified Format statement. The variables in the list take on the respective values read from the card.

As an example, assume that a card is punched as follows:

CARD COLUMNS	CONTENTS
6–7	13
22–25	– 10
26–32	+ 399124
50–51	01
78	9

In a source program the Read statement

> READ 2, I, DELTA, QUAN, NUMBR, IDEN

would cause the card to be read and the variable I to be assigned a value of 13, DELTA a value of −10, QUAN a value of +399124, NUMBR a value of 1, and IDEN a value of 9. Computations may then take place and control may pass back to the same Read statement. This would cause another card to be read and the quantities on this card assigned to the variables. Of course, the above description assumes a correct Format statement. It is the Format statement that supplies the information as to the card columns where the data is to be found.

Accept Tape Statement

General Form

ACCEPT TAPE n, list
where *n* is the statement number of a Format statement and *list* is as previously described.

Examples

ACCEPT TAPE 16, A, B, C,
ACCEPT TAPE 99, I, DELTA, A, MM

The Accept Tape statement causes quantities to be read from paper tape in accordance with the specified Format statement. The variables in the list take on the respective values read from the tape.

Accept Statement

General Form

ACCEPT n, list
where *n* is the statement number of a Format statement and *list* is as previously described.

Examples

ACCEPT 12, A
ACCEPT 1, JDEL, RADI, ARC

The Accept statement causes the carriage on the typewriter to return, and the computer awaits manual entry of data from the keyboard. Data is entered in accordance with the specified Format statement. The variables in the list take on the respective values entered from the typewriter.

OUTPUT STATEMENTS

Punch Statement

General Form

PUNCH n, list
where *n* is the statement number of a Format statement and *list* is as previously described.

Examples

PUNCH 999, ARC, SLOPE, I
PUNCH 4, COUNT, MAG

The Punch statement causes the values of the variables in the list, as determined by the program, to be punched in a card or cards in accordance with the specified Format statement.

Punch Tape Statement

General Form

PUNCH TAPE n, list
where *n* is the statement number of a Format statement and *list* is as previously described.

Examples

PUNCH TAPE 1234, A, I
PUNCH TAPE 16, SUM, VALUE, C

The Punch Tape statement causes the values of the variables in the list, as determined by the program, to be punched in paper tape in accordance with the specified Format statement.

Print Statement

General Form

PRINT n, list
where *n* is the statement number of a Format statement and *list* is as previously described.

Examples

PRINT 1, DELTA, X, Y
PRINT 42, ZDEL, X1, Y2

The Print statement causes the values of the variables in the list, as determined by the program, to be printed on the typewriter in accordance with the specified Format statement.

Type Statement

General Form

TYPE n, list
where *n* is the statement number of a Format statement and *list* is as previously described.

Examples

TYPE 6, X1, X, Y2
TYPE 888, CON1, DELTA, MIX

The Type statement causes the values of the variables in the list, as determined by the program, to be printed on the typewriter in accordance with the specified Format statement. The Type statement and the Print statement serve the same purpose and can be used interchangeably.

FORMAT STATEMENTS

In order for quantities to be transmitted correctly from the input medium to the computer, or from the computer to the output medium, it is necessary that the computer be told in what form the data exists. Special subroutines are used to convert data to and from the floating point (characteristic and mantissa) and fixed point (4-digit) forms internally used by Fortran. The subroutines must be supplied information as to what forms the data fields are in and into which form they are to be converted. The Format statement specifies this.

General Form

n FORMAT (specification)
where *n* is a statement number referenced by an I/O statement, and where *specification* is as described below. The specification must be enclosed in parentheses.

Example

2   FORMAT (F6.2,E6.1,5XI2,F6.2)
3   FORMAT (2HX = F6.2)

SPECIFICATIONS

The specification specifies what forms the data fields are in and to what form they are to be converted. There are three types of conversion for *numeric data,* as illustrated below. The conversions are used for both input and output.

INTERNAL DATA FORM	CONVERSION CODE	EXTERNAL DATA FORM
Floating Point	E	Floating Point (with exponent)
Floating Point	F	Floating Point (without exponent)
Integer	I	Integer

Let us consider the three types of numeric conversion for input data. If the input quantity on the input medium is in the floating-decimal-with-exponent form (for example, 3146.E−2, 9875.167E+13), the *E*-type conversion is specified. If the input quantity is in the floating-decimal-without-exponent form (for example, 4.678, 2., 1001.1), the *F*-type conversion is specified; and if the input quantity is in integer form, the *I*-type conversion is specified.

The conversion codes are used in a similar fashion for output. If the output quantity is to be in the floating-decimal-with-exponent form, the *E*-type conversion is specified. If the output quantity is to be in the floating-decimal-without-exponent form, *F*-type conversion is specified, and if the output quantity is to be in integer form the *I*-type conversion is specified.

The following chart illustrates how numbers *might appear* as printed output for the conversion specified. Although printing is being used as an example, the same examples could apply for card or tape output. This holds true for all examples given.

E-Type Conversion. Numbers printed by *E-type* notation are printed in the floating-decimal-with-exponent notation. Typical output might be:

NUMBER	PRINTED OUTPUT
167.12	.16712Eb03
−.0001842	−.1842E−03
91.2	.912Eb02
100039.	.10039Eb05

F-Type Conversion. Numbers printed by *F-type* conversion are printed in the "normal" decimal notation without exponent. Typical output might be:

69.21	−13627.399
1841.3	1986.
−2.1	1.01

I-Type Conversion. Numbers printed by *I*-type conversion are printed as integers. Typical output might be:

1421	2
−17	88
368	167

If the numbers in the above examples were input quantities the same type conversions would be used for the input Format statements.

The conversion codes alone do not give sufficient information to allow for the proper conversion of input or output data. Certain additional information must be supplied to the conversion subroutines. For input data the subroutine must be given the number of columns (card, tape, or typewriter) reserved for the input variables. For instance, in one problem the first input variable may be punched in card columns 1-10, whereas in another problem the first input variable may be punched in card columns 1-6 and the second variable may be punched in columns 8-15. For output data the subroutine must be given the number of columns (card, tape, or typewriter) the programmer wishes to reserve for the various output variables.

To supply this information the conversion codes when used in the specification portion of the Format statement are used in the following forms:

$$Iw$$
$$Ew.d$$
$$Fw.d$$

where I, E, or F represent the types of conversion, and w represents the field width including sign (if any) and decimal point (if any) for the converted data, and d represents the number of places to the right of the decimal point. Since d specifies the number of places to the right of the decimal, the actual decimal point need not be punched or typed on input data. The correct number of decimal places will be assigned from the Format statement. The decimal point between the w and d in the E and F specifications is *required punctuation*.

I Specifications Iw. When used as an *output* specification, w places are reserved for the number. If the number of significant digits in the quantity is less than the width specification, the number is right-justified in the output field, and the left-most spaces are filled in with blanks. If the quantity to be converted contains more than w digits, the high-order portion of the number is lost. If the quantity is negative, the space preceding the left-most digit will contain a minus sign. Included in the count w *must* be a space for the sign.

The following examples show how each of the quantities on the left is printed according to the indicated specifications.

INTERNAL	SPECIFICATION	PRINTED
613	I4	b613
12	I3	b12
9	I3	bb9
0	I3	bb0
−812	I4	−812
−1	I2	−1
8666	I3	b66°
−10	I2	−0°
6	I2	b6

* Inaccurate due to insufficient specification.

When used as an *input* specification, w columns are examined by the subroutine for the input quantity. The number must be right-justified within the input field.

If the input data is positive, it is not necessary to punch the plus sign. If this item is not present, it is not included in the count w. If a positive or negative sign is present, it is included in the count w.

The following examples show the required specification for the input quantities on the left.

INPUT DATA	SPECIFICATION
b81	I3
1421	I4
−1421	I5
−1421	I4*
10	I2
2	I1
bb42	I4**
081	I3
+67	I3

* Inaccurate due to insufficient specification.
** Notice that the number is right-justified within the input field.

F Specifications Fw.d. When used as an *output* specification, w places are reserved for the number. If the number of decimal places in a number to be converted exceeds d, the low-order positions are truncated. If the number of places reserved for the decimal portion of the number exceeds the number of decimal digits, low-order zeros are supplied. If the number of places reserved for the integer portion of the quantity is insufficient, the F specification is ignored and the number is placed on the output medium in the E14.8 specification (see E conversion). If the number of places reserved for the integer portion exceeds the number of integer digits, high-order blanks are supplied. Included in the count w must be a space for the decimal point and sign.

The following examples show how each of the quantities on the left is printed according to the indicated specifications.

INTERNAL	SPECIFICATION	PRINTED
32.1	F8.4	b32.1000
−.9	F5.2	b−.90
−8.	F5.1	b−8.0
18.67	F6.2	b18.67
9.17	F5.2	b9.17
−397.221	F8.3	−397.221
−86.221	F7.3	−86.221
12.1	F4.1	.12100000E+02
41.6745	F5.2	.41674500E+02

When used as an *input* specification, w specifies the number of places reserved for the input quantity including sign (if any) and decimal point (if any). Because the number of decimal places are specified in the d part of the specification the actual decimal point need not be punched or typed. The input quantity must be right-justified within the input field.

The following examples show the required specification for the input data on the left.

INPUT DATA	SPECIFICATION	
123.146	F7.3	
−123.146	F7.3°	
b123.146	F8.3	
+123.146	F8.3	
−96.1	F5.1	
8111.987532	F11.6	
3987	F4.2	(39.87)
b123146	F7.3	(123.196)
1	F1.0	(1.0)
00	F2.1	(0.0)
b15	F3.1	(1.5)
3100	F4.0	(3100.)

* Inaccurate due to insufficient specification.

E Specifications Ew.d. When used as an *output* specification, the field width w includes four spaces for the exponent, one for the decimal point, and one space that must be allowed for sign. The exponent is the power of 10 to which the number must be raised to obtain its true value. The exponent is written with an "E" followed by a minus sign if the exponent is negative, or a plus sign is the exponent is positive, and two spaces for the exponent. If the number of digits in the quantity exceeds the number of places reserved, the low-order positions of the number are truncated. If the number of digits in the number is less than the number of places reserved, low-order zeros are supplied. If the specification is not large enough, the program automatically converts to the E14.8 form.

The following examples show how each of the quantities on the left is printed according to the indicated specifications.

INTERNAL	SPECIFICATION	PRINTED
−67.3211	E13.7	−.6732110E+02
982.	E10.3	b9.820E+02
−6.12	E10.3	−6.120E−00
.00000132	E10.3	b1.320E−06
−642.0068	E11.4	−6.4200E+02
12345678.	E10.0	b1234.E+04°

* Last digits of accuracy are lost due to insufficient specification.

When used as an *input* specification w specifies the field width including sign (if any), decimal point (if any) and exponent. The d portion of the specification signifies how many decimal places there are. Because of this the actual decimal point need not be punched or typed.

The following examples show the required specification for the input data on the left.

INPUT DATA	SPECIFICATION
200.674E+13	E11.3
−2.98E−16	E9.2
+100.648E−16	E12.3
98.E+15	E7.0
101E+14	E7.1 (10.1×10^{14})

ADDITIONAL RULES FOR SPECIFYING FORMAT

The following rules permit variation in specifying Format:

1. If a decimal point is punched or typed in an input data field and its position is different from that indicated in the Format statement, it takes priority over the decimal as indicated in the Format statement. The following examples illustrate this:

INPUT DATA	SPECIFICATION	VALUE ASSIGNED TO INPUT VARIABLE
36.91	F5.1	36.91
900.1	F5.3	900.1
−1.6121	F7.1	−1.6121
1.81	F4.2	1.81
16.1E+17	E8.2	16.1×10^{17}

2. Field width greater than required may be specified in order to provide for spacing. Thus, if a number is to be converted by *I*-type conversion and the number is not expected to exceed five spaces including sign, a specification of I10 will reserve five *leading* blanks. Similarly with an input specification; assume that a floating point quantity is punched in columns 5–13 of a card and the first four columns are blank. The first four columns can be included in the w portion of the Format specification. Thus if the card was punched as follows:

bbbb35645.983

the following Format statement would apply

6 FORMAT (F13.3)

A Format statement of the form

6 FORMAT (F9.3)

would cause only the first nine columns to be examined and the number 35.645 would be assigned the input variable.

3. Successive specifications may be written in a single Format statement by separating them with commas. Thus (I2, E10.2) might be used to convert two separate quantities, the first an integer and the second a floating point quantity. The only limiting factor to the number of successive specifications in a Format statement is the permissible length of the Fortran statement which is 72 characters. The following are all valid Format statements:

```
  1 FORMAT (F6.4, F6.3, I2, E10.1)
  2 FORMAT (I1, I2, E18.6)
138 FORMAT (F10.2, F10.2, F10.2, F10.2, F10.2, F10.2)
```

Let us examine the Format statement numbered 1 above and consider it as being used with the Read statement below

READ 1, X, Y, INDEX, POLY

Assuming a card input (the same applies for tape or typewriter input) the first six card columns would be analyzed according to the specification F6.4, the quantity would be converted to the internal floating point form and assigned to the variable X. The quantity in columns 7 through 12, inclusive, would be converted according to specification F6.3 and assigned to the variable Y. The quantity in card columns 13 and 14 would be converted according to specification I2 and assigned to the variable INDEX. Finally, the quantity in columns 15 through 24 would be converted according to specification E10.1 and assigned to the variable POLY.

Notice that in the example given the quantities had to be punched in successive card columns. Assume that such was not the case but that the card was designed in the following manner.

CARD COLUMNS	CONTENTS
1–5	blanks
6–11	X
12–14	blanks
15–20	Y
21–24	blanks
25–26	INDEX
27–29	blanks
30–39	POLY

The following Format statement could be used.

1 FORMAT (F11.4, F9.3, I6, E13.1)

Actually all that has been done is to make each field longer by including leading blanks. Each quantity meets the requirement of being right-justified within the field.

If instead of blanks, the unused card columns had contained unused data the above solution could not be applied, since by lengthening the fields in the Format statement, the unused data would be included and would change the values of the desired variables. To cope with this situation a special conversion code is used to allow for the skipping of columns. This is the X-type conversion and will be discussed in the next section.

4. The specifications in a Format statement must have correspondence in mode with the items in the Input-output statement; integer quantities require integer conversion, and floating point quantities require floating point conversion. Thus, the following statements are compatible:

PRINT 2, A, B, I
2 FORMAT (F6.4, E10.2, I10)

The following statements are not compatible:

READ 1, A, DELT, I
1 FORMAT (F10.3, E14.2, F8.2)

The third variable in the I/O list is a fixed point variable whereas the third specification in the Format statement is for a floating point variable.

5. Successive items in the I/O list are transmitted by successive corresponding specifications in the Format statement until all items in the list are transmitted. If there are more items in the I/O list than there are specifications, control transfers to the preceding left parenthesis of the Format statement. Thus parenthesis may be included within a specification for the above purpose.

For example, suppose the following statements are written into a program:

PRINT 10, A, B, C, D, E, F, G
10 FORMAT (F10.3, E12.4, F12.2),

then the following table shows the variable transmitted in the column on the left, and the specification by which it is converted in the column on the right.

VARIABLE TRANSMITTED	SPECIFICATION
A	F10.3
B	E12.4
C	F12.2
D	F10.3
E	E12.4
F	F12.2
G	F10.3

Suppose that in the above example the Format statement had been

10 FORMAT (F10.3, (E12.4,F12.2)).

Then the table would look as follows:

Variable Transmitted	Specification
A	F10.3
B	E12.4
C	F12.2
D	E12.4
E	F12.2
F	E12.4
G	F12.2

6. A comma is used to separate successive numeric specifications and to avoid ambiguity. The comma is not necessary when the numeric specifications are separated from one another by a special character such as (and /. The example given above

$$10 \quad \text{FORMAT}(\text{F}10.3,(\text{E}12.4,\text{F}12.2}))$$

could have been written as

$$10 \quad \text{FORMAT}(\text{F}10.3(\text{E}12.4,\text{F}12.2}))$$

7. It is permissible to omit the E on input data in the floating point constant with exponent form if a plus or minus sign precedes the exponent. Thus, the following forms are valid:

$$16.8+03(16.8 \times 10^3)$$
$$18.1-02(18.1 \times 10^{-2})$$

The omission of the E is permissible only on input data. It may not be omitted in a Fortran statement. Thus, the state $A=B\star16.8+03$ is not valid; $A = B\star16.8E+03$ is valid.

X-Type Conversion for Blank Fields. Blank characters may be provided for output records or characters of an input record may be skipped by means of the X-type specification.

The general form is wX where w is the number of blanks to be provided or the number of characters to be skipped. The w must be less than or equal to 49 ($w \leqslant 49$). When X-type conversion is used in a specification, it need not be followed by a comma.

When the wX specification is used with an *input* record, w characters are skipped over no matter what they are. For example, if a card has numbers punched in columns 1–10, 13–15, and 20–30, the following Fortran statements may be used.

$$\text{READ 8, A, B, CDEL}$$
$$8 \quad \text{FORMAT (F10.3, 2XI3, 4XE11.2)}$$

When the wX specification is used with an *output* record the number of characters specified by w are left blank. As an example, suppose that four fixed point integers with five blanks between each one are to be punched. The following Fortran statements may be used.

PUNCH 7, ID1, ID2, ID3, ID4
7 FORMAT (I8, 5XI3, 5XI5, 5XI8)

H-Type Conversion for Alphameric Fields. Alphameric fields may be
read in or used as output by using the *H*-type conversion. The specification *wH* followed by *w* alphameric characters may be used in a Format
statement to provide for alphameric fields. The *w* must be less than
or equal to 49 ($w \leq 49$). When *H-type* conversion is used in a specification, it need not be followed by a comma.

The effect of the *wH* specification depends on whether it is being
used with an input or an output statement. If it is used with an *input*
statement, *w* characters are extracted from the input medium and replace the *w* characters included with the specification. If it is used
with an *output* statement the *w* characters following the specification
(or the *w* characters that replaced them as a result of input operations)
are written as part of the output record. If blanks are desired they are
included in the count *w*. If no list is associated with the I/O statement,
the comma after the Format statement number is not mandatory punctuation.

Example

    PRINT 11
11 FORMAT (21HMATRIXbMULTIPLICATION)

These statements would cause the following output to be printed:

MATRIX MULTIPLICATION

Example

    READ 1
1 FORMAT (28Hbbbbbbbbbbbbbbbbbbbbbbbbbbbb)
    PRINT 1

Assume the first card contained the following information in columns 1-28:

CONVEYORbCALCULATIONbNO.b367

This information would be printed on the typewriter or punched in an output
card if the Print statement were replaced by a Punch statement.

Example

Suppose that in the above example instead of being punched in columns 1-28,
the information was punched in columns 5-33. To read the card and print
the information as before the following Fortran statements could be used.

```
  READ 1
1 FORMAT (4X28Hbbbbbbbbbbbbbbbbbbbbbbbbbbbb)
  PRINT 1
```

Example

```
  READ 1
1 FORMAT (7HRESULT=)
  PRINT 1
```

Assume that the first card contained the following information in columns 1-7

1-7   362.111

The Print statement would cause the following to type out:

362.111

Specification for Multirecord Format. The solidus (/) is used when more than one printed line, punched card, or tape record is to be specified in one Format statement. The / may cause any of the following, depending on the I/O statement it is used with: Another card may be read, another card may be punched, another line may be printed, or another tape record may be read or punched. Using the /, several one-line Formats may be specified in one Format statement. A comma need not follow a / when it is used in a Format specification.

Example

```
  READ 3, A, B, I
3 FORMAT (F8.2/E12.4/I2)
```

Three cards would be read. The value of A would be taken from the first card, B from the second card and I from the third card.

Example

```
  PRINT 6, A, B, C, D, I
6 FORMAT (F6.2, E12.4/F8.2, F8.2, 5XI5)
```

This would cause two lines to be printed. A and B would be printed on the first line according to specifications F6.2 and E12.4, respectively. The second line would have C, D, and I according to specification F8.2, F8.2, I5, respectively.

Example

```
    PRINT 193, X, Y, Z, W
193 FORMAT (2HX = F6.2, 5X2HY = F6.2, 5X2HZ = F6.2/5X2HW = F6.2)
```

The following printed lines might result.

```
X =121.11bbbbbbY = 132.10bbbbbZ = b67.12
bbbbW = 982.11
```

Example

READ 6, A, B
6 FORMAT (F6.2//F10.4)

The value of A will be read from the first card and the value of B will be read from the third card. The second card will be read and ignored.

Example

READ 10, X, DELTA, I
10 FORMAT (5X3Hbbb6XF10.3, E14.4, 6XI4)

The values of X, DELTA, and I would be taken from one card in the following card columns:

VARIABLE	CARD COLUMNS
X	15–24
DELTA	25–38
I	45–48

The characters from columns 6–8 would replace the three blanks in the *H* specification.

The following chart may prove helpful in analyzing the control of a Format statement. The chart is read as follows: The left-hand column indicates certain characters encountered in a Format statement. The three right-hand columns indicate what functions take place when the character in the left-hand column is sensed. The column labeled "Reset for New Record" means to read or punch another card or tape record or print another line depending on the I/O statement.

CONVERSION TYPES	INTERROGATE I/O LIST FOR LAST VARIABLE	GO BACK TO LAST LEFT PARENTHESIS IF MORE VARIABLES IN LIST	RESET FOR NEW RECORD
)	Yes	Yes	Yes
/	No	No	Yes
Numeric	Yes	No	No
H and *X*	No	No	No

Note that both the right parenthesis and the solidus reset for a new record, so that in the following example the variables A and B would be printed on one line and the variables C and D on a second line.

PRINT 10, A, B, C, D
10 FORMAT (F6.2, F6.2)

In the following example each variable will be read from a different card according to the specification E14.4

READ 63, A, DELTA, X, Y, Z
63 FORMAT (E14.4)

Pause Statement

General Form
PAUSE

Example
PAUSE

When a Pause statement is executed, the computer will halt in the manual mode. Depressing the Start key on the console causes program execution to continue. The operator may take advantage of the halt to exercise manual control from the console.

Stop Statement

General Form
STOP

Example
STOP

When a Stop statement is executed, the computer halts in the manual mode. The carriage on the typewriter returns and the word "stop" types. Program execution *cannot* be continued by depressing the Start key on the console. Depressing the Start key will repeat the sequence given above.

PROCESSOR CONTROL OPERATION

End Statement

General Form
END

Example

END

The End statement *must* be the last statement in a Fortran source program. It is a signal to the compiler that the final statement of the source program has been received.

We now have all the tools at our command to write complete Fortran programs. Two examples follow.

Example

Suppose that we have a large number of quadratic equations of the form $AX^2 + BX + C = 0$ to solve. For each equation the values of A, B, and C are punched in a card as follows:

CARD COLUMNS	VARIABLE NAME	FORM
1–5	A	XXX.XX
10–14	B	XXX.XX
20–24	C	XXX.XX

It is desired to print both roots of each equation along with the values of A, B, and C. If the discriminant is negative, a message to this effect is to be printed. Provisions should also be made to allow for typewriter entry of the data. A program to accomplish the above is:

```
10   IF (SENSE SWITCH 1) 1, 2
 1   READ 21, A, B, C
21   FORMAT (F5.2, 4XF5.2, 5XF5.2)
     GO TO 6
 2   ACCEPT 21, A, B, C
 6   DISCR = B★★2 − 4.★A★C
     IF (DISCR) 7, 9, 9
 9   DENOM = 2.★A
     DISCR = DISCR★★.5
     ROOT1 = (−B + DISCR)/DENOM
     ROOT2 = (−B − DISCR)/DENOM
     PRINT 22, A, B, C, ROOT1,ROOT2
22   FORMAT (F6.2, 5XF6.2, 5XF6.2, 5XF7.2, 5XF7.2)
     GO TO 10
 7   PRINT 23, A, B, C
23   FORMAT (F6.2, 5XF6.2, 5XF6.2, 5X13HCOMPLEXbROOTS)
     GO TO 10
     END
```

Commentary

1. Format statements may be located anywhere in the program. They do not have to immediately precede or follow the associated I/O statement.
2. More than one I/O statement may reference the same Format statement.

3. By calculating DENOM = 2.★A, it was necessary to perform this calculation just once.

Example

It is desired to prepare a table of the factorials of the numbers from 1 to 15. The following Fortran program will prepare this table.

```
      PN = 15.
   8  SFACT = 1.
      A = PN
   2  SFACT = SFACT★A
      A = A − 1.
      IF (A − 1.) 4, 4, 2
   4  PRINT 271, PN, SFACT
 271  FORMAT (F4.0, 10XE14.0)
      PN = PN − 1.
      IF (PN) 3, 10, 8
  10  PRINT 17
  17  FORMAT (16HPROGRAMbCOMPLETE)
   3  STOP
      END
```

SUBSCRIPTS AND SUBSCRIPTED VARIABLES

In many mathematical problems we find ourselves working with arrays or matrices. In mathematical notation the elements of the array are subscripted for ease of notation. Thus A_{jk} might refer to the element in the jth row and kth column. Fortran provides for the subscription of variables. This facilitates the programming of many complex problems.[2]

Any variable (fixed or floating) can be made to represent any element in a one or two dimensional array by appending to it a single or double subscript. The variable is then a subscripted variable. The subscripts are fixed point quantities whose values determine which element of the array is being referred to.

SUBSCRIPTS

A subscript may be an expression in any one of the following forms:

1. An unsigned fixed point constant (for example, 3, 199, 81)
2. A fixed point variable (for example, I, JDEL, MON)
3. A fixed point variable ± a fixed point constant (for example, $I + 2$, $JDEL − 180$)

No subscript may itself be subscripted.

---

[2] All previous commentary referencing variables may be considered as accurate if the words "subscripted variables" are substituted.

SUBSCRIPTED VARIABLES

A subscripted variable is a fixed or floating point variable followed by parentheses enclosing one or two subscripts. If two subscripts are used, they are separated by a comma.

For each variable that is subscripted, the size of the array, that is, the *maximum* values which the subscripts can attain, *must* be stated in a Dimension statement (see below) preceding the first appearance of the variable.

Example

A(I)
B(M + 4)
K (2)
AB(I, J)
Z(IDEN + 7, J + 3)

Problem

Identify the following as being a subscripted variable in a correct form or incorrect form.

1. A(112)	7. TORQ (I + 3)
2. A(11, 7)	8. X (−3456)
3. FLOW (MAX)	9. Y (J★2)
4. TORQUE (MIN)	10. X1 (+2)
5. INC (I + 2, J + 3)	11. DELT (FACT)
6. TORQ (I, J, K)	12. ABS (2−J)

Dimension Statement

General Form

DIMENSION v, v, v . . .

where each *v* is a fixed or floating point variable subscripted with one or two unsigned fixed point constants. Any number of *v*'s may be given in a Dimension statement.

Example

DIMENSION A(10), B(20, 25), XY(100)
DIMENSION A(3), I(10, 3), B(17)

The Dimension statement is used to specify to the Fortran compiler how much storage is required for one and two dimensional arrays used in the source program. Every subscripted variable appearing in the source program *must* appear in a Dimension statement. If no subscripted variables appear in the source program, the Dimension statement is not necessary. One Dimension statement may be used to dimension any number of arrays. The only limiting factor is the permissible length of the Fortran statements. The programmer may find it convenient to place all Dimension statements at the beginning of his Fortran program to meet the requirement that a subscripted variable be listed in a Dimension statement before it is encountered in the program.

Example

DIMENSION A(5), B(2, 15), I(6, 6)

The Fortran compiler will reserve space for five values of A, 30 values of B, and 36 values of I.

Note: Subscripts of variables in a Dimension statement *must be unsigned fixed point constants, not variables. Dimensioning for less than one element in a one-dimensional array or two elements in a two-dimensional array is not allowed.*

To facilitate the programming of subscripted variables, the Fortran language includes two additional statements—Do and Continue.

Do Statement

General Form

DO n i $= m_1$, m_2, m_3

where n is a statement number, i is a nonsubscripted fixed point variable, and m_1, m_2, m_3 are each either an unsigned fixed point constant or a nonsubscripted fixed points variable. If m_3 is not stated, it is taken to be 1. Also $0 < m_1 \leqq m_2$.

Examples

DO 30 I $= 1$, 10
DO 21 JOB $= 2$, 18, 2

The Do statement is a command to "Repeatedly execute the statements immediately following the Do statement, up to and including the statement numbered n, first with i equal to m_1, then with i incremented by m_3 for each succeeding pass until the value of i equals or reaches the highest quantity in the sequence without exceeding m_2, and then to execute the statement following statement n."

A Do statement in which m_3 is not specified will assume m_3 to be 1. Thus, the first time the range of the Do is executed, i will be equal to m_1, subsequently $i = m_1 + 1$, $i = m_1 + 2$, ..., finally $i = m_2$.

The *range* of a Do statement is defined as "the set of statements which will be executed repeatedly; it is the sequence of consecutive statements

immediately following the Do, up to and including the statement numbered n. After the last execution of the range, the Do statement is said to
be satisfied. The index of a Do statement is the fixed point variable i,
which is controlled by the Do in such a way that its value begins at m_1
and is increased each time by m_3 until it is about to exceed m_2. Throughout the range it is available for computation, either as an ordinary fixed
point variable or as the variable of a subscript.

As an example of a Do statement, consider the following program in
which control has reached statement 10:

$$10 \quad \text{DO 11 I} = 1, 10$$
$$11 \quad \text{A(I)} = \text{B(I)} + \text{C(I)}$$
$$12 \quad \dots\dots\dots\dots\dots$$

The range of the Do is statement 11, and the index is I. The Do sets
I = 1 and control passes into the range. B(1) + C(1) is computed and
stored in A(1). Now, since statement 11 is the last statement in the
range of the Do and the Do is unsatisfied, I is increased by 1 to 2 and
control returns to the beginning of the range, statement 11. B(2) + C(2)
is computed and stored in A(2). This continues until statement 11 has
been executed with I = 10. Since the Do statement is satisfied, control
passes to statement 12.

DO'S WITHIN DO'S

One or more Do statements may be included within the range of another Do statement. This is called nesting. There are, however, certain
rules which must be observed.

1. If the range of a Do statement includes another Do statement, all
   statements in the range of the second statement must also be in the
   range of the first Do. The following diagram illustrates this rule:

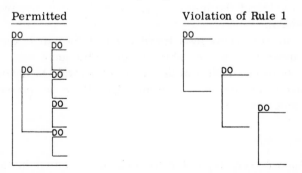

Permitted   Violation of Rule 1

A set of DOs satisfying this rule is called a nest of DOs.

2. No transfer of control by If or Go To statements is permitted into the range of any Do statement from outside its range, since such transfers would not permit the Do loop to be properly indexed. The following diagram illustrates this rule:

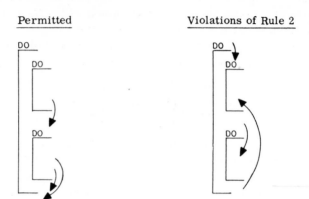

Permitted   Violations of Rule 2

3. The range of a Do cannot end with a transfer statement; that is, the statement numbered n cannot be a Go To or If type of statement.
4. The first statement in the range of a Do cannot be one of the following type of statements: Dimension, Format, or Continue.
5. The execution of a nest of Do's proceeds from the innermost Do to the outmost Do in that order.

PRESERVATION OF INDEX VALUES

When control leaves the range of a Do statement by the Do becoming satisfied ($i \gtreqless m_2$) and control passes to the next statement after the range, the exit is said to be a "normal" exit. When a "normal" exit occurs, the main value of the index (i) is lost and it may not be used unless it is redefined.

If an exit occurs by a transfer out of the range, the current value of the index remains available for any subsequent use. If the exit occurs by a transfer which is in the ranges of several Do statements, the current values of all the indices controlled by them are preserved for any subsequent use.

RESTRICTION

Almost every type of calculation is permitted in the range of a Do statement. Only one type of statement is not permitted, namely, any statement which redefines the value of the index or of any of the indexing parameters. In other words, the indexing of a Do loop must be completely set before the range is entered.

Continue Statement

General Form

CONTINUE

Example

CONTINUE

Continue is a dummy statement which does not generate any instructions in the object program. Its major use is as the last statement in the range of a Do to fill the requirement that the last statement in the range of a Do cannot be a transfer statement. As an example of a program that requires a Continue, consider the table search program:

```
10    DO 121 I = 1, 100
11    IF(A − B(I)) 121, 23, 121
121   CONTINUE
20    ..............
```

The Program will examine the 100-entry B table until it finds an entry that equals A, whereupon it will exit to statement 23 with the successful value of I available for fixed point use. If no entry in the table equals A, a normal exit to statement 20 will occur.

The following are examples of Fortran programs utilizing Do statements and subscripted variables.

Example

On page 189 a program was illustrated to sum the numbers from 1 to 1000, using an If statement to control the number of times through the loop. The following program will develop the same sum using a Do statement to control the loop.

```
     SUM = 0.0
     A = 1.0
     DO 3 I = 1, 1000
     SUM = SUM + A
3    A = A + 1.
     PUNCH 10, SUM
10   FORMAT (F10.0)
     STOP
     END
```

Example (presented without commentary for your study)

```
X = -1.0
DO 5 I = 1, 21
Y = X**3 + 3.0*X**2 - 4.0*X + 2.1
PRINT 2, X, Y
2 FORMAT (F4.1, 5XF8.3)
5 X = X + .1
STOP
END
```

Example

Assume that 1000 numbers are punched one per card. The following program will read in the numbers, sum the positive numbers, print the negative numbers, and do nothing with zeros.

```
    DIMENSION A(1000)
    DO 1 I = 1, 1000
  1 READ 15, A(I)
    SUM = 0.0
    DO 4 I = 1, 1000
    IF (A(I))3, 4, 2
  2 SUM = SUM + A(I)
    GO TO 4
  3 PRINT 15, A(I)
  4 CONTINUE
    PUNCH 16, SUM
 15 FORMAT (F8.3)
 16 FORMAT (F10.3)
    STOP
    END
```

Commentary

Notice the dimensioning of the subscripted variable. Note that all the A's are read into core storage first and then operated upon. Actually this is a waste of storage space since the values of the variables are not needed once they have been operated on. Rewrite the above example without using subscripted variables.

Example

Given X_i, Y_i, Z_j for $i = 1, 2, \ldots, 10$ $j = 1, 2, \ldots, 30$

Compute $\mathrm{PROD} = \left(\sum_{i=1}^{10} C_i \right) \left(\sum_{j=1}^{30} Z_i \right)$

Where:

$$C_i = X_i^2 + Y_i + 2X_i \text{ if } X_i > Y_i$$
$$C_i = X_i + Y_i^2 + 2Y_i \text{ if } X_i < Y_i$$
$$C_i = 0 \qquad\qquad \text{ if } X_i = Y_i$$

The 30 values of Z are punched five per card. There are ten cards with the corresponding values of X and Y on the same card. Thus X_1 and Y_1 are on the first card and X_{10} and Y_{10} are on the 10th card. The six Z cards follow. The following Fortran program is a solution:

```
   DIMENSION Z(5)
   SUMC = 0.
   DO 12 I = 1, 10
   READ 3, X, Y
 3 FORMAT (F8.3, F8.3)
   IF (X − Y) 9, 12, 11
 9 SUMC = SUMC + X + Y**2 + 2.*Y
   GO TO 12
11 SUMC = SUMC + X**2 + 2.*X + Y
12 CONTINUE
   SUMZ = 0.
   DO 15 I = 1,6
   READ 4, Z(1), Z(2), Z(3), Z(4), Z(5)
   DO 15 J = 1,5
15 SUMZ = SUMZ + Z(J)
 4 FORMAT (E14.4, E14.4, E14.4, E14.4, E14.4)
   PROD = SUMZ*SUMC
   PRINT 10, SUMC, SUMZ, PROD
10 FORMAT (E14.4, E14.4, E14.4)
   STOP
   END
```

FUNCTIONS

Frequently in programs it becomes necessary to calculate the sine or cosine of an angle or to take the natural logarithm of a number. Fortran has incorporated in it the necessary subroutines to calculate some of the more commonly required functions. It is possible in Fortran to do the following: calculate the sine of an angle, the cosine of an angle, the square root of a number, the natural logarithm of a number, the arctangent of a number, and to raise e to a power.

General Form

The name of the function being used must be written as represented below with the function name followed by the argument enclosed in parenthesis. The argument must be a floating point variable or constant. The argument may be an expression and, if desired, may contain another function. Should the argument be a floating point variable it may be subscripted. A function may be the argument of a function.

ALLOWABLE FUNCTION NAMES[3]

SIN(X) meaning sine of x (x in radians)
COS(X) meaning cosine of x (x in radians)
LOG(X) meaning $\log_e x$
EXP(X) meaning e^x
SQRT(X) meaning the square root of x
ATAN(X) meaning the $\tan^{-1} x$

Examples

COS(B)
SQRT(A★B − C)
LOGF(SIN(A))
ATAN(A(I, J))
SIN(B(I) + 2.)

For each of the functions shown, there exists a subroutine within the Fortran system that computes the function of the argument enclosed in parenthesis. These subroutines will be compiled into the object program automatically when called for by a statement containing a function.

Functions may be used in any arithmetic expression.

Examples

A = COS(DELTA) + 6.★X
IF(LOG(FIN) + SQRT(A + B))1, 2, 2
XCOOR = (SIN(R) + COS(S))/2.
BA = EXP(T(I + 2)) + X★★2.

COMMENT STATEMENT

Any statement whose first three characters are the letter "C" followed by two blanks is interpreted as a comment and does not affect the processing. Such comments are particularly helpful if one returns to a program after a prolonged period of inactivity.

Example

CbbTHIS PROGRAM CALCULATES ....

ADVANCED PROGRAMMING EXAMPLES

Example

In this example, a program is required to determine the current in an alternating-current circuit consisting of a resistance, an inductance, and a capacitance, having been given a number of sets of values of resistance, inductance, and frequency. The current is to be determined for a number of equally spaced values of the capacitance (which lie between specified limits which are input data) for voltages of 1.0, 1.5, 2.0, 2.5, and 3.0 volts.

[3] An allowable alternate name for any of the functions listed above is the permissible form of the name with a terminal "F" added. Thus, SINF, COSF, LOGF, EXPF, SQRTF and ATANF are permissable.

The equation for determining the current flowing through such a circuit is

$$i = \frac{E}{\sqrt{R^2 + \left[2\,\pi\,FL - \dfrac{1}{2\,\pi\,FC}\right]^2}}$$

where
- i = current, amperes
- E = voltage, volts
- R = resistance, ohms
- L = inductance, henrys
- C = capacitance, farads
- F = frequency, cycles per second
- π = 3.1416

The Fortran program could be written as follows:

```
 1 FORMAT (F8.2, F10.2, F8.2)
 2 FORMAT (F6.2, F8.2)
 3 FORMAT (F8.2)
10 READ 1, OHM, FREQ, HENRY
11 READ 2, FRÐ1, FRDMX
12 VOLT = 1.0
15 FARAD = FRD1
14 PUNCH 3, VOLT
16 AMP = VOLT/SQRTF(OHM**2 + (6.2832*FREQ*HENRY
     - 1./(6.2832*FREQ*FARAD))**2)
17 PUNCH 2, FARAD, AMP
18 IF (FARAD - FRDMX) 19, 21, 21
19 FARAD = FARAD + .00000001
20 GO TO 16
21 IF (VOLT - 3.0) 22, 10, 10
22 VOLT = VOLT + 0.5
23 GO TO 15
24 END
```

Commentary

Statement 10 causes the values of the resistance, the frequency, and the inductance to be read from the first card, and statement 11 causes the initial and final values of the capacitance to be read from the next card. The initial value of the voltage is introduced and punched (statements 12 and 14). Statement 15 causes the initial value of the capacitance to replace the current value of the capacitance (denoted as FARAD). The actual calculation, together with the current value of the capacitance, is then punched (statement 17).

The current value of the capacitance is compared with the final value to determine whether or not all values have been investigated (statement 18). If not, the expression is negative and the program proceeds to statement 19, which causes the value of the capacitance to be increased by the given increment. This is followed by a transfer (statement 20) to statement 16 which causes the calculation to be repeated for the new value of the capacitance. If

the expression in statement 18 is zero or positive, all values of the capacitance have been investigated and the program transfers to statement 21.

At this point the value of the voltage is compared with the upper bound to determine whether or not all specified values of the voltage have been used. If not, the expression in statement 21 is negative and the program proceeds to statement 22 which causes the value of the voltage to be increased. Following this, a transfer (statement 23) is made to statement 15, causing the new value of the voltage to be punched; and the entire process of investigating all values of the capacitance is begun again. If all values of the voltage have been used (the expression in statement 21 is zero or positive), the calculations for the current set of values of resistance, frequency, and inductance are finished. The program is returned to statement 10 so that the two cards defining the next case may be read and the program repeated. This process is repeated until all of the cases have been considered, that is, all of the cards have been read.

Example

The following is an example of a Fortran program to do matrix multiplication for matrices of a maximum size of 15 by 15. Assume that the elements are punched one per card by rows.

Given a matrix A with dimensions $N \times L$, and the matrix B with dimensions $L \times M$ the resultant product matrix C will be of size $N \times M$.

To compute any element C_{ij}, select the i row of A and the j column of B, and sum the products of their corresponding elements. The general formula for this computation is

$$C_{ij} = \sum_{k=1}^{l} A_{ik}B_{kj}$$

```
     DIMENSION A(15, 15), B(15, 15), C(15, 15)
10 FORMAT (I2, I2, I2)
11 FORMAT (F8.2)
12 FORMAT (I4, I4, F8.2)
     READ 10, L, N, M
     DO 1 I = 1, N
     DO 1 J = 1, L
 1 READ 11, A(I, J)
     DO 2 I = 1, L
     DO 2 J = 1, M
 2 READ 11, B(I, J)
     DO 4 I = 1, N
     DO 4 J = 1, M
     C(I, J) = 0.0
     DO 20 K = 1, L
20 C(I, J) = C(I, J) + A(I, K) ★ B(K, J)
 4 PRINT 12, I, J, C(I, J)
     STOP
     END
```

Example

The following Fortran program will sort up to 300 floating point numbers into ascending sequence. The exchange method of sorting is used. The numbers are punched one per card in columns 1–8. A header card is read in first; in columns 1–3 of this card is the number of numbers to be sorted. In the exchange method of sorting the first two numbers are compared. If the first number is greater than the second they are interchanged. If the second number is greater than the first the procedure continues with no interchange. The second and third numbers are then compared and if the second number is greater, they are interchanged. This process continues until finally the last number and the preceding one are compared. At this time the largest number will be at the end of the list of numbers in its proper place. The process is then repeated starting with the first number. At the completion of this second pass the next largest number will be in its proper place. Thus if N is the number of numbers a *maximum* of $N-1$ passes are required to put them in ascending sequence.

If the following items are noted the time required for the complete sort may be reduced.

1. The numbers are in sequence when no interchange has occurred in a complete pass.
2. During a pass all the numbers beyond the last interchange are in sequence. Thus if 100 numbers are being sorted and on the first past the last interchange is made between the 79th and 80th numbers in the list, on the next pass and numbers beyond the 78th and 79th need not be compared since they will be in the proper sequence.

```
Cbb FORTRAN SORT PROGRAM-EXCHANGE METHOD
    DIMENSION A(300)
 1 FORMAT (I3)
 7 FORMAT (F8.2)
11 FORMAT (F8.2, F8.2)
36 SUM = 0.0
   SUM1 = 0.0
   IND = 0
   READ 1, KOUNT
   DO 2 I = 1, KOUNT
   READ 7, A(I)
 2 SUM = SUM + A(I)
Cbb THIS IS A CHECK TOTAL TO BE COMPARED WITH
Cbb A TOTAL TAKEN AT THE END OF THE PROGRAM
   INDEX = KOUNT − 1
 3 DO 5 I = 1, INDEX
   IF (A(I + 1) − A(I))6, 5, 5
```

```
  6 SAVE = A(I + 1)
    A(I + 1) = A(I)
    A(I) = SAVE
    IHOLD = I
    IND = 1
  5 CONTINUE
    IF (IND) 9, 8, 9
  9 INDEX = IHOLD
    IND = 0
    GO TO 3
  8 DO 4 I = 1, KOUNT
    SUM1 = SUM1 + A(I)
Cbb THIS IS THE SECOND CHECK TOTAL DEVELOPED
  4 PRINT 7, A(I)
    PRINT 11, SUM, SUM1
    GO TO 36
    END
```

GENERAL INFORMATION

1. Statements may be punched anywhere in card or tape.
2. Source statements may not exceed 72 characters including blanks and statement numbers.
3. An E/L must be the last character of every Fortran statement in the tape system and is included in the 72 character count.
4. The card system does not require the record mark as a terminating character of the statement, but the presence of such a character does not affect the processing.
5. The programmer may utilize the last 8 columns of the card for any identifying information he wishes. This will not affect the processing.
6. Object time input records may not exceed 72 characters. Object time output records may not exceed 72 characters except for typewriter records which may not exceed 87 characters.

Chapter 16

Problems

SECTION 1. BASIC MACHINE LANGUAGE PROBLEMS

All problems in this section may be attempted with a knowledge of machine language coding only. Unless otherwise stated, input data is assumed to be flagged at the high-order position and, if negative, at the low-order position. A 20,000-core-position machine with card and paper tape I/O devices is assumed. Other than these features no other equipment is available. A record mark is assumed to be in position 00400 if needed. Programs may begin at any even location above 00400. Any assumptions needed for proper solution of the problems are valid.

1.1 Five positive unflagged 4-digit integers are punched in paper tape. They are separated by E/L characters and an E/L character follows the fifth and last item. Construct a program to generate and print the product of the five numbers.

1.2 Assume that the data in the previous problem is punched in columns 1–4 of five separate cards. Construct a program to type the product of the five numbers. Data is unflagged.

1.3 Five positive unflagged 4-digit integers are punched in one record on paper tape. Following the last item there is an E/L character. There are no blanks separating the data. It may be considered as a 20-digit number Generate and type the product of the five numbers.

1.4 A single card is punched with five unflagged 4-digit numbers as follows:

XXXX	Columns 1–4
XXXX	Columns 7–10
XXXX	Columns 15–18
XXXX	Columns 26–29
XXXX	Columns 75–78

Generate and type the product of the five numbers.

1.5 N cards are punched with the following information:

A (XXX.XX)   Columns 1–5
B (.XXXX)   Columns 6–9
C (X.XX)   Columns 10–12
D (XX.)   Columns 13–14

Decimal points are not punched in the cards. Thus a number of the form A may be 35.6 and will be punched as 03560. The range of the numbers is as follows:

$$-999.99 \le A \le 999.99$$
$$-.9999 \le B \le .9999$$
$$-9.99 \le C \le 9.99$$
$$-99. \le D \le 99.$$

For each input card type a single line of output information which consists of A, B, C, D and SUM, where

SUM = A + B + C + D.

Calculate SUM to two decimal places and round the result to one decimal. Terminate the program after processing the last card.

1.6 N cards are in the read hopper of the 1622. Write a program to type N ($N \le 500$). High-order zeros are not to be typed. Thus if 23 cards are in the read hopper, the result appears as 23, not as 023.

1.7 N records are on paper tape. Each record is 5 characters long (4 digits and one E/L character), except for the last, which is 6 characters long (4 digits, one record mark, and one E/L character). Write a program to type N ($N \le 8500$). High-order zeros are not to be typed as part of the result.

1.8 Five 10-digit numbers are on paper tape, separated by E/L characters. An E/L character follows the fifth and last element. Write a program to sort the data in increasing order and punch it into paper tape. The output tape is to consist of the sorted data separated by E/L characters and an E/L character is to follow the fifth and last element. No two elements are equal and the data are not necessarily all of the same sign.

1.9 N cards each contain a single 2-digit number X_i (XX.) *punched in* columns 14–15. Generate coding to calculate and print the following:

$$N \text{ and } \sum_{i=1}^{N} X_i$$

where $N \le 9999$ and $\Sigma X_i \le 99999$.

1.10 This problem is identical with the previous one, with the following two exceptions:

1. The first card has a 4-digit number P ($P \le 9999$) punched in columns 2–5.
2. There are P + 1 cards.

SECTION 2. MACROLESS SYMBOLIC CODING

All problems in this section may be attempted with a knowledge of SPS coding. Macro-instructions are not employed. For all problems, assume a 20,000-core-position 1620 with card and paper tape I/O. You may assume any alternate attachments, at the instructor's discretion. Any assumptions for the proper solution of these problems are valid. Unless otherwise stated, all data is assumed to be flagged on the input medium.

2.1 A, B, and C are on paper tape separated by E/L characters, and an E/L character lies after the third and last element.

$$A(XXX.) \leqq 300$$
$$B(XXX.) \leqq 400$$
$$C(XXX.) \leqq 200$$

Generate the coding for $G = A + B - C$
$(-500 \leqq G \leqq 900)$
If $G > 0$, print G and halt.
If $G = 0$, print A, B, C, G, and halt.
If $G < 0$, print G, A, B, C, and halt.
Do not print high-order zeros for any data.

2.2 Six cards are in the read hopper of the 1622.

Card 1: $N(X.)$—Column 1
Card 2: $A(XXX.)$—Columns 1–3
Card 3: $B(XXX.)$—Columns 1–3
Card 4: $C(XXXX.)$—Columns 1–4
Card 5: $D(XX.)$—Columns 1–2
Card 6: $E(XXX.)$—Columns 1–3

If $N = 1$, calculate and print Y where
$Y = A + B + C + D + E$ $(Y \leqq 9999)$

If $N = 2$, calculate and print Y where
$Y = A \cdot B \cdot C \cdot D \cdot E$ $(Y \leqq 99999999)$

If $N = 3$, calculate and print Y where

$Y = C - A - B - D - E$ $(Y \leqq 9999)$

If $N > 3$, print N and the following error message:

INCORRECT CODE IN FIRST CARD

2.3 On tape, in a single record, are A_i $(i = 1,100)$. $A_i \leqq 999$ for all i. An E/L character follows A_{100}. Each A_i is three characters. Calculate and print:

$$\sum_{i=1}^{100} A_i$$

2.4   On 510 cards, A_i, B_i $(i = 1{,}510)$.

Each A_i, B_i occupies a single card.
  A_i: Columns 1–3 $(A_i \leq 800)$
  B_i: Columns 5–8 $(B_i \leq 9000)$

Generate 510 cards such that:

  A_i: Columns 5–7
  B_i: Columns 1–4
  C_i: Columns 75–78 $(C \leq 5000)$ *

where $C_i = A_i + B_i$

2.5   This problem is identical with the previous one with the following three exceptions:

  1.   There are N (≤ 5000) cards.
  2. $i = 1, N$
  3.   After producing the N-th card, punch an $(N + 1)$st card with N in columns 77–80.

2.6   There are two records on paper tape.
The first consists of A_i $(i = 1{,}75)$.

The second consists of B_j $(j = 1{,}38)$.

$$A_i \; (XX.) \leq 99$$
$$B_j \; (XXX.) \leq 999$$

Calculate and print:

$$\sum_{\substack{i = 1 \\ j = 1}}^{\substack{38 \\ 75}} A_i B_j \qquad (\leq 99999999)$$

An E/L character separates the two records and an E/L character termi-

---

* In many computer problems, the theoretical final result does not agree with the actual final result. In this case it seems that C_i might obtain a maximum value of 9800. A comparison might be made to a payroll operation where an employer has 100 employees, and each makes a maximum of $100 per week. This does not necessarily imply that the employer must have $10,000 ready to meet his payroll. Previous experience has told him that his payroll has never exceeded $5,000 in any one week, even though it is theoretically possible for it to be twice as high. This is one of the great problems in fixed point arithmetic: extremely tight bounds on all input data must be known, and checks are generally established along the program's path to assure that all data stay within these bounds. Determining the historical background of a data processing or scientific problem can often take much longer than the actual program construction.

nates the second record. The first record is 151 characters in length. The second record is 115 characters in length.

2.7 On tape there are six records.

Record 1: M (2 digits)
Record 2: N (2 digits)
Record 3: P (2 digits)
Record 4: A_i ($i = 1, M$. Each $A_i \leq 999$.)
Record 5: B_j ($j = 1, N$. Each $B_j \leq 99$.)
Record 6: C_k ($k = 1, P$. Each $C_k \leq 99$.)

Calculate and print:

$$\begin{array}{c} P \\ N \\ M \\ \sum_{\substack{i=1 \\ j=1 \\ k=1}} A_i B_j C_k \;(\leq 10^{10}) \end{array}$$

The count of the number of digits in each record given above does not include the E/L character. Therefore, Record 1 is 3 characters long, and so forth.

2.8 Analyze and comment on the following program. Give a timing estimate at the object level.

LINE	LABEL	OPERATION	OPERANDS & REMARKS		
0,1,0		D,O,R,G	4,0,2,		
0,2,0	S,T,A,R,T,	T,F,M	C,O,U,N,T,		
0,3,0		A,M	C,O,U,N,T,,,1,		
0,4,0		B,N,V,	*,-,1,2,		
0,5,0		H,			
0,6,0	C,O,U,N,T,	D,S,	,*,		
0,7,0		D,E,N,D	S,T,A,R,T,		
0,8,0					

2.9 One hundred cards are in the read hopper of the 1622. Each card has a 4-digit number punched in columns 1–4. There is a record mark in column 80 of each card. Reproduce this deck in ascending, sorted order. No data is necessarily unique.

2.10 Write a program to generate and print the following:

0000	1100
0001	1101
0011	1111
0010	1110
0110	1010
0111	1011
0101	1001
0100	1000

The above binary-type coding is to be generated through the use of iterative coding, not through the use of 16 DC statements.

2.11 Generate and print the following:

0123456789
1234567890
2345678901
3456789012
4567890123
5678901234
6789012345
7890123456
8901234567
9012345678

Similarly, do not use 10 DC statements, but rather iterative coding.

SECTION 3. FULL SYMBOLIC CODING WITH MACRO-INSTRUCTIONS

All problems in this section may be attempted with a knowledge of full symbolic coding. For all problems, assume a 20,000-core-position 1620 with card and paper tape I/O. You may assume any alternate attachments, at the instructor's discretion. Any assumptions for the proper solution of these problems are valid. Unless otherwise stated, all data is assumed to be flagged on the input medium. All problems done in floating point assume a 10-digit floating point word. With adequate modifications of the statement of the problem, any floating point word size may be assumed.

3.1 N cards are in the read hopper of the 1622. Each card contains three floating point numbers punched as follows:

    A: 1–10
    B: 11–20
    C: 21–30

For each input card punch a single output card with the following information:

$$A: \quad 1\text{–}10$$
$$B: \quad 11\text{–}20$$
$$C: \quad 21\text{–}30$$
$$X_1: \quad 31\text{–}40$$
$$X_2: \quad 41\text{–}50$$
$$\text{Blank:} \quad 51\text{–}80$$

where X_1 and X_2 are the solutions to the quadratic system:

$$AX^2 + BX + C = 0$$

If the discriminant of the quadratic is negative, punch the following information to avoid complex roots:

$$A: \quad 1\text{–}10$$
$$B: \quad 11\text{–}20$$
$$C: \quad 21\text{–}30$$
$$\text{Discriminant:} \quad 31\text{–}40 \quad (B^2 - 4AC)$$
$$\text{Blanks:} \quad 41\text{–}80$$

3.2 Given a matrix A_{mn} punched in cards by rows, where each element of the matrix is a floating point word and each card contains a maximum of 8 words. This matrix has 9 rows and 7 columns. Calculate a matrix B_{mn} where:

1. $b_{1j} = a_{1j}$ $\quad (j = 1, 7)$
2. $b_{9j} = a_{9j}$ $\quad (j = 1, 7)$
3. $b_{i1} = a_{i1}$ $\quad (i = 2, 9)$
4. $b_{i7} = a_{i7}$ $\quad (i = 2, 9)$
5. $b_{ij} = \tfrac{1}{4}a_{i-1,j} + \tfrac{1}{4}a_{i+1,j} + \tfrac{1}{4}a_{i,j-1} + \tfrac{1}{4}a_{i,j+1}$
$$\text{for } i = 2, 8$$
$$j = 2, 6$$

The B_{mn} matrix is developed by superimposing itself on the A_{mn} matrix. At the conclusion of the program, the A_{mn} matrix has been overlain completely. Punch the resultant matrix on cards packed 8 words per card, except for the last card which is blank in the last 10 columns.

3.3 This problem is identical with the previous one, with the following exceptions:

1. Preceding the matrix is a single card with the following information:

(a) Columns 1–2: m $(\bar{X}X) \leq 40$

(b) Columns 3–4: n $(\bar{X}X) \leq 40$

2. m and n are not necessarily equal.

Calculate the matrix B_{mn} where:

1. $b_{1j} = a_{1j}$ $(j = 1, n)$
2. $b_{mj} = a_{mj}$ $(j = 1, n)$
3. $b_{i1} = a_{i1}$ $(i = 2, m)$
4. $b_{in} = a_{in}$ $(i = 2, m)$
5. $b_{ij} = \frac{1}{4}a_{i-1,j} + \frac{1}{4}a_{i+1,j} + \frac{1}{4}a_{i,j-1} + \frac{1}{4}a_{i,j+1}$
   for $i = 2, m - 1$
   $j = 2, n - 1$

3.4 Calculate and print the following tabulation with alphabetic headings. All calculation and all output is in floating point form.

   X(RADIANS)   SIN(X)   COS(X)
where:

   $0 \le X \le 2\,\Pi$
   $\Delta X = .0001$ radians

3.5 A 2-digit record ($\bar{X}X \le 40$) is terminated by an E/L character on paper tape. A second record consists of the upper half of a square symmetrical matrix: (by rows)

$$a_{11}a_{12} \ldots a_{1j}a_{22}a_{23} \ldots a_{2j}a_{33} \ldots a_{3j} \ldots a_{jj}$$

where $a_{ij} = a_{ji}$.

The second record consists of $\dfrac{j(j+1)}{2}$

elements, each one of which is a floating point number. The first record is j. The second record is terminated by an E/L character.

Generate and punch the complete square symmetrical matrix from the information given about the upper half. Data are to be punched in paper tape in a single record. The complete matrix is to be punched as follows:

$$a_{11}a_{12} \ldots a_{1j}a_{21}a_{22}a_{23} \ldots a_{2j} \ldots a_{j1}a_{j2} \ldots a_{jj}$$

Thus, if $j = 3$, the input information is:

$$a_{11}a_{12}a_{13}a_{22}a_{23}a_{33}$$

$$\begin{matrix} a_{11} & a_{12} & a_{13} \\ & a_{22} & a_{23} \\ & & a_{33} \end{matrix}$$

and the output information is:

$$a_{11}a_{12}a_{13}a_{21}a_{22}a_{23}a_{31}a_{32}a_{33}$$

$$\begin{matrix} a_{11} & a_{12} & a_{13} \\ a_{21} & a_{22} & a_{23} \\ a_{31} & a_{32} & a_{33} \end{matrix}$$

3.6 Assume a machine without divide hardware for the following problem. Tabulate a list of X and $1/X$ for $1 \le X \le 1000$ with $\Delta X = 1$. Calculate all reciprocals to three decimals. Use fixed point arithmetic.

X	1/X
1	1000
2	500
3	333
4	250
.	.
.	.
.	.
1000	001

3.7 Evaluate and print X *and* F (X) for the following polynomial:

$$F(X) = 2.7X^7 + 3.2X^6 - 2.1X^5 + X^4 + 3X^3 - 2X^2 + X + 17$$
$$0 \leq X \leq 10 \qquad \Delta X = .1$$

Hint: Nest the polynomial as follows:

$$((\ldots ((2.7X + 3.2)X - 2.1)X + \ldots)X + 17$$

All calculation and output is to be done in floating point form, with the following tabulation:

X   F (X)

3.8 Write a program to generate $\sqrt{a}$ using the Newtonian method of successive approximation:

$$x_{n+1} = \tfrac{1}{2}(x_n + a/x_n)$$

where x_{n+1} is the $(n+1)$st approximation to $\sqrt{a}$.
Calculate and print all a and $\sqrt{a}$ for $1 \leq a \leq 1000$ with $\Delta a = 1.0$. Do not use the square root macro. Do all arithmetic in floating point.

3.9 Construct a generalized float routine with input from paper tape and each number is separated from the next by an E/L character. Punch the floated data on tape in the same form (separated by E/L characters). Data may be signed or unsigned with a maximum of 8 decimal digits. A decimal point is always present. Thus a maximum record is 11 characters, including E/L character. A minimum record is 3 characters, including E/L character. The desired output record for each input record is the input number expressed in floating point form. Input data is not flagged, namely.

123.4E/L−.001E/L75.9832E/L.1E/L...

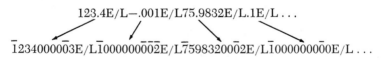

1234000003E/L1000000002E/L7598320002E/L1000000000E/L...

3.10 Construct a generalized fix routine with input from paper tape in a fashion identical with the output of the previous problem. Positive data are to be printed unsigned, and negative data are to be printed with sign. The range of the characteristic of the floating point number will not exceed $\bar{0}7$ or be less than $\bar{0}\bar{7}$. Print the number with decimal point and 8 digits, namely:

$\bar{1}2340000\bar{0}3$	yields	123.40000
$\bar{1}000000\bar{0}\bar{0}\bar{2}$	yields	$-.00100000$
$7598320\bar{0}\bar{0}2$	yields	75.983200
$\bar{9}99999990\bar{7}$	yields	9999999.9
$\bar{1}2345678\bar{0}\bar{7}$	yields	.00000001

SECTION 4.   FORTRAN PROBLEMS

All problems in this section may be attempted with a knowledge of basic 1620 Fortran.

4.1   Any centesimal year not divisible by 400 is not a leap year. Type a list of all leap years from the year 1599 to the present year. If the present year is a leap year, include it in the list.

4.2   Calculate and print the following tabulations with alphabetic headings.

$$X(RADIANS) \qquad SIN(X) \qquad COS(X)$$

for $0 \leq X \leq 2$ and $\Delta X = .001$ radians.

4.3   Assume typewriter input for all necessary parameters. Design a Fortran program to evaluate

$$\int_A^B Ln(x)\,dx$$

by Simpson's rule.[1]

$A + nh = B$

$$\int_A f(x)\,dx = h/3\,(f(x_0) + 4f(x_1) + 2f(x_2) + 4f(x_3) + 2f(x_4) + \ldots$$

$$+ 2f(x_{n-2}) + 4f(x_{n-1}) + f(x_n))$$

where

1. $x_i + h = x_{i+1}$
2. $A = x_0$
3. $B = A + nh = x_n$

[1] For a complete discussion of numerical integration see:
  (a) Milne, W. E., *Numerical Calculus*. Princeton, N. J.: Princeton University Press, 1949. pp. 100-200.
  (b) Hildebrand, F. B., *Introduction to Numerical Analysis*. New York: McGraw-Hill Publishing Company, Inc., 1956. pp. 64-84.
  (c) Scarborough, J. B., *Numerical Mathematical Analysis*. Baltimore, Md.: The Johns Hopkins Press, 1958. pp. 131-167.

4.4 Design a Fortran program to perform the numerical integration of the preceding problem employing Weddle's rule.[2]

$$A + nh = B$$
$$\int_A^{A+nh=B} f(x)\,dx = 3h/10 \quad \left(\sum_{i=0}^{n} kf(x_i) \right)$$

where $k = 1, 5, 1, 6, 1, 5, 2, 5, 1, 6, 1, 5, 2, \ldots, 1$

4.5 Design a Fortran program to perform the same numerical integration as the previous two problems, employing Gauss' Quadrature formula.[3]

$$\int_A^B f(x)\,dx = (B - A)(R_1\phi(u_1) + R_2\phi(u_2) + \ldots + R_n\phi(u_n)).^{\circ}$$

using the transformations

$$x = (B - A)u + \frac{a + b}{2}$$

$$y - f(x) = f((B - A)u + \frac{a + b}{2}) = \phi(u)$$

4.6 Write a Fortran program to generate $\sqrt{a}$ using the Newtonian method of successive approximation:

$$x_{n+1} = \frac{1}{2}(x_n + a/x_n)$$

where x_{n+1} is the $(n + 1)$st approximation to $\sqrt{a}$. Calculate and print all a and $\sqrt{a}$ for $1 \le a \le 1000$ with $\Delta a = 1.0$. Do not use the Fortran subroutine SQRT or SQRTF.

4.7 Examine the following Fortran program for error. It is designed to yield two roots of a quadratic if the discriminant is positive and not zero. If the discriminant is zero, it types one value for the double root. If the discriminant is negative an unconditional halt is obtained.

```
6 READ 1, A, B, C
1 FORMAT (F8.2)
5 FORMAT (F8.4)
  X = B★★2 − 4.★A★C
  IF (X) 2, 3, 4
2 STOP
```

[2] Ibid.

[3] Ibid.

° For values of R and u for extensive n see Scarborough, pp. 148-149. For the most extensive tables of Gauss coefficients ever published, see "Tables of the Zeros of the Legendre Polynomials of Order 1-16 and the Weight Coefficients for Gauss' Mechanical Quadrature Formula," by A. N. Lowan, Norman Davids and Arthur Levinson, in Bulletin of the American Mathematical Society, vol. 48, no. 10, October 1942, pp. 739-743.

```
3 X = −B/2.★A
  PRINT 5, X
  GO TO 6
4 ROOT 1 = (−B + SQRT(X))/2.★A
  ROOT 2 = (−B − SQRT(X))/2.★A
  PRINT 5, ROOT 1, ROOT 2
  GO TO 6
```

4.8   There are $I+J+K+1$ cards in the read hopper of the 1620.
The I cards have a_i $(I \leq 10)$
The J cards have b_j $(J \leq 15)$
The K cards have c_k $(K \leq 17)$
The first card in the sequence has I, J, K punched in colunms 1–2, 3–4,
5–6 respectively. All a_i, b_j, c_k are of the form ± XXX.XXX and are
punched, one per card, in columns 1–8 of the $I+J+K$ cards. Calculate
and print:

$$\sum_{\substack{i=1 \\ j=1 \\ k=1}}^{\substack{K \\ J \\ I}} a_i b_j c_k$$

4.9   Generate a Fortran program to construct a matrix a_{ij} where $a_{ij} = 1/(i+j+1)$. Parameters i and j may be entered into the system in any fashion.

$$1 \leq i \leq 30; \ 1 \leq j \leq 30$$

4.10 Calculate one root of the following polynomial using a technique of examination of sign changes of $f(x)$.

$$x^4 - 5x^3 + 5x^2 + 5x - 6 = 0$$

All roots lie between −3 and 1 inclusive.

Additional Instructions

The three instructions discussed in this chapter are not considered as part of the standard 1620 hardware and therefore are not included among the 1620 basic instructions.

The Move Flag, Transfer Numerical Strip, and Transfer Numerical Fill instructions are extremely useful where it is necessary to read and write all data in the alphameric mode.

Instruction: Move Flag

Operation Code: 71

Symbolic Name: MF

Description:

The flag bit at the core storage position specified by the Q address is transmitted to the core storage position specified by the P address. If the core position specified by the Q address contains a flag, a flag is placed at the core position specified by the P address and the flag at the Q address is cleared. If no flag is present at the Q address, the flag at the core position specified by the P address is cleared. The digits at the P and Q addresses are not altered.

Execution Time in Microseconds: 240 (constant)

Example: 71 19000 00409

2. ◄─────────────┐ $\overline{0}$ ◄─────────────┐

Core location 19000   Core location 00409 before
before Move Flag   Move Flag

$\overline{2}$ ◄─────────────┐   0 ◄─────────────┐

Core location 19000   Core location 00409 after
after Move Flag   Move Flag

Example: 71 15000 16000

3 ◄─────────────┐   7 ◄─────────────┐

Core location 15000   Core location 16000 before
before Move Flag   Move Flag

3 ◄─────────────┐   7 ◄─────────────┐

Core location 15000   Core location 16000 after
after Move Flag   Move Flag

Example: 71 13876 14998

$\overline{8}$ ◄─────────────┐   5 ◄─────────────┐

Core location 13876   Core location 14998 before
before Move Flag   Move Flag

8 ◄─────────────┐   5 ◄─────────────┐

Core location 13876   Core location 14998 after
after Move Flag   Move Flag

Example: 71 13810 16950

$\overline{5}$ ◄─────────────┐ $\overline{4}$ ◄─────────────┐

Core location 13810   Core location 16950 before
before Move Flag   Move Flag

$\overline{5}$ ◄─────────────┐   4 ◄─────────────┐

Core location 13810   Core location 16950 after
after Move Flag   Move Flag

Example: 71 12998 13000

00$\overline{4}$169 ◄─────────────┐

Core location 13003
before Move Flag

$\overline{0}$04169 ◄─────────────┐

Core location 13003
after Move Flag

The preceding example shows how a Move Flag instruction is used to lengthen a field.

The Transfer Numerical Strip and Transfer Numerical Fill instructions facilitate programming where all input and output is in the double-digit alphameric code. They greatly simplify the conversion of the double-digit representation of numerical data to single-digit coding required for use in arithmetic operations, and the reconversion to double-digit coding for alphameric output.

During the discussion of these two instructions the terms "P field" and "alphameric field" will be used. Though technically the term "field" is incorrect because, as will be discussed, no field-defining flag is necessary, the terms will be used to avoid a repetitive verbose description of the areas referenced. The terms "P field" and "alphameric field" used interchangeably will refer to the core position specified by the P address and all contiguous lower numbered core positions which contain data used by the instruction.

The symbol D_P' will be used to represent the number of digits in the "P field" as described above.

Instruction: Transfer Numerical Strip

Operation Code: 72

Symbolic Name: TNS

Description:

This instruction converts double-digit alphameric data into single-digit numerical data with sign. The units position of the alphameric field is specified by the P address of the instruction and must always be an odd-numbered core location. The units position of the numerical field is specified by the Q address. The digits in the odd-numbered core storage locations of the alphameric field (P field) are transmitted without change to the adjacent positions of the numerical field.

Transmission of data proceeds from the position addressed, through successively lower numbered core storage locations, until a flag is sensed in the *numerical* field in other than the units position. The flag must be placed in the numerical field prior to the Transfer Numerical Strip instruction to define the high-order position. It remains unchanged by the instruction. Except for the field-defining flag, all previous contents of the numerical field are erased by the new contents. The erasure includes the units position sign flag that designates a previous negative value. The alphameric field remains unchanged.

The zone digits in the even-numbered core storage locations of the alphameric field are ignored except for a 5, 2, or a 1 in the units zone position. A 5 in a units zone position of an alphamerically coded numerical field indicates a negative number read from an input card, a paper tape, or a typewriter. A 2 in a units zone position occurs when an X alone, representing a negative zero, is read from input card or paper tape. A 1 occurs when a negative zero (X,0) is read from paper tape. A 5, a 2, or a 1 in the units zone position is converted by the Transfer Numerical Strip instruction to a flag which is placed over the units digit of the numerical field. Any number other than a 5, 2, or 1 results in no flag over the units digit.

Flags in the even-numbered zone positions of the alphameric field are ignored. However, flags present in the odd-numbered core locations of the alphameric field are transmitted with the digit to the corresponding positions of the numerical field. Because such flags, when transmitted, may effect the length or sign of the numerical field, all flags in the odd-numbered core positions of the alphameric field should be cleared by instructions at the beginning of the program. Such extraneous flags may be the result of the previous use of the core storage locations or the fact that the Read Alphamerically instruction does not destroy any flags which are in core.

Note carefully that the TNS instruction transmits data from the P-address location to the Q-address location. This is directly opposite to the general philosophy of all other 1620 instructions.

Execution Time in Microseconds: $160 + 40D_p$

Example: 72 16235 17464

71727354 ◄───────┐
Core location 16235
before and after
Transmit Numerical Strip

7890 ◄───────────┐
Core location 17464 before
Transmit Numerical Strip

1234 ◄───────────┐
Core location 17464 after
Transmit Numerical Strip

Execution Time: 480 microseconds

Example: 72 09813 09000

787379757176◄──┐
Core location 09813
before and after
Transmit Numerical Strip

21300 ◄──────────┐
Core location 09000 before
Transmit Numerical Strip

39516 ◄──────────┐
Core location 09000 after
Transmit Numerical Strip

Execution Time: 560 microseconds

Instruction: Transfer Numerical Fill

Operation Code: 73

Symbolic Name: TNF

Description:

This instruction moves and expands single-digit numerical data with a sign into double-digit alphameric data. The units position of the alphameric field is specified by the P address of the instruction and must always be an odd-numbered core location. The units position of the numerical field is specified by the Q address.

The digits in the field whose units position is specified by the Q address are transmitted without change to the corresponding odd-numbered positions of the field specified by the P address. The contents, including flags of the odd-numbered core positions of the P field, are replaced by the Q field data. The even-numbered positions of the P field are filled with 7's, giving the double-digit representation of the single-digit numerical Q field data.

Transmission of data proceeds from the units position of the Q field data through successively lower numbered core locations, until terminated by the sensing of the flag defining the high-order position of the Q field data. The flag terminating data transmission is *not* transmitted to the P field. The Q field data is not altered by this instruction.

If the numerical field specified by the Q address is negative, a 5 is placed in the even-numbered units zone position of the alphameric (P) field. During a Write Alphamerically instruction, a negative zero, represented by a zone digit five and a numerical digit zero, is converted to X coding in paper tape, to X, 0 coding in an output card, and to a minus sign (−) on the typewriter. All other negative units positions having a zone digit 5 type and punch as the letters J through R ($\bar{1}$ through $\bar{9}$)

Execution Time in Microseconds: $160 + 40D_P$

Example: 73 16257 17394

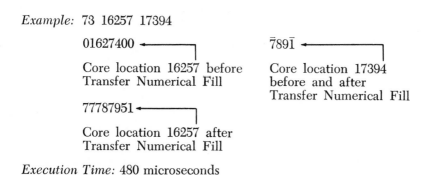

01627400 ←

Core location 16257 before Transfer Numerical Fill

$\bar{7}89\bar{1}$ ←

Core location 17394 before and after Transfer Numerical Fill

77787951 ←

Core location 16257 after Transfer Numerical Fill

Execution Time: 480 microseconds

Example: 73 06421 19003

$$00\bar{0}\bar{0}00000\bar{0}\bar{0}\bar{0}\bar{0}\bar{0} \qquad\qquad \bar{7}842162$$

Core location 06421 before
Transfer Numerical Fill

Core location 19003
before and after
Transfer Numerical Fill

77787472717672

Core location 06421 after
Transfer Numerical Fill

Execution Time: 720 microseconds

Problems

For all Problems the following core content is assumed:

CORE LOCATION LOW-ORDER DIGIT	CONTENTS
13123	777871727374
07000	$\bar{0}00\bar{0}$
05555	$\bar{7}\bar{3}797851$
06000	$\bar{9}99$
15321	$\bar{6}431$

For each problem show the contents of the P field and Q field after the instruction(s) have been executed.

The core content listed above is to be assumed for every problem and the results of any one problem are independent of all others.

1. 72 13123 07000
2. 73 13123 07000
3. 71 06998 06999
    71 06997 06998
    72 13123 07000
4. 72 05555 06000
5. 72 05555 15321
6. 73 13123 05555

Appendix **II**

Direct Divide

Although the division subroutine is adequate, some computer installations cannot afford to relinquish the core storage required by the subroutine. Also, when many divisions are required, it may be desirable to increase the processing speed of division. The Divide feature increases the processing speed of division by two to four times that of the subroutine, and saves storage since only one instruction need be given to divide. The Divide feature also simplifies programming since it provides the programmer with four additional commands to facilitate the positioning of the dividend and divisor in core storage.

The Divide feature imposes no limitations upon the size of the dividend, divisor, or quotient. The quotient and remainder are developed in the fixed product area (00080–00099). When a quotient length plus remainder length exceeds 20 digits, core storage positions below 00080 (00079, 00078, etc.) must be cleared to zeros by programming prior to the execution of the Divide instruction. This is similar to the multiply operation when a product greater than 20 digits is required. As an example, suppose that 30 positions are required for the quotient and remainder. Core positions 00070–00079 must be set to zeros by programming before the Divide instruction is given.

The four instructions provided with the Divide feature are: Load Dividend, Load Dividend Immediate, Divide, and Divide Immediate. When the timing of these instructions is discussed, the following abbreviation will be used: Q_T = number of digits in the quotient.

The dividend must be placed in the fixed product area before a Divide command is given. The Load Dividend and Load Dividend Immediate instructions may be used to satisfy this requirement.

Instruction: Load Dividend

Operation Code: 28

Symbolic Name: LD

Description:

The Load Dividend instruction automatically resets the fixed product area (00080–00099) to zeros. The data (the dividend) that is located at the Q address is transmitted serially to the core location specified by the P address and to successively lower core positions. The flag in the high-order position of the Q field data terminates the transmission.

The P address of the Load Dividend instruction is 00099 minus the number of zero positions desired to the right of the dividend. For example, if it were desired to add 3 places to the dividend 2634, the dividend would be transmitted to core location 00096. The algebraic sign of the dividend is automatically placed in 00099 regardless of where the low-order dividend digit is placed by the P address.

Execution Time in Microseconds: $400 + 40D_q$

Example: 28 00096 00748

$098\overline{2}000\overline{0}0001114\overline{2}9\overline{8}76$⬅⌐

Core location 00099 ⎯⌋
before Load Dividend

$00000000000\overline{3}4782000\overline{0}$⬅⌐

Core location 00099 ⎯⌋
after Load Dividend

$\overline{3}478\overline{2}$ ⬅⎯⎯⎯⎯⎯⌐

Core location 00748 before
and after Load Dividend

Execution Time: 600 microseconds

Example: 28 00099 00909

97000000001623000000⬅⌐

Core location 00099 ⎯⌋
before Load Dividend

$0000000000000\overline{0}29754$⬅⌐

Core location 00099 ⎯⌋
after Load Dividend

$\overline{0}29754$ ⬅⎯⎯⎯⎯⌐

Core location 00909 before
and after Load Dividend

Execution Time: 640 microseconds

Note:

If a Load Dividend instruction is *not* used to position the dividend in the fixed product area, it is the programmer's responsibility to clear the remainder of the fixed product area to zeros. This is also applicable to the Load Dividend Immediate instruction.

Instruction: Load Dividend Immediate

Operation Code: 18

Symbolic Name: LDM

Description:

The Load Dividend Immediate instruction automatically resets the fixed product area (00080–00099) to zeros. The data (the dividend) whose units position is the Q_{11} digit of the instruction is transmitted serially to the location specified by the P address and to successively lower core positions. The flag in the high-order position of the dividend terminates the transmission of data. The P address is determined in the same manner as in the Load Dividend instruction.

The algebraic sign of the dividend is automatically placed in 00099 regardless of where the low-order dividend digit is placed by the P address.

Execution Time in Microseconds: $400 + 40D_q$

Example: 18 00098 $0\overline{9850}$

             00000111129874621004 ⟵⟶

             Core location 00099 before
             Load Dividend Immediate

             $00000000000000\overline{0}0985\overline{0}\overline{0}$ ⟵⟶

             Core location 00099 after
             Load Dividend Immediate

Execution Time: 600 microseconds

Instruction: Divide

Operation Code: 29

Symbolic Name: D

Description:

The dividend whose high-order position is specified by the P address is divided by the field whose units position is specified by the Q address. Division is accomplished by successive subtractions of the divisor from the dividend. The P address of the Divide instruction positions the divisor for the first subtraction from the high-order position(s) of the dividend, as in manual division.

Each successful subtraction causes the quotient digit to be increased by 1. Quotient digits are developed in the units position of a special register. An overdraw initiates a correction (the divisor is added once) and the next subtraction occurs one place to the right. The first (high-order) quotient digit is stored at the address specified by the P address of the Divide instruction minus the length of the divisor. A flag is generated and stored with the first quotient digit. Division is terminated after a quotient digit is developed, by subtractions, with the units position of the divisor at 00099.

The quotient and remainder replace the dividend in the product area. The address of the quotient is 00099 minus the length of the divisor. The algebraic sign of the quotient (determined by the signs of the dividend and divisor) is automatically placed in the low-order position of the quotient. The address of the remainder is 00099 and a flag is automatically placed in the high-order position. The remainder has the sign of the dividend and the same number of digits as the divisor.

The High/Positive indicator is turned on or off, depending on whether the quotient is positive or negative. The Equal/Zero indicator is turned on if the quotient is zero. The quotient must be at least two digits in length. Improper positioning of the divisor with respect to the dividend can cause an overflow condition which is discussed in detail on page 245.

Execution Time in Microseconds: $160 + 520D_qQ_T + 740Q_T$ assuming an average value of 4.5 for each quotient digit

Example:

Figure AII. 1 shows the manner in which the 1620 solves the problem $4906 \div 23 = 213$ with a remainder of 7.

Instruction: Divide Immediate

Operation Code: 19

Symbolic Name: DM

Description:

The dividend whose high-order position is specified by the P address is divided by the field whose units position is the Q_{11} digit of the Divide Immediate instruction.

Division is accomplished as described in the Divide instruction.

Execution Time in Microseconds: $160 + 520D_qQ_T + 740Q_T$, assuming an average value of 4.5 for each quotient digit.

Instruction	Data At Memory Addresses	Description	00092	00093	00094	00095	00096	00097	00098	00099
28 00099 00500	00500 4906̄ 00600 2̄3	Load Dividend	0	0	0	0	4̄	9	0	6
29 00096 00600		Subtract divisor					−	2	3	
		Overdraw					9	8	1	
		Add divisor back to correct overdraw.					+	2	3	
							0	0	4	
		Store first (high-order) digit of quotient (0) and flag bit	0	0	0̄	0	4	9	0	6
		Subtract divisor one place to the right				−	2	3		
		No overdraw					2	6		
		Subtract divisor					−	2	3	
		No overdraw					0	0	3	
		Subtract divisor					−	2	3	
		Overdraw					9	8	0	
		Add divisor back to correct overdraw					+	2	3	
							0	0	3	
		Store second digit of quotient (2)	0	0	0̄	2	0	3	0	6
		Subtract divisor one place to the right					−	2	3	
		No overdraw					0	0	7	
		Subtract divisor					−	2	3	
		Overdraw					9	8	4	
		Add back divisor to correct overdraw					+	2	3	
							0	0	7	
		Store third digit of quotient (1)	0	0	0̄	2	1	0	7	6
		Subtract divisor one place to the right						−	2	3
		No overdraw						0	5	3
		Subtract divisor						−	2	3
		No overdraw						0	3	0
		Subtract divisor						−	2	3
		No overdraw						0	0	7
		Subtract divisor						−	2	3
		Overdraw						9	8	4
		Add back divisor to correct overdraw						+	2	3
								0	0	7
		Store fourth digit of quotient (3) and flag bit, if negative. Operation stops with quotient (213) and remainder (07) in product area.	0	0	0̄	2	1	3	0̄	7

Fig. AII.1. Example of Divide Command.

Example:

Figure AII.2 shows the 1620 solution of the divide problem
$-212 \div 24 = -8.83$ with a remainder of 8.

Instruction	Description	00090	00091	00092	00093	00094	00095	00096	00097	00098	00099
	Data										
18 00097 00̄2̄1̄2̄	Reset 00080 – 00099 to zeros. Transmit Dn to 00097. Dn sign to 00099.	0	0	0	0	0	2̄	1	2	0	0̄
19 00095 00024̄	Subtract Dv from Dn starting at 00095.					−	2	4			
	Overdraw					9	7	8			
	Correction					+	2	4			
						0	0	2			
	Store first quotient digit (0) & flag bit	0	0	0	0	⊛0	2	1	2	0	0̄
	Subtract one place to the right						−	2	4		
	Overdraw						9	9	7		
	Correction						+	2	4		
							0	2	1		
	Store 2nd quotient digit (0)	0	0	0	0	0̄	⊛0	2	1	2	0	0̄
	Subtract one place to the right							−	2	4	
	Successful subtraction							1	8	8	
	Seven more successful subt (7 × 24 = 168)							−1	6	8	
								0	2	0	
								−	2	4	
	Overdraw							9	9	6	
	Correction							+	2	4	
								0	2	0	
	Store quotient digit (8)	0	0	0	0	0̄	0	⊛2	0	0	0̄
	8 successful subtractions (8 × 24 = 192)							−1	9	2	
	(Overdraw & Correction Not Shown)								0	0	8
	Store quotient digit (8)	0	0	0	0	0̄	0	8	⊛0	8	0̄
	3 successful subtractions (3 × 24 = 72)								−7	2	
									0	8	
									−	2	4
	Overdraw								9	8	4
	Correction								+	2	4
									0	0	8
	Store quotient digit (3)	0	0	0	0	0̄	0	8	8	⊛0	0̄8̄
	Store flag over high-order position of remainder. Sign of quotient over units position (00099 − Dv, where Dv is length of divisor).	0	0	0	0	0̄	0	8	8	3̄	0̄8̄

Fig. AII.2. Example of Divide Immediate Command.

INCORRECT DIVISOR POSITIONING

The following error conditions are caused by an incorrect P address in the Divide instruction:

1. Overflow. As illustrated in Figure AII.3, an incorrectly positioned divisor can cause more than nine successful subtractions and an incorrect quotient. The Overflow indicator is turned on, but processing does not stop unless the Overflow switch is set to "stop."

Instruction	Description	00650	00090	00091	00092	00093	00094	00095	00096	00097	00098	00099
		2̄ 1	0	0	0	0	0	2̄	1	2	0	0̄
D 29 00097 00650	Successful Subtraction No. 1							—	2	1		
								1	9	1		
	" " No. 2							—	2	1		
								1	7	0		
	" " No. 3							—	2	1		
								1	4	9		
	" " No. 4							—	2	1		
								1	2	8		
	" " No. 5							—	2	1		
								1	0	7		
	" " No. 6							—	2	1		
								0	8	6		
	" " No. 7							—	2	1		
								0	6	5		
	" " No. 8							—	2	1		
								0	4	4		
	" " No. 9							—	2	1		
								0	2	3		
	" " No. 10							—	2	1		
			0	0	0	0	0	0	0	2	0	0̄

Fig. AII.3. Incorrect Divisor Positioning.

2. Loss of one or more dividend high-order digits. The high-order digit of the dividend is assumed by the 1620 to be one position to the left

of the high-order digit of the divisor. Figure AII.4 shows how the high-order digits of the dividend are lost if the divisor is positioned too far to the right. Processing continues with no indication of an incorrect quotient.

Instruction	Description	00650	00095	00096	00097	00098	00099
29 00098 00650	Divide (Incorrect P Address)	1̄9	2̄	0	2	3	0
					−	1	9
					0	0	4
					−	1	9
					9	8	5
					+	1	9
					0	0	4
			2̄	⊠	0	4	0
					−	1	9
					0	2	1
					−	1	9
					0	0	2
					−	1	9
					9	8	3
					+	1	9
					0	0	2
			2̄	1̄	⊠	0̄	2

Fig. AII.4.   Incorrect Divisor Positioning.

SUMMARY OF AUTOMATIC DIVISION RULES

1. Load Dividend (28—LD or 18—LDM)
   (a) P address = 00099 minus the number of zeros desired to the right of the units position of the dividend.
   (b) Q address = units position of the dividend.
2. Divide (29—D or 19—DM)
   (a) P address = 00100 minus the length of the quotient. The quotient length must be at least two digits.
   (b) Q address = units position of the divisor.
3. Quotient address = 00099 minus the length of the divisor.
4. Remainder address = 00099

5. Sign of quotient—determined by the algebraic signs of the dividend and divisor.

6. Sign of remainder—same as that of the dividend.

Problems

For all Problems the following core content is assumed:

CORE LOCATION (LOW-ORDER DIGIT)	CONTENTS
13124	$\bar{6}3780$
14000	$\bar{0}04$
00900	$\bar{1}3684221$

For each problem give the contents of the fixed product area (00080–00099) including flags after the Divide or Divide Immediate instruction has been executed.

The core content listed above is to be assumed for every problem and the results of any one problem are independent of all others.

1. 28 00096 13124
   29 00092 14000

2. 25 13124 13120
   28 00098 13124
   29 00094 14000

3. 18 00098 $\bar{1}234\bar{5}$
   19 00094 0000$\bar{5}$

4. 15 13999 00002
   28 00095 13123
   19 00092 000$\bar{3}$2

5. 28 00095 00900
   19 00087 0000$\bar{3}$

6. 22 00900 13124
   28 00098 00900
   29 00091 14000

Indirect Addressing

Indirect Addressing saves program steps and computer time by providing a direct method of address modification. Its primary use is in programs where multiple instructions have the same P or Q addresses and this address is to be modified in each of the instructions by the program. With the utilization of the Indirect Addressing special feature, it is not necessary to modify directly each instruction separately, instead one 5-digit address can be modified—this, in effect, serves to modify each of the multiple instructions.

Normally, an instruction address (P and/or Q) is the location of data to be used during the execution of the instruction. This is known as "direct addressing," since the address refers directly to the location of the data. However, if an instruction address (P and/or Q) is an Indirect address, it does not refer directly to data. Rather it is the location of a second address; this second address is the location of the data to be used by the instruction. In effect, this second address is a substitute for the Indirect address at instruction execution time.

For example, suppose that in the Add instruction 21 15000 17000, the Q address 17000 is an Indirect address. Locations 16996–17000 contain the 5-digit field 18000. When the instruction is under execution the data at location 18000 is added to the field at 15000. If the Q address had been a Direct address, the data at location 17000 would have been added to the field at 15000.

A flag in position P_6 and/or Q_{11} indicates that the P and/or Q addresses of an instruction are Indirect. Thus the P address of an instruction is Indirect if there is a flag in the P_6 position of the instruction. The Q address of an instruction is Indirect if there is a flag in the Q_{11} position of the instruction. Any P and/or Q address can be Indirect if it is the address of an instruction, digit, field, or record. Any 1620 instruction can have Indirect addresses except Branch Back, Control, Halt, and No Operation. Table AIII.1 shows which instructions can contain both P and/or Q, or P only, Indirect addresses.

Table AIII.1

Indirect Address Operation Codes

	MNEMONIC	CODE	P AND/OR Q	P ONLY
Arithmetic Instructions				
Add	A	21	X	
Add Immediate	AM	11		X
Subtract	S	22	X	
Subtract Immediate	SM	12		X
Multiply	M	23	X	
Multiply Immediate	MM	13		X
Compare	C	24	X	
Compare Immediate	CM	14		X
Internal Data Transmission Instructions				
Transmit Digit	TD	25	X	
Transmit Digit Immediate	TDM	15		X
Transmit Field	TF	26	X	
Transmit Field Immediate	TFM	16		X
Transmit Record	TR	31	X	
Branch Instructions				
Branch	B	49		X
Branch No Flag	BNF	44	X	
Branch No Record Mark	BNR	45	X	
Branch On Digit	BD	43	X	
Branch Indicator	BI	46		X
Branch No Indicator	BNI	47		X
Branch and Transmit	BT	27	X	
Branch and Transmit Immediate	BTM	17		X
Branch Back	BB	42		
Input-Output Instructions				
Read Numerically	RN	36		X
Write Numerically	WN	38		X
Dump Numerically	DN	35		X
Read Alphanumerically	RA	37		X
Write Alphanumerically	WA	39		X
Control	K	34		

(*continued*)

	Mnemonic	Code	P and/or Q	P Only
Miscellaneous Instructions				
Set Flag	SF	32		X
Clear Flag	CF	33		X
Halt	H	48		
No Operation	NOP	41		
Additional Instructions				
Move Flag	MF	71	X	
Transmit Numeric Strip	TNS	72	X	
Transmit Numeric Fill	TNF	73	X	
Load Dividend	LD	28	X	
Load Dividend Immediate	LDM	18		X
Divide	D	29	X	
Divide Immediate	DM	19		X

If the P address of an immediate instruction is Indirect, the Q data cannot be more than 6 digits in length because the flag in the units position of the P operand would also serve to define the high order digit in the immediate field.

The data field specified by the Indirect address is always interpreted as being 5 digits in length regardless of the presence or absence of flags within the field. Thus, no high-order flag is necessary to define the high-order position of the field at the Indirect address. Should the field specified by the Indirect address contain a flag in its units position, it also is treated as an Indirect address. This chaining effect continues until a flag is not present in the units position of the field specified by an Indirect address; this field is then treated as a Direct address.

An instruction with the P and/or Q addresses Indirect *is in no way altered* in core storage as the result of Indirect addressing. Only internal registers are changed.

Execution Time: Each address that is interpreted as an Indirect address requires four additional memory cycles. An instruction with one Indirect address requires an additional 80 microseconds processing time. An instruction with two Indirect addresses requires an additional 160 microseconds and so forth.

Example: 21 1500$\overline{0}$ 16091

10032 ←⎤
Core location 15000 before and after Add

$\overline{1}$247 ←⎤
Core location 16091 before and after Add

$\overline{0}$0213 ←⎤
Core location 10032 before Add

$\overline{0}$1460 ←⎤
Core location 10032 after Add

Execution Time: 640 microseconds

Example: 11 0090$\overline{0}$ 31416

13168 ←⎤
Core location 00900 before and after Add Immediate

$\overline{0}$0198421 ←⎤
Core location 13168 before Add Immediate

$\overline{0}$0229837 ←⎤
Core location 13168 after Add Immediate

Execution Time: 880 microseconds

Example:

00910 ←⎤
Core location 13500

16225 ←⎤
Core location 17005

1350$\overline{0}$ ←⎤
Core location 09225

18005 ←⎤
Core location 15000

Instructions In Core Storage	Effective Instructions
21 15000 17005	21 15000 17005
21 15000 1700$\overline{5}$	21 15000 16225
21 1500$\overline{0}$ 17005	21 18005 17005
21 1500$\overline{0}$ 1700$\overline{5}$	21 18005 16225
21 0922$\overline{5}$ 1500$\overline{0}$	21 00910 18005

Example: 49 1300$\overline{0}$ 00000

04$\overline{\overline{6}}$86

Core location 13000 before and after Branch

The program will branch to 04686 for the next instruction.

Example:

A program to list all core storage locations which contain a record mark refers to each location in the Branch No Record Mark instruction and also in the Write Numerically instruction when the addresses are typed. Both need to be modified. Following are two programs to do this—one utilizing Indirect addressing and the other without Indirect Addressing.

WITHOUT INDIRECT ADDRESSING				WITH INDIRECT ADDRESSING			
00600	16	00623	$\overline{0}0000$	00600	16	00690	$\overline{0}0000$
00612	45	00660	$\overline{0}0000$	00612	45	00648	$0069\overline{0}$
00624	26	00702	00623	00624	34	00000	00102
00636	34	00000	00102	00636	38	00686	00100
00648	38	00698	00100	00648	11	00690	$0000\overline{1}$
00660	11	00623	$0000\overline{1}$	00660	14	00690	$\overline{2}0000$
00672	14	00623	$\overline{2}0000$	00672	47	00612	01200
00684	47	00612	01200	00684	48	$\overline{0}0000$	‡
00696	48	$\overline{0}0000$	‡				

Example:

Each element A_t in a table of 8-digit numbers with addresses from 13016 to 13808 (units positions) is to be replaced by $A_t/5$ if the element exceeds 5,000,000.

Solution:

01600	16	01623	$\overline{1}3016$	Initialize
01612	24	01726	13016	Compare field to 5,000,000
01624	46	01672	01300	Branch if 5,000,000 $\geqslant A_t$
01636	28	00099	$0162\overline{3}$	Position dividend $\overline{X}XXXXXXX$
01648	19	00092	$0000\overline{5}$	Divide
01660	26	$0162\overline{3}$	00097	Move quotient $\overline{X}XXXXXXX$
01672	11	01623	$0000\overline{8}$	Change address
01684	14	01623	$\overline{1}3816$	Test if done
01696	47	01612	01200	Branch if not done
01708	48	00000	00000	Terminate program
01720	$\overline{5}000000$			

Floating Point Hardware

It is possible to obtain a special device that performs floating point calculations.[1] The advantage of this feature is that, like the division hardware, the core storage required for macro-generated subroutines may be used by the main program. In addition, the linkage instructions are eliminated and, in their place, a single machine language instruction is employed. Lastly, the hardware commands are substantially faster.

The arithmetic that one enjoys through the use of the floating point hardware is, for all practical purposes, completely variable in mantissa size. The actual maximum limit to the length of the mantissa is 99 digits. The characteristic (synonymously termed exponent) is only and always 2 digits, with or without sign and/or field-terminating flag. The minimum mantissa length is 2 digits.

The length of the floating point number is generally specified by the mantissa length. Thus the maximum floating point number is said to be 99 digits instead of 101.

One restriction is imposed upon floating point hardware arithmetic: arithmetic is permissible only on floating point numbers of equal mantissa lengths. This restriction is easily complied with since the hardware contains mantissa shortening and lengthening commands as part of its standard instruction repertoire. It is permissible to perform a series of calculations on floating point numbers with identical mantissa lengths, alter the mantissa lengths, perform subsequent calculations, alter the mantissa lengths, and so forth. Thus, the restriction as stated above is imposed only on any single calculation.

[1] This chapter presupposes a knowledge of the material contained in Chapter 12.

With the exception of two commands, all floating point hardware instructions address the units characteristic position of the specified floating point numbers. These will be referred to as A and B for the P and Q operands respectively. There are eight commands in the floating point hardware repertoire:

> Floating Add
> Floating Subtract
> Floating Multiply
> Floating Divide
> Floating Transmit Field
> Floating Branch and Transmit
> Floating Shift Right
> Floating Shift Left

Instruction: Floating Add

Operation Code: 01

Symbolic Name: FADD

Description:

The floating point number specified by B is added to the floating point number specified by A. The floating point sum replaces A. The floating point number specified by B remains unchanged.

Execution Time in Microseconds: $400 + 100L$ (average)
Recomplementation Time in Microseconds: $80L$

where L is the mantissa length. See Chapter 5 for a discussion of recomplementation.

Example: 01 10000 15000

$\overline{1}000\overline{2}$ ⟵⟶
Core location 10000 before
Floating Add

$\overline{3}0000\overline{1}$ ⟵⟶
Core location 15000 before
and after Floating Add

$\overline{1}300\overline{2}$ ⟵⟶
Core location 10000 after
Floating Add

Example: 01 17000 19000

$\overline{5}0000000\overline{1}0$ ⟵⟶
Core location 17000 before
Floating Add

$\overline{2}5000000\overline{1}1$ ⟵⟶
Core location 19000 before
and after Floating Add

$\overline{3}0000000\overline{1}1$ ⟵⟶
Core location 17000 after
Floating Add

Example: 01 02000 03000

$\overline{1}10\overline{1}$ ◄———————┐
Core location 02000 before
Floating Add

$99\overline{0}1$ ◄———————┐
Core location 03000 before
and after Floating Add

$\overline{1}10\overline{2}$ ◄———————┐
Core location 02000 after
Floating Add

Instruction: Floating Subtract

Operation Code: 02

Symbolic Name: FSUB

Description:

The floating point number specified by B is subtracted from the floating point number specified by A. The floating point difference replaces A. The floating point number specified by B remains unchanged. The execution time is identical with that of FADD.

Example: 02 10000 15000

$\overline{1}2\overline{0}0$ ◄———————┐
Core location 10000 before
Floating Subtract

$\overline{2}00\overline{1}$ ◄———————┐
Core location 15000 before
and after Floating Subtract

$\overline{1}0\overline{0}0$ ◄———————┐
Core location 10000 after
Floating Subtract

Instruction: Floating Multiply

Operation Code: 03

Symbolic Name: FMUL

Description:

The floating point number specified by A is multiplied by the floating point number specified by B. The resultant floating point product, with length identical to that of A and B, appears at A and not at 00099.

The fixed product area is employed to generate a product whose length is 2L, and the L most significant digits are chosen by the hardware as the mantissa of the floating point product. Thus, should the mantissas of the multiplier and multiplicand be greater than 10 digits, it is the programmer's responsibility to clear a sufficient area below core location 00080.

As an example, the multiplication of two 14-digit floating point numbers would require core locations 00072–00079 to be cleared to zeros before the FMUL command.

Execution Time in Microseconds: $1120 + 80L + 168L^2$ (average)

Example: 03 10000 15000

$\overline{1}2\overline{3}03$ ◄————————┐

Core location 10000 before Floating Multiply

$\overline{1}15\overline{0}2$ ◄————————┐

Core location 15000 before and after Floating Multiply

$\overline{1}4\overline{1}04$ ◄————————┐

Core location 10000 after Floating Multiply

Example: 03 17000 19000

$\overline{9999}9\overline{15}$ ◄————————┐

Core location 17000 before Floating Multiply

$\overline{8888}8\overline{1}2$ ◄————————┐

Core location 19000 before and after Floating Multiply

$\overline{8888}7\overline{0}3$ ◄————————┐

Core location 17000 after Floating Multiply

Instruction: Floating Divide

Operation Code: 09

Symbolic Name: FDIV

Description:

The floating point number specified by A is divided by the floating point number specified by B. The resultant floating point quotient, with length identical to that of A and B appears at A and not at 00099. The fixed product area is employed to generate a quotient and remainder, each of length L. Thus, should the mantissas of the divisor and dividend be greater than 10 digits, it is the programmer's responsibility to clear a sufficient area below core location 00080.

Attempt at division by zero causes the overflow check indicator (14) to be turned on. The mantissa of A is not altered but the characteristic of $A(C_A)$ is changed to $C_A - C_B$.

Execution Time in Microseconds: $880 + 940L + 520L^2$ (average)

Example: 09 10000 15000

$\overline{4500}2$ ◄─────────┐ $\overline{2500}3$ ◄─────────┐

Core location 10000 before   Core location 15000 before
Floating Divide   and after Floating Divide

$\overline{1800}6$ ◄─────────┐

Core location 10000 after
Floating Divide

Instruction: Floating Transmit Field (Transmit Floating Field)

Operation Code: 06

Symbolic Name: TFL

Description:

The characteristic and mantissa of the floating point number specified by B are transmitted so that the units characteristic position occupies the core location specified by A and the units mantissa position occupies the core location specified by A−2.

Execution Time in Microseconds: 240 + 40L

Example: 06 10000 15000

$\overline{1}2345678\overline{90}1$ ◄─────┐ $\overline{1}34\overline{1}\overline{2}$ ◄─────────┐
Core location 10000 before   Core location 15000 before
Transmit Floating   and after Floating Transmit

$\overline{1}2345\overline{6}1\overline{3}4\overline{1}\overline{2}$ ◄─────┐

Core location 10000 after
Transmit Floating

Instruction: Floating Branch and Transmit (Branch and Transmit Floating)

Operation Code: 07

Symbolic Name: BTFL

Description:

The description of this operation is identical with that of Branch and Transmit with the exception that the argument, specified by the B address, is assumed to be in floating point form. This argument is transmitted to the location specified by P less 1. The mantissa of the argument therefore appears at location P-3. Exit from a subroutine entered through the use of BTFL is, of course, by a Branch Back (BB) command.

Execution Time in Microseconds: 280 + 40L

Instruction: Floating Shift Right

Operation Code: 08

Symbolic Name: FSR

Description:

The field whose units position is specified by the Q address is shifted right so that this units position occupies the location specified by the P address. Thus, the effect of this instruction is to shrink the mantissa of a floating point number. Vacated high-order positions are set to zeros. An existing flag bit at the units position of the original mantissa is retained for algebraic sign. The high-order mantissa flag is transmitted with the mantissa field.

Execution Time in Microseconds: $200 + 40L$

Example: 08 10000 09995

$\overline{1}234567890\overline{7}$ ←———┐

Core location 10002 before
Floating Shift Right

$00000\overline{1}234\overline{0}7$ ←———┐

Core location 10002 after
Floating Shift Right

Example: 08 00521 00520

$\overline{1}\overline{2}\overline{3}01$ ←————————┐

Core location 00523 before
Floating Shift Right

$01\overline{2}\overline{0}1$ ←————————┐

Core location 00523 after
Floating Shift Right

Example: FSR P-2, P-4

$\overline{9}876\overline{5}\overline{4}3$ ←————————┐

Symbolic core location P
before Floating Shift Right

$00\overline{9}8\overline{7}\overline{4}3$ ←————————┐

Symbolic core location P
after Floating Shift Right

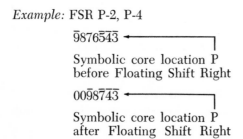

Instruction: Floating Shift Left

Operation Code: 05

Symbolic Name: FSL

Description:

The field whose units position is specified by the Q address is shifted left. This shift is terminated when the high-order digit of the field in question is at the core location specified by P. Thus, the effect of this instruction is to expand the mantissa of a floating point number.

At the conclusion of the shift, the old field-defining high-order flag bit is removed and a zero fill operation begins at the new mantissa units position plus 1. This zero fill operation is terminated by a flagged digit.

Thus, if the mantissa is expanded to a length greater than 2L, any extraneous flags in core between the old high-order mantissa position and the new low-order mantissa position must be removed. An existing flag bit at the Q address is retained for algebraic sign.

Execution Time in Microseconds: $200 + 40L + 40L'$
where L' is the amount of increase in the field size introduced by the shift.

Example: 05 09998 10000

$\qquad$ . . . $7\overline{\overline{8}}05$ ⟵ ⌐

Core location 10002 before
Floating Shift Left

$\qquad$ . . $\overline{7}80\overline{\overline{0}}5$ ⟵ ⌐

Core location 10002 after
Floating Shift Left

Example: FSL P-5, P-2

$\qquad$ . . $12\overline{6}\overline{4}5\overline{1}5$ ⟵ ⌐

Symbolic core location P
before Floating Shift Left

$\qquad$ . . $1\overline{4}500\overline{1}5$ ⟵ ⌐

Symbolic core location P
after Floating Shift Left

Example: FSL P-10, P-2

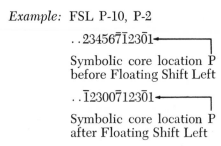

Symbolic core location P
before Floating Shift Left

Symbolic core location P
after Floating Shift Left

Comment: Failure to clear the flag at location P-5 caused the zero fill operation to terminate when the flagged 7 was encountered. This is therefore an incorrect mantissa 'expansion.

Example: CF   P-5
          FSL P-10, P-2

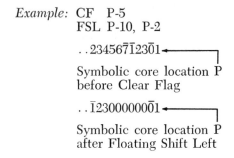

Symbolic core location P
before Clear Flag

Symbolic core location P
after Floating Shift Left

GENERAL INFORMATION ON FLOATING POINT HARDWARE

When a floating point computation results in a zero mantissa, a special floating point zero is created of the form $\overline{00}\ldots\overline{0099}$. Zeros entered as floating point data should be in the special floating point zero form.

The H/P, E/Z, and H/P–E/Z indicators reflect the status of arithmetic operations performed by floating point hardware. Thus, a floating point computation which produces a positive mantissa will cause the H/P indicator to be turned on and the E/Z indicator to be turned off. The E/Z indicator is turned on and the H/P off if a floating point computation produces a zero mantissa.

The exponent check indicator (15) is turned on by exponent overflow or underflow. This condition arises when an exponent greater than 99 or less than −99 is generated. When the former condition occurs, the mantissa is set to all 9's. The sign is determined by the algebra of the operation. The H/P indicator will be set accordingly.

Should the latter condition occur, the mantissa is set to plus zero. The E/Z indicator is also turned on. In case of exponent overflow, the exponent is automatically set to 99. In case of exponent underflow, the exponent is automatically set to −99.

An exponent underflow is not indicated if a zero mantissa is developed through a normal fashion (addition of two numbers that have the same absolute value but unlike signs; multiplication of a number by zero, and so forth).

Program operation, in the event of an exponent overflow or underflow is determined by the console overflow check switch. The symbolic commands for testing the exponent overflow indicator are

1. BXV (Branch on Exponent Overflow)
2. BNXV (Branch No Exponent Overflow)

All floating point hardware commands may be indirectly addressed at P and/or Q.

Appendix **V**

Input-Output Devices

The 1620 Data Processing System can process either punched cards or paper tape or both. The 1622 Card Read-Punch is the input-output device for punched card processing, whereas the 1621 Paper Tape Reader and the 1624 Paper Tape Punch are the input-output devices for paper tape processing. The console typewriter is also an input-output device allowing for typewritten output documents and the manual entry of information into the system.

This chapter will discuss the functions of the keys, lights, and switches necessary for the manual and automatic control of each input-output device.

1621 PAPER TAPE READER

The Paper Tape Reader reads an 8-channel paper tape at the rate of 150 characters per second. A photoelectronic device senses the characters; they are then automatically converted to the 6-bit numeric code and placed in the core storage positions specified by the Read instruction.

If a parity error is detected in the input area, or if an invalid character is detected on the input tape, the Read Check indicator light on the console of the 1620 is turned on. Reading of tape continues until an E/L character is sensed. If the I/O Check switch on the console is set to the "Stop" position, the computer then stops. If the switch is set to

the "Program" position, processing continues. Sensing of the E/L character from the paper tape causes a record mark to be placed in storage
as the right-most character of the input record.

The front panel of the Paper Tape Reader (Fig. AV.1) consists of the
following components:

Fig. AV.1. Tape Reader.

1. The Read Head. The paper tape must be properly positioned over
   the read head in order to be sensed by the photoelectronic reader.
2. Photoelectronic Reader. This device senses the characters in the
   paper tape.
3. Tape Guides. Two tape guides help position the paper tape over
   the read head.
4. Tape Rollers. Two rollers guide the tape as it is being read.
5. Stationary Buffer Rollers and Buffer Arm Rollers. One stationary
   buffer roller and one buffer arm are located on each side of the read
   head to apply a steady tension to the tape.
6. Take-up Reel. This reel takes up the paper tape after it has been
   read.

7. Supply Reel. This reel guides the paper tape as it approaches the read head.
8. Idler Roller. The roller positions the tape on the supply reel.
9. Tape Guide Stand. This stand guides the tape from the center roll feed.

OPERATING KEYS, SWITCHES, AND LIGHTS

10. Reel Power Key. Depression of this key operates the supply and take-up reels to position the paper tape for reading. The buffer arms are lowered to apply tension.
11. Power Switch. This switch when turned to the "On" position supplies all necessary power to the tape reader.
12. Reel-Strip Switch. This switch controls the manner in which tape is read. When short strips of tape are to be read, they may be loaded directly over the read head. The switch should then be set to the "Strip" position. The "Reel" position is used when the paper tape is loaded in the conventional manner, as will be discussed.
13. Non-Process Run-Out Key. Depression of this key causes paper tape to feed. No information is transferred into storage. The tape continues feeding until the end of the tape is sensed by the read head.
14. Power-On Light. This light is turned on when the Power switch is on.

LOADING THE PAPER TAPE READER

Paper tape can be loaded in three different forms: center roll feed, strip feed, and reel feed.

CENTER ROLL FEED

Paper tape is wound inside out making the starting end of the paper tape roll the inner end. The center roll feed device is attached to the front of the Paper Tape Reader and eliminates the necessity for rewinding the paper tape rolls.

The roll of tape is placed surrounding the circular guide in the middle of the center roll feed with the inside end going in a counterclockwise direction. The inner edge of the paper tape is passed into the center guide and partially around the center spindle exiting from the space on the right of the center guide. The tape then goes over the supply reel, around the read head, and onto the take-up reel. The exact procedure for loading tape is as follows:

1. Position the Reel-Strip switch to "Reel."
2. Position the tape roll on the center roll feed device as described above and unwind approximately 5 feet of tape to work with.

3. Raise the reel buffer arms until they latch.
4. Open the tape guides and form an inverted U (∩) with the center section of the first 5 feet of tape. Wrap the paper tape around the read head meshing the tape feed holes with the pins on both sides of the read head. The tape should be mounted so that there is a minimum of free play.
5. Close the tape guides.
6. Pass the leading section of the tape under the guide roller and between the stationary buffer rollers and the latched buffer arm rollers. Then fix the front end of the tape on the take-up reel.
7. Thread the paper tape from the right side of the read head, under the guide roller, between the stationary buffer rollers and the latched buffer arm rollers, over the supply reel, and through the tape guide stand. Figure AV.2 shows the positioning of the tape at this point.

Fig. AV.2. Threading Tape from Center Roll Feed.

8. Lower the idler roller onto the supply reel.
9. Gently lower the buffer arms.
10. Depress the Reel Power key. The buffer arms should swing down-

ward to a neutral position applying tension to the paper tape. Figure AV.3 shows a tape fully loaded.

Fig. AV.3.   Center Roll Feed—Loaded.

STRIP FEED

Small strips of paper tape may be loaded directly onto the read head. The procedure is as follows:

1. Position the Reel-Strip switch to "Strip."
2. Position the paper tape over the read head as described in step 4 of the center roll feed procedure.
3. Close the tape guides.

REEL FEED

A reel of paper tape may be mounted by removing the rubber drive hub from the supply reel and mounting the reel of tape in its place. Figure AV.4 shows a loaded paper tape reel.

Fig. AV.4.   Reel Feed.

TAPE HANDLING TIPS

1. To avoid mounting a tape backwards on the paper tape reader, check to see that an E/L character is *not* the first character on the tape. If the first character is an E/L character, the tape is backwards.
2. Check the tape on the read head to make sure that the tape is mounted correctly. Loosely positioned tape will cause a Reader No Feed condition.
3. Lower the buffer arm rollers *gently;* do not let them snap down.
4. A dirty read head may cause a read check. Wipe it off with a clean handkerchief.
5. Be sure that there is sufficient tape on the tape punch to punch all results.
6. Have approximately 5 feet of leader on tape being punched.
7. The feed holes are closer to the bottom of the tape than to the top. In this way it is possible to tell if the tape is upside down.
8. **Label all tapes.**

1624 PAPER TAPE PUNCH

The Paper Tape Punch punches data received from core storage at the rate of 15 characters per second. Each character is automatically translated from the 6-bit numeric code to the coding used on paper tape. When a Write Numerically or a Write Alphamerically command on the paper tape punch is given, the record mark in core storage which stops data transmission is punched as an E/L character in the paper tape. If an invalid character is transmitted from core storage, it is punched but the tape feed *does not advance*. The computer stops in the automatic mode and the Punch No Feed and Write Check lights on the console are turned on.

Incorrect punching of a valid character causes the computer to stop in the automatic mode. The tape feed does not advance and the Punch No Feed light on the console is turned on. Program processing can continue if the following procedure is employed:

1. Position the 1624 Tape Feed switch on. This is a two-position switch. When turned to the "On" position, it causes the tape to feed and the tape feed code (a punch in channels 1–7) is punched. The tape reader passes tape punched with the tape feed code but no characters are transmitted into storage. When the switch is turned on, the feed code (all punches) is punched over the incorrectly punched character and the Punch No Feed light on the console is turned off. The computer is returned to manual mode.

2. Depress the Start key. The correct character is punched and the computer continues processing.

If the 1624 runs out of paper tape, the computer stops in the automatic mode and the Punch No Feed light on the console turns on. The above procedure is used to resume operation after a new roll of tape is loaded.

LOADING THE PAPER TAPE PUNCH

Place the roll of unpunched tape on the turntable and thread as shown in Figure AV.5. The tape retainer (F) must be rotated to the left by pushing back on its extended left edge. This also moves the tape lever (D) forward. The tape is then threaded as follows:

1. Through tape guide (A).
2. Inside tape guide (B).
3. In front of tape tension guide (C).
4. In back of tape lever (D).
5. Between the punching mechanism and the punch guide block (E) which can be seen in front of the tape.
6. Between the guides on the tape retainer (F).

With the end of the tape held to the left, the tape retainer (F) is returned to normal position, which causes the pins on the feed roll to punch

Fig. AV.5. Paper Tape Punch.

through the blank tape. The tape lever simultaneously returns to its normal position with the top guide above the tape.

The Tape Feed switch (G) is used to repetitively punch the tape feed code to provide a lead section of paper tape. Approximately 60 inches of lead are needed for threading paper tape on the Paper Tape Reader. The lead section is threaded into the take-up reel so that the top edge of the tape is at the outside of the reel.

1622 CARD READ-PUNCH

The 1622 Card Read-Punch (Fig. AV.6) provides punched card input and output for the 1620 Data Processing System. The reader and punch units are both housed in the 1622, but they function independently and are entirely separate units. Each unit has its own card feed, control switches and lights, checking circuits, stackers, and buffer. The reader can read cards at the rate of 250 per minute; the card punch can punch cards at the rate of 125 per minute.

Fig. AV.6.   1622 Card Read-Punch.

Each unit has its own buffer storage so that reading, punching, and processing can occur simultaneously. When a card is read, the information is transmitted to the buffer and then into core storage. Thus, information from a card is read into the buffer before it is called for by the stored program. When a read command is given, the information from the buffer is transmitted into core storage and the next card is read into the buffer. Data is transmitted from buffer to core storage in 3.4 milliseconds. A read cycle takes 240 milliseconds (250 cards a minute). Since only 3.4 milliseconds are required to transmit information from buffer to core storage, the remaining 236.6 milliseconds are available for processing.

After cards are read or punched, they fall into radial stackers located on the front of the unit. Properly read cards are stacked in the right-most stacker. If a read error is detected, the card causing the error is selected into the second stacker from the right. The same principle applies to the punch side. Properly punched cards fall into the left-most stacker and improperly punched cards are selected into the second stacker from the left. The middle stacker is not used.

Figure AV.7 is a schematic diagram of the keys, lights, and card feeds on the 1622 Card Read-Punch unit.

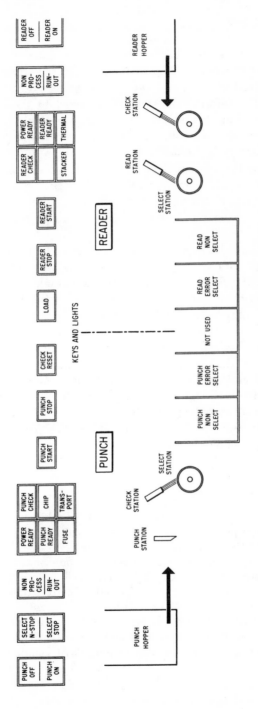

Fig. AV.7. Keys, Lights, and Card Feeds of 1622 Card Read-Punch.

CARD READER

The Card Reader is the unit on the right side of the 1622. Cards to be read are placed in the read hopper 9-edge first, face down. Depression of the reader Start key or Load key causes the first card to be read and checked, and the information to be transferred to the buffer. Thereafter, all card feeding is under stored program control.

Each card is read at two different stations; a check station and a read station. The card is first read at the check station and the information is stored. When this card is read at the read station, the information is compared with the information stored at the check station. If an unequal comparison or a parity error is detected, the reader stops, the Reader Check light is turned on, and the Ready status of the card reader is terminated.

A read command transfers data from the input buffer to core storage. The transferred data is parity checked. If a parity error is detected in core storage the Read Check light on the console is turned on. The Read Check indicator (06) is also turned on. If the I/O check switch on the console is set to the "Stop" position, processing terminates. If the switch is set to the "Program" position, processing continues.

After data has been correctly transferred to core storage, a card feed cycle follows immediately to reload the input buffer with the information previously read and checked at the read station. At the same time new data is read at the read station, and the following card data is read at the check station and stored for comparison on the next card feed cycle when it will be read at the read station. Figure AV. 8 illustrates the data flow in a read operation.

OPERATING KEYS, SWITCHES, AND LIGHTS

1. Power Switch (Reader Off-Reader On Switch). This switch is used to supply power to the reader. The 1620 Power switch must be on to make the 1622 Power switch active.

2. Load Key. This key causes data from the first card to be checked, read into buffer storage, and automatically transferred in numerical mode to core storage positions 00000–00079. Upon completion of this data transfer, another card feed cycle occurs which loads buffer storage with data from the second card. The 1620 then executes the instruction at core position 00000. Thus the instructions from the first card, now in core storage 00000–00079, can be used to continue

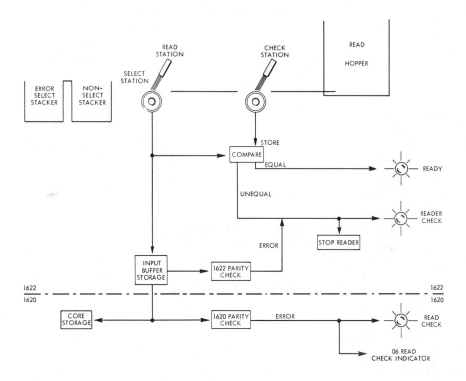

Fig. AV.8. Data Flow in a Read Operation.

loading the program or begin processing. The 1620 *must be reset
and in manual mode* or a 48(H) must appear in the OP register to
make the Load key active.

3. Reader Start Key. Depression of this key causes one card to be read
   and the information checked and read into buffer storage. The information in the buffer is transmitted to core storage *only* when a
   Read Numerically or Read Alphamerically instruction is executed.
   When the feed hopper runs out of cards, a Reader No Feed condition
   initiates. To read in and process the cards remaining in the feed, the
   Reader Start key is depressed. The Reader Start key is also used to
   restore a Ready status after the reader has been stopped with the
   Reader Stop key, an empty hopper, a full stacker, or an error condition.

4. Reader Stop Key. This key is used to stop the read feed at the end
   of the card cycle in progress and/or to remove the reader from a
   Ready status. The computer continues processing; the next read card
   command causes a Reader No Feed stop.

5. Non-Process Run-Out Key. This key is used to run cards out of the read feed after a Reader Check error, or after the Stop key has been used to stop the reader. The cards are run-out into the read error select stacker without a buffer storage to core storage transfer. The Reader Check light and check circuits are turned off. *Cards must be removed from the hopper* to make the Non-Process Run-Out key active.

6. Power Ready Light. This light is turned on to indicate that power has been supplied to the reader by setting the Power switch to the "Reader On" position.

7. Reader Ready Light. This light is turned on to indicate that the first card has been loaded into buffer storage with the Reader Start key or Load key, without a reader check error. It remains on until one of the following conditions occur: depression of the Stop key, an empty hopper, a full stacker, a reader check error, a transport jam, or a misfeed.

8. Reader Check Light. This light is turned on by an unequal comparison between the read and check stations or by incorrect parity detected in buffer storage. The reader is stopped, Ready status is terminated, and the buffer storage data just read cannot be transferred to core storage on the next Read command.

CARD PUNCH

The Card Punch is the unit on the left side of the 1622. Cards are placed in the punch hopper 12-edge first, face down. A write command causes data to be transferred from core storage to output buffer storage.

The data is parity checked in the 1620 core storage. If a parity error is detected, the Write Check light on the console and the Write Check indicator (07) are turned on. If the I/O Check switch on the console is set to "Stop," processing terminates before the data is punched. If it is set to the "Program" position, processing continues.

If no parity error is detected, the data is stored for comparison, its parity is checked and the data punched into the card. If a 1622 parity error is detected, the data is punched and, if the Select Stop switch is set to "Stop," the punch stops, Ready status is terminated and the Punch Check light is turned on. The error card is selected into the error select stacker. When the Select Stop switch is set to the "N-Stop" position, processing continues, the punch remains in a Ready status, and the error card is selected into the error select stacker. If no parity error is detected the card that was punched is read at a check station and compared with the data stored. An unequal comparison has the same effect as a 1622 parity error. An equal comparison causes processing to continue. Figure AV. 9 illustrates the data flow in a punch operation.

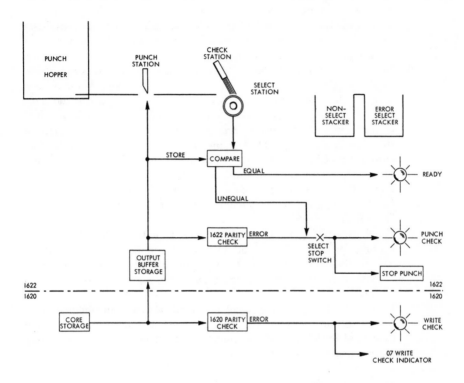

Fig. AV.9. Data Flow in a Punch Operation.

OPERATING KEYS, SWITCHES, AND LIGHTS

1. Power Switch (Punch off–Punch on Switch). This switch is used to supply power to the punch. The 1620 Power switch must be on to make the 1622 Power switch active.
2. Punch Start Key. This key is used to feed cards to the punch station initially or after an error and non-process run-out condition, and to re-establish the Ready status after a Punch Stop key depression, an empty hopper, a full stacker, a transport jam, or a misfeed.
3. Punch Stop Key. This key is used to stop the punch feed at the end of the card cycle in progress and/or to remove the punch from a Ready status.
4. Check Reset Key. This key is used to reset error circuits and turn off the Punch Check light. A Punch Start key or Non-Process Run-

Out key depression follows, as described in the "Error Restart Procedures" section.

5. Select Stop—Select N-Stop Switch. This switch is used to control the punch Ready status when error cards are selected into the punch error select stacker. With the switch set to "Stop," the punch feed stops with the error card in the select stacker. With the switch set to "N-Stop," the error cards are selected into the punch error select stacker and processing continues.

6. Non-Process Run-Out Key. This key is used to run cards out of the punch feed after a punch check error or after the Stop key has been used to stop the punch. The cards are run out into the left-most stacker. This key must be used to run out and check the last punched card of a job. Cards *must be removed from the punch hopper* to make the Non-Process Run-Out key operative. If a punch error has occurred the Check Reset key must be depressed *before* the Non-Process Run-Out key is operative.

7. Power Ready Light. This light is turned on to indicate that power has been supplied to the punch by setting the Power switch to the "Punch On" position.

8. Punch Ready Light. This light is used to indicate that the 1622 is waiting for and will respond to a write command from the 1620. The ready light is turned off by a Stop key depression, an empty hopper, a full stacker, a punch check error, a transport jam, or a misfeed.

9. Punch Check Light. This light is turned on when an unequal comparison occurs between the data punched and the data read (one card feed cycle later at the punch check station), or when a 1622 parity error is detected.

OPERATOR LIGHTS COMMON TO BOTH READ AND PUNCH UNITS

1. Chip Light. This light turns on when the chip box is full.

2. Stacker Light. This light is turned on when any stacker is full. Both feeds are stopped and removed from the Ready status. When the full stacker is either entirely or partially emptied, operation automatically resumes.

3. Transport Light. The Transport light is turned on when a card in either the read or punch feed does not feed properly. When this occurs, both feeds are stopped and removed from a Ready status. Both Start keys must be depressed to resume operation after the condition is corrected.

4. Fuse Light. This light turns on to indicate a blown fuse.

5. Thermal Light. This light is turned on if the internal temperature of the 1622 becomes excessive. After several minutes delay, the 1620 console Reset key may be depressed to turn off the Thermal light.

If depression of the Reset key turns off the Thermal light, the 1620 Power switch must be turned off and then on again. Operation may be resumed after the Power Ready light is turned on.

ERROR RESTART PROCEDURES—CARD INPUT AND OUTPUT

READER CHECK ERROR

Cause: An unequal comparison between the data at the read and check stations of the Card Reader or an input buffer storage parity error. The reader stops with the error card in the select stacker (last card). The data from the error card has not been transferred to core storage.

Indicators: 1622 Reader Check light on; 1622 Ready Light off.

Restart Procedure:

1. Remove the remaining cards from the read hopper.
2. Depress the Non-Process Run-Out key.
3. There will be three cards in the select stacker: the error card and the following two cards which were at the check and read stations respectively. Remove these three cards from the stacker.
4. Place these three cards in front of the cards removed from the read hopper and replace the deck in the hopper.
5. Depress the Start key. The card that caused the error is read into the buffer storage again and if an equal comparison is obtained, the interlocked read instruction is executed and processing continues.[1]

1620 READ CHECK ERROR

Cause: A parity error detected on information just transmitted into core storage from the input buffer. The reader stops with the error card in the *nonselect* stacker (the last card).

Indicators: 1620 Read Check light on. 1622 Reader Ready light on. Read Check indicator (06) on.

Restart Procedure:

1. Remove the cards from the read hopper.
2. Depress the Non-Process Run-Out key. The two cards in the read feed at the time of the error will be run out into the select stacker.
3. Remove the last card from the nonselect stacker and the two cards from the select stacker.
4. Place these three cards in front of the cards removed from the read hopper. The error card from the nonselect stacker is to be read in first.

---

[1] However, if a card is punched with an invalid code, it will *never* be correctly read. The card must be corrected.

5. Use manual restart procedures to return the stored program to the instruction that transfers the error card data from the input buffer storage to core storage.

PUNCH CHECK ERROR

Cause: An unequal comparison between the data punched and the data read (one card feed cycle later, at the punch check station), or a 1622 parity error while punching data from the output buffer storage. If the Select Stop N-Stop switch is set to "Stop," the punch stops with the error card in the select stacker. Another card has been punched.

Indicators: 1622 Punch Check light on. 1622 Punch Ready light off.

RESTART PROCEDURE

1. Depress the Check Reset key.
2. For manual correction of error card.
   (a) Remove the remaining cards from the punch hopper.
   (b) Depress the punch Non-Process Run-Out key. Three cards will be run out into the nonselect stacker. The first card out will be the first card punched after the error card was punched. The last two cards are blank cards.
   (c) Remove the error card from the punch error select stacker. Correct the error card (if possible) and place it in front of the last three cards in the nonselect stacker. Remove the last two cards from the nonselect stacker. These will be blank cards run out when the Non-Process Run-Out key was depressed.
   (d) Place blank cards in the punch hopper.
   (ε) Depress the Start key. The interlocked write command for the second card following the error card can now be executed.

1620 WRITE CHECK ERROR

Cause: A parity error. The error has *not* been punched into a card.
Indicators: 1620 Write Check light on. Write Check indicator (07) on.

A type-out of the core storage positions that were transferred to the output buffer indicates whether the trouble is in core storage or the punch.

CONSOLE TYPEWRITER

The typewriter (Fig. AV. 10) is used as both an input and an output device. The keyboard is similar to that of a standard typewriter except for the positioning of the digits 0–9 and the inclusion of the special characters required by the system. Except when data is being entered, the typewriter keyboard is locked preventing its use as an off-line device.

Fig. AV.10. 1620 Console Typewriter.

The typewriter is equipped with a shift key. When this key is depressed, only *numeric* data may be entered. A Read Numerically instruction specifying the typewriter, automatically causes the keyboard to be locked in the shift position. A typing line contains a maximum of 88 positions. Margins and tab stops may be set manually.

A Write command specifying the typewriter as the output device causes data to be transmitted from core storage to the typewriter which types it. Transmission of data is terminated by the sensing of a record mark in core storage; the record mark is *not* typed. As data is transmitted from core storage to the typewriter, it is parity checked. If a character with incorrect parity is detected, the Write Check indicator (07) is turned on, and a character[2] is printed with a horizontal bar across its center; for example, C̶, D̶, 2̶, O̶. The output operation is completed, and processing is continued or terminated depending upon the position of the console I/O Check switch. If an *invalid* character with correct parity is sensed, a special symbol character (⌧) is printed.

A Read command specifying the typewriter allows for the manual insertion of data. The input data is parity checked before it enters core storage. If a character with incorrect parity is detected the Read Check indicator (06) is turned on. After completion of the input operation, processing continues or terminates depending upon the setting of the I/O Check switch.

[2] The 1620 will print the character that it is best able to interpret.

Depression of the Insert key on the console unlocks the keyboard and locks it in the shift position, permitting *numeric* data to be entered into core storage, starting at location 00000. Each depression of a typewriter key enters the character into core storage one location higher than the previous character. Each character is parity checked. After the 100th character is entered, the computer automatically enters the manual mode locking the keyboard. Depression of the Start key causes the instruction at core location 00000 to be executed. If less than 100 characters are entered, the Release key on the console is depressed to give an end-of-record indication. The keyboard locks and the computer enters the manual mode.

The 1620 Console

The console (Fig. AVI.1) is an integral part of the 1620 Data Processing System. It consists of control keys and lights, switches, an indicator panel, and a typewriter.[1] The main function of the console is to serve as a communication link between the operator and the computer.

This communication takes various forms. Lights on the indicator panel provide a visual indication of the status or contents of the various registers and indicators within the 1620. The control keys allow for manual or automatic operation of the system. They allow the operator complete flexibility in running under stored program control and then interrupting the program to perform desired operations from the console. Control may then be returned to the stored program.

The console typewriter provides the operator with the means of inserting data or instructions directly into core storage. It also allows the operator to examine portions of the memory by having the contents of the desired core locations typed out on the typewriter.

This chapter will describe in detail the console components and the part they play in the overall picture of program writing, debugging, and, finally, running the corrected program. The following chapter will describe the console procedures to follow when assembling SPS or Fortran and performing other operations from the console.

---

[1] The typewriter is considered as a part of the console even though it is physically removed from the console.

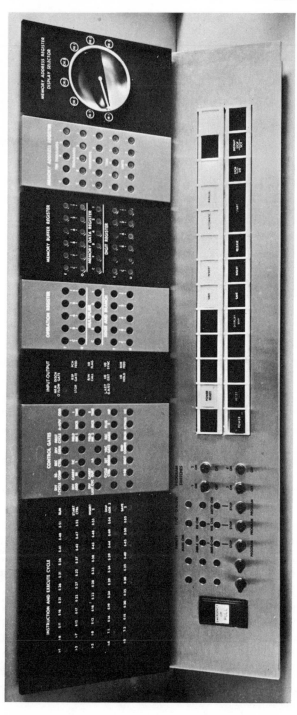

Fig. AVI.1. The Complete 1620 Console.

Fig. AVI.2. Console Panel.

CONSOLE PANEL

The console panel (Fig. AVI.2) consists of a display selector and six sections of indicator lights. They are as follows:

Fig. AVI.3. Instruction and Execute Cycle Lights.

SECTION NUMBER 1 (Fig. AVI.3)

INSTRUCTION AND EXECUTE CYCLE INDICATOR LIGHTS

This set of indicator lights is used primarily for diagnostic testing by customer engineers.

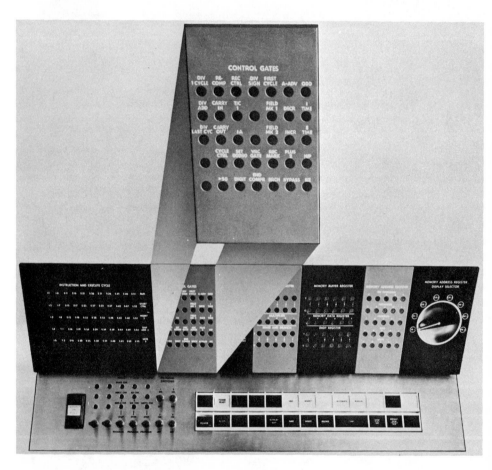

Fig. AVI.4. Control Gate Indicators.

SECTION NUMBER 2 (Fig. AVI.4)

CONTROL GATE INDICATOR LIGHTS

This set of indicator lights is used primarily for diagnostic testing by customer engineers. However, during manual single instruction execution of a program, certain of these lights display information that may be useful for debugging purposes.

1. H/P (High-Positive) Indicator Light. This light shows the status of the internal H/P indicator as determined by the last arithmetic or compare operation. The light will be on if and only if the H/P indicator is on.
2. E/Z (Equal-Zero) Indicator Light. This light shows the status of the internal E/Z indicator as determined by the last arithmetic or compare operation. The light will be on if and only if the E/Z indicator is on.
3. RECOMP (Recomplement) Light. This light indicates that the result of an add or subtract operation will be recomplemented upon completion of the computation.
4. REC MARK (Record Mark) Light. This light shows that a record mark was sensed in core storage.
5. BRCH (Branch) Light. This light is turned on if a branch is to be taken in a conditional Branch instruction. If the light is not on, the next instruction in sequence will be executed. This is true for the BI instruction set. For the BNI instruction set, the above sequence is reversed.

SECTION NUMBER 3

INPUT-OUTPUT INDICATOR LIGHTS

The input-output indicator lights are used primarily for diagnostic testing by customer engineers.

SECTION NUMBER 4 (Fig. AVI.5)

OPERATION REGISTER

These two rows of five lights each display the bit configuration of the 2-digit operation code of the instruction *last* executed. The flag bits are not displayed. The row of lights labeled "T," displays the O_0 digit; the row labeled "U," displays the O_1 digit.

MULTIPLIER

This 5-light register displays each multiplier digit as it is used during a multiply operation. As in the operation register, flag bits are not displayed. This register is useful for displaying the multiplier digits when executing a Multiply instruction with the SCE (single cycle execution) key.

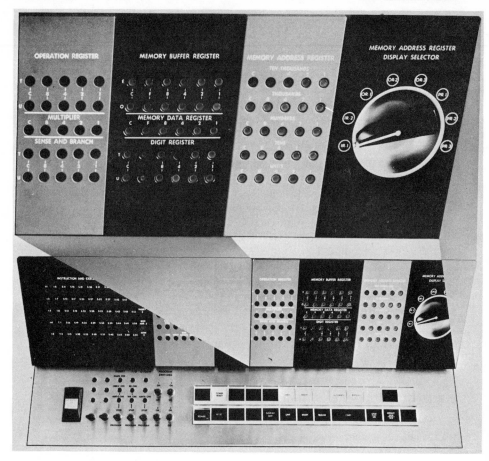

Fig. AVI.5.   Register Display Indicators.

SENSE AND BRANCH

Two rows of five lights each display the Q_8 and Q_9 positions of each Branch Indicator, Branch No Indicator, all Input-Output instructions, and the Control instruction. The row of lights labeled "T" displays the Q_8 position; the row of lights labeled "U" displays the Q_9 position.

SECTION NUMBER 5 (Fig. AVI.5)

MEMORY BUFFER REGISTER (MBR)

Two rows of six lights each display the contents of the two core locations effected by a core storage address. If the core storage address is odd, its digit is displayed in the row of lights labeled "O" (odd); the digit in the next lower core location is displayed in the row of lights labeled "E" (even). Should the core storage address be even, its digit is displayed by the lights in the row labeled "E"; the digit in the next higher core location is displayed in the row of lights labeled "O". This register is especially useful in the alphabetic mode, since the complete 2-digit representation of an alphamerical character is displayed at one time.

MEMORY DATA REGISTER (MDR)

One row of six lights displays the bit configuration of the digit in the core storage position addressed. This same digit will also be displayed in the Memory Buffer Register in either the E or O row depending on whether the addressed digit is located at an even or odd core location.

DIGIT REGISTER

These two rows of six lights each are used primarily for diagnostic testing by customer engineers.

SECTION NUMBER 6 (Fig. AVI.5)

MEMORY ADDRESS REGISTER

Five rows of five indicator lights display the bit configuration of the 5-digit address in any one of the eight MAR registers. The specific register to be displayed is selected by the Memory Address Register Display Selector switch; a depression of the Display MAR key then causes the address to be displayed in the lights.

MEMORY ADDRESS REGISTER DISPLAY SELECTOR

This is an 8-position rotary switch that permits the selection of any one of the eight MAR registers for display in the Memory Address Register lights. The position of this switch may be changed at any time without altering the display; it is the depression of the Display MAR key that causes the Memory Address Register lights to display the contents of the selected register. The display selector switch should not be repositioned simultaneously with the depression of the Display MAR key. The following registers may be chosen by this selector:

IR-1. Contains the address of the next instruction.
OR-1. Contains the Q address of the instruction in OP register.
OR-2. Contains the P address of the instruction in OP register.

IR-2. Contains the address saved by a Branch and Transmit or Branch and Transmit Immediate instruction.

PR-1. Contains the address saved by a depression of the Save key.

OR-3, PR-2, PR-3. Used in the multiply operation.

Fig. AVI.6.   Indicator Displays and Switches.

CONSOLE SWITCHES AND INDICATOR LIGHTS (Fig. AVI.6)

PARITY CHECK SWITCH

This is a 2-position switch that is manually set to either the "Stop" or "Program" position. When the switch is in the "Stop" position and a parity error occurs, the computer immediately terminates processing. If the switch is set to the "Program" position, processing continues.

PARITY CHECK INDICATOR LIGHTS

1. MBR-E CHK (Memory Buffer Register-Even) Light. This light reflects the status of the Memory Buffer Register-Even Check indicator (16). The indicator is turned on when a parity error is detected in

the even address digit in the MBR register. Processing continues or terminates depending upon the setting of the Parity Check switch. The indicator and light are turned off if the indicator is interrogated by a Branch Indicator or Branch No Indicator instruction.

2. MBR-O CHK (Memory Buffer Register-Odd) Light. This light reflects the status of the Memory Buffer Register-Odd Check indicator (17). The indicator is turned on when a parity error is detected in the odd address digit in the MBR register. Processing continues or terminates depending upon the setting of the Parity Check switch. The indicator and light are turned off if the indicator is interrogated by a Branch Indicator or Branch No Indicator instruction.

3. MARS CHK (Memory Address Register Storage) Light. This light is turned on when a digit in the MAR has a parity error. It is also turned on when the MAR receives a nonexistent address or a nonexistent OP code in some later versions of the 1620. When this light is turned on the computer immediately stops processing regardless of the setting of the Parity Check switch.

I/O CHECK SWITCH

This is a 2-position switch that is manually set to either a "Stop" or "Program" position. When this switch is set to the "Stop" position and a parity error is detected in an input or output operation, the computer terminates processing *after* the I/O operation is completed. When the switch is set to the "Program" position and an error is detected, processing does *not* stop but continues.

I/O CHECK LIGHTS

1. RD CHK (Read Check) Light. This light reflects the status of the Read Check indicator (06). The Read Check indicator is turned on when an input character with a parity error is detected prior to conversion of the input data to the BCD coding. Processing continues or terminates depending upon the setting of the I/O Check switch.

2. WR CHK (Write Check) Light. This light reflects the status of the Write Check indicator (07). The Write Check indicator is turned on when an output character with a parity error is detected after the conversion of the output data from BCD coding to the output code. Processing continues or terminates depending upon the setting of the I/O Check switch. However, if a parity error occurs while paper tape is being punched, the computer will terminate processing immediately, regardless of the setting of the I/O Check switch.

OVERFLOW CHECK SWITCH

This is a 2-position switch set manually to either a "Stop" or "Program" position. When this switch is set to a "Stop" position and an overflow occurs as the result of an arithmetic operation, the computer terminates processing at the end of the instruction being executed and the manual mode is initiated. Depression of the Start key causes the computer to continue processing.

When the Overflow Check switch is set to the "Program" position, and an overflow condition is detected, processing continues.

OVERFLOW LIGHTS

    1. ARITH CHK (Arithmetic Check) Light. This indicator light reflects the status of the internal overflow indicator. When the indicator is on, the light is on. The Overflow indicator (14) is turned on whenever an overflow condition is detected. It is turned off in only two ways: (1) depression of the Reset key or (2) interrogation of the indicator with a Branch Indicator or Branch No Indicator instruction.

    2. EXP CHK (Exponent Check) Light. This indicator light reflects the status of the internal exponent overflow indicator. When the indicator is on, the light is on. The Exponent Overflow indicator (15) is turned on whenever an attempt is made to generate an exponent greater than 99 or less than −99. It is turned off in a fashion identical with that of indicator 14.

PROGRAM SWITCHES

There are four program switches numbered 1 through 4, which may be set to either an "On" or "Off" position by the operator. It is these switches that are interrogated by the Branch Indicator and Branch No Indicator instructions with a modifier of 01, 02, 03, or 04. (See page 69). These switches belong exclusively to the operator as the only way to set or alter their position is to move them physically to an "On" or "Off" position. Their position may be altered at any time during program execution.

CONSOLE KEYS AND SIGNAL LIGHTS (Fig. AVI.7)

POWER SWITCH

This is a 2-position (on and off) switch that is used to apply electrical power to the computer when it is turned to the "On" position.

POWER ON LIGHT

This light is turned on when the power switch is on.

POWER READY LIGHT

The Power Ready light comes on after the Power switch has been turned on and when the internal machine temperature and voltages

Fig. AVI.7   Control Keys and Signal Lights.

reach proper operating values. There is a delay from the time the Power switch is turned on until operating conditions are obtained. The time delay varies with room temperature and the time elapsed since power was last turned off. When the computer is turned on the first thing in the morning, the delay may be from 5 to 15 minutes.

RESET KEY

Depression of the Reset key restores all machine status indicators and signal lights to their initial or reset condition and initiates the manual mode. This key is inactive when the computer is in the automatic mode.

THERMAL LIGHT

This light is turned on if the internal temperature of the computer becomes too high. Power is turned off and the Power Ready light is turned off. Depression of the Reset key turns off the Thermal light *after* the internal temperature has returned to normal. To apply power to the 1620, the Power switch must be turned off and then on again.

PUNCH NO FEED LIGHT

This light is turned on by the following conditions: (1) When a Write command is executed and there are no cards in the punch hopper or there is no tape on the paper tape punch. (2) When a Write command is executed and the card punch is not in a Ready status. (3) When a parity check occurs while paper tape is being punched. All the above conditions stop the computer in the automatic mode with both the Automatic and Punch No Feed lights turned on. When a parity error occurs, the I/O Write Check light is also turned on. Depression of the Reset key, while in the manual mode, turns off the Punch No Feed and I/O Write Check light. Manual correction and restart procedures can begin after depression of the Release and Reset keys.

READER NO FEED LIGHT

This light is turned on when the computer attempts to execute a read from the paper tape reader or card reader and the reader is not in a Ready status. Improperly mounted paper tape, failure to depress the Reel Power key, no tape mounted in the reader, no cards in the read hopper, failure to depress the Reader Start key, and an end-of-file condition, all will cause the Reader No Feed light to go on.[2]

DISPLAY MAR KEY

Depression of the Display MAR key causes the register to which the MAR Display Selector switch is set to be displayed in the Memory Address Register lights. This key is operative only when the Manual light is on and the Automatic light is off. The MAR display selector should not be turned simultaneously with the depression of the Display MAR key.

SAVE KEY

Depression of the Save key causes the address of the next sequential instruction to be saved in a special register. A subsequent Branch Back instruction will cause the computer to go to the core location saved for the next instruction. However, a multiply operation will cause the saved address to be lost. The Save key function takes priority over a Branch and Transmit or Branch and Transmit Immediate instruction when a Branch Back instruction is executed. If preceding the execution of a

---

[2] Due to the high speed of internal processing this light appears to be continually on as cards are being read. Actually it is being turned on and off at a high rate of speed. This action does *not* indicate that a reader no feed condition exists.

Branch Back instruction, the Save key had been depressed and a Branch and Transmit or Branch and Transmit Immediate had been executed, the Branch Back instruction would branch to the address saved by the Save key depression.

SAVE LIGHT

The Save light is turned on by the depression of the Save key.

INSERT KEY

The Insert key is operative only when the computer is in the manual mode (when the Manual light is on). Depression of the Insert key activates the typewriter in the *numeric* shift so that direct entry of instructions can be made. The first digit typed goes into core location 00000; the succeeding digits typed go into successively higher core locations. Up to 100 digits (8–12 digit instructions) may be typed in, after the 100th digit is entered an automatic release occurs and the manual mode is entered.

INSERT LIGHT

The Insert light is turned on by the depression of the Insert key.

RELEASE KEY

Depression of the Release key will terminate any input-output operation. The manual mode is initiated and the manual light turned on. When instructions are entered from the typewriter in the insert mode, depression of the Release key after the entry of the last digit causes the insert mode to be terminated and the manual mode is initiated. The Release key is operative only when the computer is in the automatic mode.

START KEY

The Start key is used to start program processing. Depression of the Start key puts the computer in the automatic mode. It is operative only when the computer is in the manual mode. Depression of the Insert, Release, and Start keys in that order causes the computer to go to core location 00000 for the first instruction to be executed. Therefore, if any instructions were entered while the computer was in the insert mode they would be executed since the first instruction entered went into core location 00000.

AUTOMATIC LIGHT

The Automatic light is on when the computer is in the automatic mode. This occurs when the stored program is being executed or when information is being entered into core storage from the typewriter.

MANUAL LIGHT

The Manual light is on when the computer is in the manual mode. The computer is in the manual mode when all operation has been terminated. Operator intervention may take place at this time. The manual mode is initiated in the following ways: the execution of a Halt instruction, depression of the Release key, or the depression of the Stop key. The manual mode is terminated in the following ways: depression of the Start key, depression of the Insert key, or depression of the Display MAR key. The Save light and/or a no feed light can be on when the Manual light is on.

Both the Manual and Automatic lights are on when an instruction is single cycled with the SCE key.

STOP/SIE (SINGLE INSTRUCTION EXECUTE) KEY

Depression of the Stop SIE key during program execution causes the computer to stop in the manual mode at the end of the instruction being executed when the key was depressed. This key also serves as a single instruction execute key, since successive depressions of this key cause one instruction to be executed for each depression.

INSTANT STOP/SCE (SINGLE CYCLE EXECUTE) KEY

Depression of the Instant Stop SCE key causes the computer to stop at the end of the 20-microsecond machine cycle in progress at the time the key is depressed. Successive depressions of this key cause single machine cycles to take place. Both the Manual and Automatic lights are on.

CHECK STOP LIGHT

This light is turned on when the 1620 stops because of a parity check. One or more of the Parity or I/O Check indicators will also be on, indicating what condition caused the stop. The Check Stop light will be turned off when the check indicator(s) is/are reset (by depressing the Reset key), or when the Parity or I/O switch is set to the "Program" position.

EMERGENCY OFF SWITCH (Fig. AVI.8)

This switch is for *emergency use only*. If this switch is turned off, all power in the computer is turned off. The blowers that cool the electronic circuits are stopped.

Fig. AVI.8. Emergency Off Switch.

Console Operating Procedures

This chapter describes console procedures. They are designed to aid the console operator when he is performing certain functions from the console. The procedures may be modified as required to meet individual requirements.

Instruct the Computer from the Typewriter.

Operator Action	*Explanation*
1. Depress Instant Stop key	Processing is halted.
2. Depress Reset key	Indicators are reset and the manual mode is initiated.
3. Depress Insert key	The typewriter is conditioned to enter *numeric* data into core storage beginning at core location 00000.
4. Type instructions	Instructions are entered into core storage at location 00000 and successively higher core locations. The operator may enter a *maximum* of 100 digits of information. After the 100th digit is entered, an automatic release initiates and the computer enters the manual mode.
5. Depress Release key	The typewriter is released and the computer enters the manual mode.
6. Depress Start key	The computer begins executing instructions sequentially starting with the instruction at location 00000.

Clear Core Storage to Zeros

Operator Action	*Explanation*
1. Depress Instant Stop key	Processing is halted.
2. Set the Parity Check switch and the I/O Check switch to the "program" position.	Instruction execution is to continue even if a parity error is detected.
3. Depress Reset key	Indicators are reset and the manual mode is initiated.
4. Depress Insert key	The typewriter is conditioned to enter *numeric* data into core storage beginning at location 00000.

5. Type one of the following:
    26 00008 00009
    16 00010 00000
    31 00003 00002
	Enter any *one* of these three instructions to clear core to zeros.

6. Depress Release key	The typewriter is released.
7. Depress Start key	The instruction entered in step 5 is executed. Approximately 0.8 seconds are required to clear 20,000 core positions.
8. Depress Instant Stop key	The operation is stopped at the end of the machine cycle in progress.

Program Entry from the Typewriter

Operator Action	*Explanation*
1. Clear core to zeros (if desired)	
2. Depress Reset key	
3. Depress Insert key	

4. Type:
    36 XXXXX 00100
    49 XXXXX
	Enter instructions to read numerically from the typewriter into the first position of program storage XXXXX and branch to the first program instruction.

5. Depress Release key	
6. Depress Start key	The Read Numerically instruction entered in step 4 is executed.
7. Type program instructions and data	The characters are entered into location XXXXX and successively higher core storage positions.
8. Depress Release key	Terminates the Read instruction.
9. Depress Start key	The Branch instruction, entered in step 4 is executed and program execution begins.

Print Core Storage Data on Typewriter

Operator Action	Explanation
1. Depress Insert key	
2. Type one of the following:	
39 XXXXX 00100 48	Write alphamerically beginning at location XXXXX (must be odd) and continuing until a record mark is sensed.
38 XXXXX 00100 48	Write numerically beginning at location XXXXX and continuing until a record mark is sensed.
35 XXXXX 00100 48	Dump numerically beginning at location XXXXX and continuing until the content of core location 19999 is typed or the Release key is depressed.
3. Depress Release key	
4. Depress Start key	The instruction entered in step 2 is executed.

Program Alteration and/or Data Entry

Operator Action	Explanation
1. Depress Stop key	Processing is halted and the manual mode is initiated.
2. Depress Save key	The address of the next instruction in sequence is saved in PR-1.
3. Depress Insert key	

4. Type:
    36 XXXXX 00100
    42
	Enter instruction to read numerically from the typewriter beginning at the first position of data entry (XXXXX), and branch to the address saved in PR-1 by the depression of the Save key in step 2.

5. Depress Release key	
6. Depress Start key	The Read instruction entered in step 4 is executed.
7. Type instructions and/or data	
8. Depress Release key	
9. Depress Start key	The next sequential instruction which is the Branch Back instruction entered in step 4 is executed and a branch to the instruction at the address saved in step 2 is effected.

Single Instruction Execution of a Program

Operator Action	*Explanation*
1. Depress Stop/SIE key	Processing is halted and the manual mode is initiated.
2. Depress Stop/SIE key	Each depression causes the execution of one instruction. The OP code of the instruction *just executed* is displayed in the OP register lights.
3. Depress Instant Stop/SCE key.	One machine cycle is executed. The OP code and the address of the instruction that is about to be executed are displayed in the OP register and MAR lights respectively.
4. Depress Stop/SIE key	The instruction displayed in step 3 is executed. Steps 3 and 4 can be alternated to display succeeding instructions.

PROCEDURE TO TURN OFF THERMAL LIGHT

If the Thermal light comes on when the Power switch is turned on, depress the Reset key. Then turn the Power switch off and back on again. If the Thermal light remains on there is a possibility that the Emergency Off switch has been pulled. Notify the supervisor of your machine installation.

PROCEDURE FOR ASSEMBLING SPS PROGRAMS ON A 1620 TAPE SYSTEM

ASSEMBLING AN SPS SOURCE PROGRAM

The symbolic assembly system consists of six tapes: the SPS processor tape, two SPS subroutine tapes for computers with the automatic division special feature (one tape for variable-mantissa-size floating point subroutines and the other for fixed-mantissa-size floating point subroutines), and two subroutine tapes for computers without the automatic division feature (one tape for variable-mantissa-size floating point subroutines and the other for fixed-mantissa-size floating point subroutines). The fifth subroutine tape is for a computer with floating-point hardware.

The assembly system is a 2-pass system—the source statements must be read in twice. The first pass builds up the table of labels; no punching occurs in Pass I. The second pass actually assembles the source statement. The sequence of operations in obtaining an object program is as follows:

Pass I

1. Clear the core memory to zeros.
2. Set the Overflow Check switch to "Program" and the I/O and Parity Check switches to "Stop."
3. Set the console program switches. The function of the program switches during pass I are as follows:

   Switch 1 On—The input is from the paper tape reader.
             Off—The input is from the typewriter.
   Switch 2 On—If an error is detected by the processor, the entire state-
             ment may be re-entered from the typewriter.
             Off—If an error is detected, it is noted but ignored and the
             processing continues (to be explained in section on errors,
             pages 303 and 304).
   Switch 3 Not used by tape SPS.
   Switch 4 On—Normally off, but used for correcting statements keyed in
             improperly at the typewriter. When the programmer de-
             tects such an entry he should
             (a) throw switch 4 on,
             (b) depress Release and Start keys,
             (c) throw switch off,
             (d) re-enter complete statement.

4. Load the tape punch with approximately 5 feet of leader.
5. Mount the processor tape in the Paper Tape Reader. The following procedure is used to read the processor tape:
   (a) depress Reset key,
   (b) depress Insert key,
   (c) type 36 00000 00300,
   (d) depress Release key,
   (e) depress Start key.

6. The processor tape will be read, and the computer will halt in the manual mode.
7. Mount the source tape (only applicable if source statements are on paper tape).
8. Depress Start key. Pass I processing will begin.
9. Two methods of source program input may be used under control of program switch 1.
   (a) If the source statements are entered from the typewriter (switch 1 off), the processor will transfer control to the console typewriter to await the first statement. Type one source statement followed by a record mark. Depress the Release and Start keys. The statement will be processed and the typewriter carriage will return to await entry of the next statement. As each statement is processed, it is punched on the tape punch so that at the end of Pass I an exact copy of the source statements entered from the typewriter have been punched on tape. This tape is then used as input to Pass II.

(b) If the source statements are being entered from paper tape (switch 1 on), each statement is read and processed individually.

10. Sensing of the DEND statement signals the processor that the entry of source statements is completed. The computer will halt in the manual mode and the following message will be typed:

END OF PASS I

Pass II

11. Set the program switches for Pass II. The functions of the program switches for Pass II are as follows:

Switch 1 On—A complete listing is typed out; that is, entire input statement together with the machine language instructions.
        Off—No listing is typed out.
Switch 2 On—Same as Pass I.
        Off—Same as Pass I.
Switch 3 On—Same as Pass I.
        Off—Same as Pass I.
Switch 4 On—No object program is punched except loader and arithmetic tables.
        Off—Object program is punched.
    Note: The purpose of Switch 4 is to allow the assembly process to take place for the purpose of error detection only.

12. If a complete listing is to be typed, set typewriter margins and tab stop. Recommended settings are as follows:
Margins: extreme right and left
Tab Stops: tab stop at 55.

13. Mount the source tape (the original or that which was produced from the typed-in statements) on the paper tape reader.

14. If source statements were entered from the typewriter in Pass I, the paper tape punch will require reloading. This should be done leaving about 5 feet of leader.

15. Depress the Start key on the console. Pass II processing will begin. Each source statement will be read in and processed. The machine language statements will be punched. Error messages are typed out when certain errors are detected. The setting of program switch 2 determines the course of action to be taken. See pages 303 and 304.

16. When all the source statements have been processed, the computer will halt in the manual mode and one of the following messages will be typed:

END OF PASS II

LOAD SUBROUTINES

17. If "END OF PASS II" is typed omit the next two steps.
18. Mount the *appropriate* subroutine tape on the paper tape reader.

19. Depress the Start key on the console. If the subroutine tape with the variable-mantissa-size floating point subroutines is used, the following message will be typed:

ENTER MANTISSA LENGTH

The operator must then type in the mantissa size with a flag over the high-order digit ($\overline{X}X$). Depress Release and Start keys. The subroutines will be read in and those requested through the use of macro-instructions will be selected and punched. The following message will be typed:

END OF PASS II

20. A table of all the labels and their associated addresses will then be typed. If it is desired to suppress the typing of this table, turn switch 4 on— but turn it on *only* after the message "END OF PASS II" begins to type.
21. Depress the Tape Feed switch on the paper tape punch and let about 2 feet of tape be punched with the tape feed code. Remove the tape from the punch. This is the complete object program tape.

ERROR DETECTION IN SOURCE PROGRAM

Error messages will be typed out when certain errors are detected in the form of the input statements. The messages are of the form "ERn" where *n* identifies the error. When an error is detected during the first or second pass, the error message will refer to the last defined label plus the number of statements from this labeled statement to the statement in error. If, however, during the second pass, a full typewriter listing is requested, error reporting is of the following nature: the source statement is typed followed by the error message. At that point, the setting of Switch 2 determines the subsequent course of action.

The following errors are detected by the system:

ER1   A record mark is in the label or operation code field.
ER2   For address adjustment, a product greater than 10 digits has resulted from a multiplication.
ER3   An invalid operation code has been detected.
ER4   A dollar sign ($), which is being used as a Head indicator, is incorrectly positioned in an operand.
ER5   (a) The symbolic address contains more than six characters.
      (b) The actual address contains more than five characters.
      (c) An undefined symbolic address or an invalid special character is used in an operand.
ER6   A DSA statement has more than 10 operands.
ER7   A DSB statement has the second operand missing.
ER8   (a) A DC, DSC, DAC, or DNB has a length operand greater than 50.
      (b) A DC, DSC, or DAC has no constant specified.

(c) A DC or DSC has a specified length less than the number of digits in the constant.

(d) A DAC has a specified length different than the number of characters in the constant.

ER9   The table of labels is full.

ER10   A label has been defined more than once.

ER11   An assembled address is greater than five digits.

ER12   A Head statement contains an invalid special character as a heading character.

ER13   A Head statement contains more than one character.

ER14   An invalid special character is used in a label.

PROCEDURES FOR HANDLING ERRORS

Program Switch 2 On

The entire statement should be entered correctly from the typewriter. The statement must be terminated by a record mark. The carriage automatically returns to accept the corrected statement. It should be noted that, when the source statements are entered at the tape reader, errors detected during the first pass will again be detected, and will again require correction, during the second pass. When the input is from the typewriter, however, first pass error correction will be incorporated in the symbolic tape being prepared.

Program Switch 2 Off

Errors are handled as follows:

ER1   The label is treated as blank and a NOP instruction, 410000000000, is assembled and the next statement is read in.

ER2   The operand is assembled as 00000 and the processing continues.

ER3   The label is treated as blank and a NOP instruction, 410000000000, is assembled and the next statement is read in.

ER4   The operand is assembled as 00000 and the processing continues.

ER5   The operand is assembled as 00000 and the processing continues.

ER6   Only the first 10 operands are assembled and the remaining are ignored.

ER7   The statement is assembled as a DS with a length of 50.

ER8   (a) If the declarative is a DC, it will be treated as a DS with a length operand of 50.

(b) If the declarative is a DSC, it will be treated as a DSS with a length operand of 50.

(c) If the declarative is a DAC, it will be treated as a DAS with a length operand of 50.

(d) If the declarative is a DNB, its length operand is chosen to be 50.

ER9   The label is treated as a blank label.

ER10   The label is treated as a blank label.

ER11   The operand is assembled as 00000 and the processing continues.
ER12   The Head character is assumed to be a blank.
ER13   The first nonblank character is assumed to be the Head character.
ER14   The label is treated as a blank label.

RUNNING THE OBJECT PROGRAM

The object tape contains a load routine, all the constants and instructions, the required subroutines, and the arithmetic tables. The object program is run in the following manner:

1. Mount the object tape on the tape reader.
2. Clear core memory to zeros.
3. (a) Load the tape punch if the output is to be punched.
   (b) Set margins and tab stops if the output is to be typed.
4. Set Overflow Check switch to "Program" and the parity and I/O Check switches to "Stop".[1]
5. Depress Reset key.
6. Depress Insert key.
7. Type 36 00000 00300.
8. Depress Release key.
9. Depress Start key.
10. After the object tape is read in, the computer will halt in the manual mode.
11. If data is being entered from tape, mount the data tape on the tape reader.
12. Depress the Start key. If the DEND statement contained an operand, the computer will perform a branch to the address specified in the operand. If no operand was present in the DEND statement, the operator must manually branch to the first instruction he wishes executed in his object program.

ERROR MESSAGES AT OBJECT TIME

In the 1620 floating point subroutines, the presence of certain special conditions will cause an error message of the following form to be typed out:

$$\underbrace{\text{XXXXX}}_{R}\text{O}\underbrace{\text{OXX}}_{S}$$

R is the address of the next instruction in sequence in the *main program* and S is a code which identifies the special condition.

Except in the case of characteristic overflow or underflow where the subsequent course of action depends on the digit at 401, a subroutine

---

[1] These are only suggested settings. The programmer may position them at his discretion. However, the subroutines utilize the Overflow indicator by branching on its condition; therefore, if macro-instructons are used, the Overflow check switch must be set to the "Program" position.

will always halt immediately after typing the error message. The code in the error message tells the operator why the subroutine has stopped. He may then use the return address and insert a Branch instruction at location zero that will return control to the main program, or in some cases he may continue execution of the subroutine by pressing the Start key on the console.

The following are the special conditions that can arise in the floating point subroutines and the error code associated with each one:

01	FA, FS	Characteristic overflow.
02	FA, FS	Characteristic underflow.
03	FM	Characteristic overflow.
04	FM	Characteristic underflow.
05	FD	Characteristic overflow.
06	FD	Characteristic underflow.
07	FD	Attempt to divide by a floating point number with a zero mantissa. May not continue execution of the subroutine.
08	FSQR	Attempt to take the square root of a negative number. May press the Start key to continue execution of the subroutine, finding the square root of the absolute value of the number, or may branch back to the main program.
09	FSIN, FCOS	Input argument has a characteristic greater than L (mantissa length). May not continue execution of the subroutine as all significance would be lost in the result.
10	FSIN, FCOS	Input argument has a characteristic greater than or equal to $\overset{-}{0}3$ and less than or equal to L (mantissa length). May continue execution of the subroutine with some loss of significance in the result.
11	FEX FEXT	Characteristic overflow. Course of action depends on digit at location 401.
12	FEX FEXT	Characteristic underflow. Course of action depends on digit at location 401.
13	FLN FLOG	Input argument has zero mantissa. May not continue execution of the subroutine.
14	FLN FLOG	Input argument is negative. May continue to execute the subroutine, computing with the absolute value of the number.

PROCEDURE FOR COMPILING FORTRAN PROGRAMS ON A 1620 PAPER TAPE SYSTEM

COMPILING A FORTRAN PROGRAM

Four tapes are provided for the 1620 Fortran system: the Fortran compiler tape, the Fortran subroutine tape for computers with the automatic division special feature, a subroutine tape for computers without the automatic division feature, and a subroutine tape for computers with the floating point hardware special feature. The sequence of operations in obtaining an object program is as follows:

1. Load the tape punch with about 5 feet of leader.
2. Clear core memory to zeros.
3. Set the Overflow Check switch to "Program" and the I/O and Parity Check switches to "Stop".
4. Mount the compiler tape in the paper tape reader. The following procedure is used to read in the compiler tape:
   (a) Depress Reset key
   (b) Depress Insert key
   (c) Type 36 00000 00300
   (d) Depress Release key
   (e) Depress Start key.
5. The compiler tape will be read in and punching will occur. The load routines are punched. When the loading of the compiler tape is completed, the computer will halt in the manual mode, and the following message will be typed:

ENTER SOURCE PROGRAM, PUSH START

6. If the source program is to be entered from the paper tape reader, mount the source tape.
7. Set the console program switches. The functions of the program switches at compile time are as follows:

   Switch 1 On—Causes the source statements and the object time address of the first compiled instruction to be listed at the console as they are processed. Statements will be listed with the object time address of the first instruction compiled from the source statement.
   Off—Source statements are not listed.
   Switch 2 On—Causes trace instructions to be compiled. (The trace feature is discussed on page 309.)
   Off—Trace instructions are not compiled.
   Switch 3 On—Input to the compiler (that is, the source statements) is being entered via the console typewriter.
   Off—Source program entered from the paper tape reader.
   Switch 4 This switch is used in conjunction with switch 3 if and only if switch 3 is in the "on" position. It provides the operator with the ability to restart the typing of a statement if an error has been made. Switch 4 is normally Off. When a typing error is made in a source statement and is to be corrected, Switch 4 is placed on, the Release and Start keys are depressed, and then Switch 4 is turned Off. The operator can now retype the statement.

8. Depress the Start key. Compilation will begin.

9. Two methods of source program input may be used under control of program switch 3.
    (a) If the source statements are entered from the typewriter (switch 3 on), the compiler will transfer control to the console typewriter to await the first statement. Type one source statement followed by a record mark. Depress the Release and Start keys. The statement will be compiled and the machine language instructions punched. The typewriter carriage will return after each statement has been processed to await the entry of the next statement. This routine is repeated until an End statement is sensed.
    (b) If the source statements are being entered from paper tape (switch 3 on) each statement is entered individually. It will be compiled and the machine language instructions punched.
10. Sensing of the End statement signals the compiler that the entry of source statements is completed. The computer halts in the manual mode and the following message will be typed:

PROG SW1 ON FOR SYMBOL TABLE, PUSH START

11. If it is desired to get a listing of the symbol table put program switch 1 on. If the listing is not desired, turn program switch 1 off.
12. Depress the Start key on the console. If program switch 1 is on, a listing of the symbol table is typed.
13. The computer will halt in the manual mode and the following message will be typed:

SW1 OFF TO IGNORE SUBROUTINES, PUSH START

14. The operator is given a choice. He may process the subroutines at this time, or he may wait until he runs the object program to process the subroutines.
15. If it is desired to process the subroutines at this time, turn program switch 1 on. If program switch 1 is turned off depress the Start key on the console. The message in step 18 is typed and the procedure in step 19 should be followed.
16. Mount the *appropriate* subroutine tape on the paper tape reader.
17. Depress the Start key on the console. The subroutine tape will be read in and the required subroutines will be selected and punched.
18. After the required subroutines have been punched, the computer will halt in the manual mode and the following message will be typed:

PROCESSING COMPLETE

19. Depress the Tape Feed switch on the paper tape punch and let about two feet of tape punch with the tape feed code. Remove the tape from the tape punch. This tape is the object program tape.

ERRORS IN THE SOURCE PROGRAM

During compilation, a number of tests are made for source program errors. If an error is found in a source statement an error message in the

form "ERROR NO. n" is typed, where *n* is the error code, and processing
continues. The errors detected are as follows:

ERROR NO.   CONDITION

1   Incorrectly formed statement.
2   Subscripted variable for which no Dimension statement has
            previously appeared in the program, or a dimensioned variable
            is used without subscripts, or a variable used in a Dimension
            statement has already appeared in the source program.
3   Floating point number not in allowable range of values, or fixed
            point number contains more than 4 digits.
4   Symbol table full.
5   Mixed mode expression.
6   Variable name in an expression contains more than 5 characters.
7   Switch number has been omitted in an If (Sense Switch) state-
            ment or the first character following the right parenthesis in an
            If statement or If (Sense Switch) statement is not a digit.
8   A comma follows the statement number in a Do statement. (for
            example, DO 1, I = 1, 10)
9   A Dimension statement ends with a comma, or more than two
            dimensions have been specified in a Dimension statement (for
            example, DIMENSION A (10, 10, 10))
10   A Format statement does not have a statement number.
11   Incorrect representation in a Format statement.
            (a) Used special characters ($=$, $+$, $-$, and so forth) in a
                numerical field specification.
            (b) Alphabetical characters other than E, F, or I in a numerical
                field specification.
            (c) A decimal point is omitted in E- or F-type numerical field
                specifications.
            (d) Number of positions to the right of the decimal has not
                been given in an E- or F-type numerical field specification.
            (e) A record mark appears in the numerical field specification
                or an alphameric field specification.
            (f) The first character following the word "Format" is not a
                left parenthesis.
12   The total record width specified in a Format statement is greater
            than 87 characters.
13   A Format statement number has been omitted in an I/0 state-
            ment.

Another error message is typed if the compiled instructions and
required data storage *not* including relocatable subroutines will, at object
time, exceed the storage capacity of the 1620. This message is typed at
the point in the compilation of the source program where overlap occurs.

Compilation will continue, and the message will be typed after each statement thereafter.

If the inclusion of any of the relocatable subroutines causes an overlap the following message is typed as the subroutines are loading

OVERLAP XXXXX POSITIONS

The XXXXX is the number of core storage positions of overlap between the end of the object program and the data storage area.

FORTRAN TRACE FEATURE

The Fortran processor will, under console switch control (console switch 2 on), compile certain instructions into the object program that will enable the operator to trace the flow of the program and check its correctness. When the object program is executed, console switch 4 performs the following functions:

> Switch 4 On—Causes compiled trace instructions to be executed.
> Off—Trace instructions are not executed.

The trace output provided is the evaluated left-hand side of each executed *arithmetic* statement, typed at the left margin. Normal output, resulting from Punch, Print, and Type statements, is not inhibited. The output format of the trace data is E14.8 in the case of floating point results or I(w-i) where w is the specified width.

Note that console switch 4 serves a dual function during execution of the object program, that is, provision of trace data and correction of input data incorrectly entered at the console keyboard. Thus when running in the trace mode, the operator should turn off CS4 before typing input data. Following the entry of the last item on the list, he should (after depressing Release) depress SIE three times, turn the switch on, and depress the Start key.

RUNNING THE OBJECT PROGRAM

The object tape contains a load routine, all the constants and instructions, the arithmetic tables, and the required subroutines if they were processed at compile time. The object program is run in the following manner:

1. (a) Clear core memory to zeros.
   (b) Set the Overflow Check switch to "Program" and the I/O and Parity Check switches to "Stop".
   (c) Mount the object tape.
   (d) Depress Reset key.
   (e) Depress Insert key.
   (f) Type in 36 00000 00300.

(g) Depress Release key.

(h) Depress Start key. The object tape will read in.

Note: Once a source program has been debugged and compiled, it is necessary to load the object tape only to run the program at some future date. The process of compilation does not have to be repeated.

2. After the object tape has been read in, one of two of the following messages will be typed and the computer will halt in the manual mode.

LOAD DATA or

ENTER SUBROUTINES, PUSH START

3. The message "LOAD DATA" will type if the subroutines were processed at compile time. If this message types, omit the next three steps.

4. If the message "ENTER SUBROUTINES, PUSH START" types, mount the *appropriate* subroutine tape on the paper tape reader.

5. Depress the Start key on the console. The subroutine tape will be read in, and the required subroutines selected and stored for use by the object program.

6. After the required subroutines have been selected and stored, the computer halts in the manual mode and the following message is typed:

LOAD DATA

7. If data is being entered from tape, mount the data tape on the paper tape reader.

8. Set margins and tab stops on the typewriter as desired. This will apply only if the output is to be typed. If the output is to be punched, load the tape punch with approximately 5 feet of leader.

9. Set the program switches.

Program switches 1, 2, and 3 are completely at the operator's disposal at object time. If the source program contained If (Sense Switch) statements, the switches are set accordingly.

Program switch 4 has a dual function at object time.

Switch 4 On—If trace instructions were compiled (program switch 2 on at compile time), they will be executed.

Off—Compiled trace instructions are not executed.

When data is entered from the typewriter (through use of the accept statement) this switch provides the ability to correct a typing error. Switch 4 is normally off.[2] If an error is made, set switch 4 on, depress the Release and Start keys, and turn switch 4 off. The data may now be retyped.

10. Depress Start key. Program execution will begin.

TYPEWRITER ENTRY OF DATA

When data is to be entered from the typewriter, the typewriter carriage returns and control is transferred to the typewriter. Enter the data

---

[2] If switch 4 is on to execute trace instructions, it must be turned off prior to data entry from the typewriter. After the data has been correctly entered and the Release key has been depressed, depress the Stop/SIE key three times. Switch 4 may then be turned on again and the Start key depressed.

according to the format specification. Depress the Release and Start keys on the console. Processing will continue.

ERROR MESSAGES AT OBJECT TIME

A number of error checks have been built into the Fortran subroutines. The basic philosophy that has been followed with respect to an error situation is to have an error message typed out, to set the result of the operation equal to the most reasonable value under the circumstances, and to have the program continue. Listed below are the error checks that exist in the subroutines, the error codes that are typed out, and the value to which FAC is set before the program continues. In the list, it will be noted that the terms overflow and underflow occur several times. Overflow means that the characteristic of the result has exceeded 99. Underflow means that the characteristic of the result is less than −99.

Error Check	Error Code	Contents of FAC
Overflow in FAD or FSB.	E1	$\overline{9}9999999\overline{9}9$
Underflow in FAD or FSB.	E2	$\overline{0}0000000\overline{9}\overline{9}$
Overflow in FMP.	E3	$\overline{9}9999999\overline{9}9$
Underflow in FMP.	E4	$\overline{0}0000000\overline{9}\overline{9}$
Overflow in FDV or FDVR.	E5	$\overline{9}9999999\overline{9}9$
Underflow in FDV or FDVR.	E6	$\overline{0}0000000\overline{9}\overline{9}$
Zero divisor in FDV or FDVR.	E7	$\overline{9}9999999\overline{9}9$
Zero divisor in FXD or FXDR.	E8	$\overline{9}999$
Argument in FIX ≤ -10000*	E9	$\overline{9}99\overline{9}$
Argument in FIX ≥ 10000*	E9	$\overline{9}999$
Loss of all significance in FSIN or FCOS.	F1	$\overline{9}9999999\overline{9}9$
Zero argument in FLN.	F2	$\overline{9}9999999\overline{9}9$
Negative argument in FLN.	F3	Ln $|x|$
Overflow in FEXP or FEXN.	F4	$\overline{9}9999999\overline{9}9$
Underflow in FEXP or FEXN.	F5	$\overline{0}0000000\overline{9}\overline{9}$
Negative argument in FAXB.	F6	$|A|^B$
Negative argument in FSQR.	F6	$\sqrt{|x|}$
Input data in incorrect form or is outside the allowable range.	F7	
Output data outside allowable range or in a form not acceptable to the applicable format specification.	F8	

* Floating point hardware system only.

Input or output tape or typewriter
  record is longer than 87 characters,
  or there is an element in an input
  or output list for which there is no
  specification in the corresponding
  Format statement.   F9

PROCEDURE FOR ASSEMBLING SPS PROGRAMS ON A 1620 CARD SYSTEM

ASSEMBLING AN SPS SOURCE PROGRAM

The symbolic assembly system consists of six card decks: the SPS processor deck, two SPS subroutine decks for computers with the automatic division special feature (one deck for variable-mantissa-size floating point subroutines and the other for fixed-mantissa-size floating point subroutines), and two subroutine decks for computers without the automatic division feature (one deck for variable-mantissa-size floating point subroutines and the other for fixed-mantissa-size floating point subroutines). The fifth subroutine deck is for a computer with floating point hardware.

The assembly system is a 2-pass system—the source statements must be read in twice. The first pass builds up the table of labels; no punching occurs in Pass I. The second pass actually assembles the source statements. The sequence of operations in obtaining an object program is as follows:

Pass I

1. Clear the core memory to zeros.
2. Set the Overflow Check switch to "Program" and the I/O and Parity Check switches to "Stop."
3. Set the console program switches. The function of the program switches during Pass I are as follows:

    Switch 1 On—The input is from the card reader.
            Off—The input is from the typewriter.
    Switch 2 On—If an error is detected by the processor, the entire statement may be re-entered from the typewriter.
            Off—If an error is detected, it is noted but ignored and the processing continues (to be explained in section on errors, page 316.)
    Switch 3   Must be off in Pass I.
    Switch 4 On—Normally off, but used for correcting statements keyed in improperly at the typewriter. When the programmer detects such an entry he should:
        (a) throw switch on,
        (b) depress Release and Start,
        (c) throw switch off,
        (d) re-enter the complete statement.

4. Depress Reset key.
5. Place the processor deck in the read hopper.
6. Depress the Load key. The processor deck will be read in and the computer will halt in the manual mode (a 48 will appear in the operation register lights).
7. If the source program is on cards, place the source deck in the read hopper and depress the Reader Start key.
8. If the source program is to be entered from the typewriter, place blank cards in the punch hopper and depress the Punch Start key.
9. Depress the Start key on the console. Pass I processing will begin.
10. Two methods of source program input may be used under control of program switch 1.

    (a) If the source statements are entered from the typewriter (switch 1 off), the processor will transfer control to the console typewriter to await the entry of the first statement. Type one source statement followed by a record mark. Depress the Release and Start keys. The statement will be processed and the typewriter carriage will return to await entry of the next statement. As each statement is processed it is punched on a card so that at the end of Pass I, an exact copy of the source statements entered from the typewriter have been punched on cards. These cards are then used as the input to Pass II.

    (b) If the source statements are be entered from cards (switch 1 on), each statement is read in and processed individually.

11. Sensing of the DEND statement signals the processor that the entry of source statements is completed. The computer will halt in the manual mode and the following message will be typed:

END OF PASS I

Pass II

12. Set the program switches for Pass II. The functions of the program switches for Pass II are as follows:

    Switch 1 On—A complete listing is typed out; that is, entire input statement together with the machine language instructions.
    Off—No typed listing.
    Switch 2 On—Same as Pass I.
    Off—Same as Pass I.
    Switch 3 On—A compressed deck is produced.
    Off—A listing deck is produced. This is a deck which may be listed on peripheral printing equipment.
    Switch 4 On—No object program is punched except loader and arithmetic tables. If switch 4 is on, switch 3 *must* be on.
    Off—Object program is punched.
    Note: The purpose of switch 4 is to allow the assembly process to take place for the purpose of error detection only.

13. If a complete listing is to be typed, set typewriter margins and tab stop. Recommended settings are as follows:

Margins: extreme right and left

Tab stops: tab stop at 55

14. Place the source deck (the original or that which was produced from the typed-in statements) in the read hopper and depress the Reader Start key.

15. Place blank cards in the punch hopper and depress the Punch Start key.

16. Depress the Start key on the console. Pass II processing will begin. Each source statement will be read in and processed. The machine language statements will be punched. Error messages are typed out when certain errors are detected. The setting of program switch 2 determines the course of action to be taken. See page 316.

17. When all the source statements have been processed the computer will halt in the manual mode and one of the following messages will be typed:

END OF PASS II or

LOAD SUBROUTINES

18. If "END OF PASS II" is typed omit the next two steps.

19. Place the *appropriate* subroutine deck in the read hopper and depress the Reader Start key.

20. Depress the Start key on the console. If the subroutine deck with the variable mantissa size floating point subroutines is used, the following message is typed:

ENTER MANTISSA LENGTH

The operator must then type in the mantissa size with a flag over the high-order digit ($\overline{X}X$). Depress Release and Start keys. The subroutines will be read in and those requested through the use of macro-instructions will be selected and punched. The following message will be typed:

END OF PASS II

21. A table of all the labels and their associated addresses will then type out. If it is desired to suppress the typing of this table, turn switch 4 on, but turn it on only after the message "END OF PASS II" begins typing.

22. With the Non-Process Run-Out key run the cards out of the punch feed. *The object deck is in the punch stacker.* Remove the last two cards which will be blanks.

ERROR DETECTION IN SOURCE PROGRAM

Error messages will be typed out when certain errors are detected in the form of the input statements. The messages are of the form "ERn" where *n* identifies the error.

When an error is detected during the first or second pass, the error message will refer to the last defined label plus the number of statements from this labeled statement to the statement in error. If however, during the second pass, a full typewriter listing is requested, error reporting is of the following nature: the source statement is typed followed by the error message. At that point, the setting of Switch 2 determines the subsequent course of action.

The following errors are detected by the system:

ER1   A record mark is in the label or operation code field.

ER2   For address adjustment, a product greater than 10 digits has resulted from a multiplication.

ER3   An invalid operation code has been detected.

ER4   A dollar sign ($), which is being used as a Head indicator, is incorrectly positioned in an operand.

ER5   (a) The symbolic address contains more than six characters.
      (b) The actual address contains more than five characters.
      (c) An undefined symbolic address or an invalid special character is used in the operand.

ER6   A DSA statement has more than 10 operands.

ER7   A DSB statement has the second operand missing.

ER8   (a) A DC, DSC, DAC, or DNB has a length operand greater than 50.
      (b) A DC, DSC, or DAC has no constant specified.
      (c) A DC or DSC has a specified length less than the number of digits in the constant.
      (d) A DAC has a specified length different than the number of characters in the constant.

ER9   The table of labels is full.

ER10 A label has been defined more than once.

ER11 An assembled address is greater than five digits.

ER12 A Head statement contains an invalid special character as a heading character.

ER13 A Head statement contains more than one character.

ER14 An invalid special character is used in a label.

PROCEDURES FOR HANDLING ERRORS

Program Switch 2 On

The entire statement should be entered correctly from the typewriter. The statement must be terminated by a record mark. The carriage automatically returns to accept the corrected statement. It should be noted that when the source statements are entered at the card reader, errors detected during the first pass will be again detected, and will again require correction, during the second pass. When the input is from the typewriter, however, first pass error correction will be incorporated in the symbolic deck being prepared.

Program Switch 2 Off

Errors are handled as follows:

ER1   The label is treated as blank and a NOP instruction, 410000000000, is assembled and the next statement is read in.

ER2   The operand is assembled as 00000 and the processing continues.

ER3   The label is treated as blank and a NOP instruction, 410000000000, is assembled and the next statement is read in.

ER4   The operand is assembled as 00000 and the processing continues.

ER5   The operand is assembled as 00000 and the processing continues.

ER6   Only the first 10 operands are assembled and the remaining ones are ignored.

ER7   The statement is assembled as a DS with a length of 50.

ER8   (a) If the declarative is a DC, it will be treated as a DS with a length operand of 50.

          (b) If the declarative is a DSC, it will be treated as a DSS with a length operand of 50.

          (c) If the declarative is a DAC, it will be treated as a DAS with a length operand of 50.

          (d) If the declarative is a DNB, its length operand is chosen to be 50.

ER9   The label is treated as a blank label.

ER10   The label is treated as a blank label.

ER11   The operand is assembled as 00000 and the processing continues.

ER12   The Head character is assumed to be a blank.

ER13   The first nonblank character is assumed to be the Head character.

ER14   The label is treated as a blank label.

RUNNING THE OBJECT PROGRAM

The object deck contains a load routine, all the constants and instructions, the required subroutines, and the arithmetic tables. The object program is run in the following manner:

1. Clear core memory to zeros.
2. Place the object deck in the read hopper.
3. (a) If the output is to be punched, place blank cards in the punch hopper and depress the Punch Start key.

   (b) If the output is to be typed, set the margins and tab stops.
4. Set the Overflow Check switch to "Program" and the Parity and I/O Check switches to "Stop".[3]
5. Depress the Load key. The object deck is read in and the computer will halt in the manual mode.
6. If data is being entered from cards, place the data cards in the read hopper and depress the Reader Start key.

_____

[3] These are only suggested settings. The programmer may position them at his discretion. However, the subroutines utilize the Overflow indicator by branching on its condition; therefore, if macro-instructions are used, the overflow Check switch must be set to the "Program" position.

7. Depress the Start key on the console. If the DEND statement contained an operand, the computer will execute a branch to the address specified in the operand. If no operand was present in the DEND statement, the operator must manually branch to the first instruction he wishes executed in his object program.

ERROR MESSAGES AT OBJECT TIME

In the 1620 floating point subroutines, the presence of certain special conditions will cause an error message of the following form to be typed out:

$$\underbrace{\text{XXXXX}}_{R}\underbrace{\text{OOXX}}_{S}$$

R is the address of the next instruction in sequence in the main program and S is a code that identifies the special condition.

Except in the case of characteristic overflow or underflow where the subsequent course of action depends on the digit at 401, a subroutine will always halt immediately after typing the error message. The code in the error message tells the operator why the subroutine has stopped. He may then use the return address and insert a branch instruction at location zero that will return control to the main program, or in some cases he may continue execution of the subroutine by pressing the Start key on the console.

The following are the special conditions that can arise in the floating point subroutines and the error code associated with each one:

01	FA, FS	Characteristic overflow.
02	FA, FS	Characteristic underflow.
03	FM	Characteristic overflow.
04	FM	Characteristic underflow.
05	FD	Characteristic overflow.
06	FD	Characteristic underflow.
07	FD	Attempt to divide by a floating point number with a zero mantissa. May not continue execution of the subroutine.
08	FSQR	Attempt to take the square root of a negative number. May press the Start key to continue execution of the subroutine, finding the square root of the absolute value of the number, or may branch back to the main program.
09	FSIN, FCOS	Input argument has a characteristic greater than L (mantissa length). May not continue execution of the subroutine as all significance would be lost in the result.
10	FSIN, FCOS	Input argument has a characteristic greater than or equal to 03 and less than or equal to L (mantissa length). May continue execution of the subroutine with some loss of significance in the result.
11	FEX FEXT	Characteristic overflow. Course of action depends on digit at location 401.

12	FEX FEXT	Characteristic underflow. Course of action depends on digit at location 401.
13	FLN FLOG	Input argument has zero mantissa. May not continue execution of the subroutine.
14	FLN FLOG	Input argument is negative. May continue to execute the subroutine, computing with the absolute value of the number.

PROCEDURES FOR COMPILING FORTRAN PROGRAMS ON A 1620 CARD SYSTEM

COMPILING A FORTRAN PROGRAM

Four card decks are provided for the 1620 Fortran system: the Fortran compiler deck, the Fortran subroutine deck for computers with the automatic division special feature, a subroutine deck for computers without the automatic division feature, and a subroutine deck for computers with the floating point hardware special feature. The sequence of operations in obtaining an object program is as follows:

1. Clear core memory to zeros.
2. Depress Reset key.
3. Set the Overflow Check switch to "Program" and the I/O and Parity Check switches to "Stop."
4. Place blank cards in the punch hopper and depress the Punch Start key.
5. Place the Fortran compiler deck in the read hopper.
6. Depress the Load key. The compiler deck will be read in and the load routine will be punched.
7. When the compiler deck has been read in, the following message will be typed, and the computer will halt in the manual mode.

ENTER SOURCE PROGRAM, PUSH START

8. Set the console program switches. The functions of the program switches at compile time are as follows

> Switch 1 On—Causes the source statements and the object time address of the first compiled instruction to be listed at the console as they are processed. Statements will be listed with the object time address of the first instruction compiled from the source statement.
> Off—Source statements are not listed.
> Switch 2 On—Causes Trace instructions to be compiled. The Trace feature is discussed on page 322.
> Off—Trace instructions are not compiled.
> Switch 3 On—Input to the compiler (that is the source statements) is being entered via the console typewriter.
> Off—Source program entered from card reader.

Switch 4—This switch is used in conjunction with switch 3 if and only if switch 3 is in the "On" position. It provides the operator with the ability to restart the typing of a statement if an error has been made. Switch 4 is normally off. When a typing error is made in a source statement and is to be corrected, switch 3 is placed on, the Release and Start keys depressed, and then switch 4 turned off. The operator can now retype the statement.

9. If the source program is to be entered from cards, place the source deck in the read hopper. Depress the Reader Start key.

10. Depress the Start key on the console.

11. Two methods of source program input may be used under control of program switch 3.

(a) If the source statements are entered from the typewriter (switch 3 on), the compiler will transfer control to the console typewriter to await the first statement. Type one source statement followed by a record mark. Depress the Release and Start keys. The statement will be compiled and the machine language instructions punched. The typewriter carriage will return after each statement has been processed to await the entry of the next statement. This routine is repeated until an End statement is sensed.

(b) If the source statements are being entered from cards, each statement will be entered separately. It will be compiled and the machine language instructions punched.

12. Sensing of the End statement signals the compiler that the entry of source statements is completed. The computer halts in the manual mode and the following message will be typed:

PROG SW1 ON FOR SYMBOL TABLE, PUSH START

13. If it is desired to get a listing of the symbol table, put program switch 1 On. If the listing is not desired, turn program switch 1 off.

14. Depress the Start key on the console. If program switch 1 is on, a listing of the symbol table is typed.

15. The computer will halt in the manual mode and the following message will be typed:

SW1 OFF TO IGNORE SUBROUTINES, PUSH START

16. The operator is given a choice. He may process the subroutines at this time, or he may wait until he runs the object program to process the subroutines.

17. If it is desired to process the subroutines at this time, turn program switch 1 on. If program switch 1 is turned off depress the Start key on the console. The message in step 20 is typed and the procedure in step 21 should be followed.

18. Place the *appropriate* subroutine deck in the read hopper. Depress the Reader Start key.
19. Depress the Start key on the console. The subroutine deck will be read in and the required subroutines will be selected and punched.
20. After the required subroutines have been punched the computer will halt in the manual mode and the following message will be typed:

PROCESSING COMPLETE

21. With the Non-Process Run-Out key run the cards out of the punch feed. The object deck is in the punch stacker. Remove the last two cards as they will be blanks.

ERRORS IN THE SOURCE PROGRAM

During compilation a number of tests are made for source program errors. If an error is found in a source statement, an error message in the form "ERROR NO. n" is typed, where *n* is the error code, and processing continues. The errors detected are as follows:

ERROR No.	CONDITION
1	Incorrectly formed statement.
2	Subscripted variable for which no Dimension statement has previously appeared in the program, or a dimensioned variable is used without subscripts, or a variable used in a Dimension statement has already appeared in the source program.
3	Floating point number not in allowable range of values, or fixed point number contains more than 4 digits.
4	Symbol table full.
5	Mixed mode expression.
6	Variable name in an expression contains more than 5 characters.
7	Switch number has been omitted in an If (Sense Switch) statement or the first character following the right parenthesis in an If statement or If (Sense Switch) statement is not a digit.
8	A comma follows the statement number in a Do statement (for example, DO 1, I = 1, 10).
9	A Dimension statement ends with a comma, or more than 2 dimensions have been specified in a Dimension statement (for example DIMENSION A (10, 10, 10)).
10	A Format statement does not have a statement number.
11	Incorrect representation in a Format statement.

    (a) Used special characters (=, +, −, and so forth) in a numerical field specification.

    (b) Alphabetic characters other than E, F, or I in a numerical field specification.

    (c) A decimal point is omitted in E- or F-type numerical field specifications.

    (d) Number of positions to the right of the decimal has not been given in an E- or F-type numerical field specification.

(e) A record mark appears in the numerical field specification or an alphameric field specification.

(f) The first character following the word Format is not a left parenthesis.

12   The total record width specified in a Format statement is greater than 87 characters.

13   A Format statement number has been omitted in an I/O statement.

Another error message is typed if the compiled instructions and required data storage *not* including relocatable subroutines will, at object time, exceed the storage capacity of the 1620. This message is typed at the point in the compilation of the source program where overlap occurs. Compilation will continue, and the message will be typed after each statement thereafter.

If the inclusion of any of the relocatable subroutines causes an overlap the following message is typed as the subroutines are loading:

OVERLAP XXXXX POSITIONS

The XXXXX is the number of core storage positions of overlap between the end of the object program and the data storage area.

SEQUENCE CHECKING THE FORTRAN COMPILER AND SUBROUTINE DECKS

FORTRAN COMPILER

The cards comprising the Fortran compiler deck are punched with sequence numbers in columns 76 through 80 and the deck must be loaded in sequence. If the first card read is not card number 1, the machine will stop with an operation code of 00 displayed in the Operation Register lights. If cards 2 through 24 are not read in the proper sequence, the message "CARDNN," where NN is the number of the missing card, will be typed on the console typewriter and the computer will halt. The cards must be removed from the reader and placed in proper order. Core storage *must be cleared to zeros* before the deck is read in again starting with card 1.

Beginning with card number 25, if any card is out of sequence, the console typewriter carriage will be returned, and the following message will be typed,

CARD 0NNNN OUT OF SEQUENCE

and the computer will halt. When this occurs, the card numbered 0NNNN has been read in out of sequence. Remove the cards from the reader and put the proper card in place of the one out of sequence.

Put that part of the deck that has not yet been loaded into the read hopper, starting with the card replacing card number 0NNNN. Depress the Reader Start key, and continue reading by depressing the Start key on the 1620 console.

FORTRAN SUBROUTINES

The cards in the subroutine deck have a sequence number punched in columns 76 through 80, and they must be loaded in sequential order, If cards numbered from 1 through 8 are not read in proper sequence, the computer will halt with an invalid operation code displayed in the Operation Register lights. If this occurs, remove the cards from the reader, place them in proper sequence, and replace the deck in the read hopper. Depress the Reset key and then the Load key.

Any other card out of sequence will cause the message.

CARD OUT OF SEQUENCE

to be typed on the console typewriter, and the computer will halt. The card which has been read out of sequence is the second card from the back in the read stacker. All preceding cards have been loaded properly. Remove from the reader the cards that have not been loaded, put them into the correct sequence, and replace the deck in the read hopper. To continue reading the subroutine deck, depress Reader Start and Start keys.

Note: Once a source program has been debugged and compiled it is necessary to load the object deck only to run the program at some future date. The process of compilation *does not have to be repeated.*

FORTRAN TRACE FEATURE

The Fortran processor will, under console switch control (console switch 2 on), compile certain instructions into the object program that will enable the operator to trace the flow of the program and check its correctness. When the object program is executed, console switch 4 performs the following functions:

> Switch 4 On—Causes compiled trace instructions to be executed.
> Off—Trace instructions are not executed.

The trace output provided is the evaluated left-hand side of each executed *arithmetic* statement, typed at the left margin. Normal output, resulting from Punch, Print, and Type statements is not inhibited. The output format of the trace data is E14.8 for floating point data or $I(w-1)$ where w is the specified width.

Note that console switch 4 serves a dual function during execution of the object program, that is, provision of trace data and correction of input data incorrectly entered at the console keyboard. Thus when running in the trace mode, the operator should turn off CS4 before typing input data. Following the entry of the last datum on the list, he should (after depressing the Record Mark and Release keys) depress SIE two or three times, turn the switch on, and depress the Start key.

RUNNING THE OBJECT PROGRAM

The object deck contains a load routine, all the constants and instructions, the arithmetic tables, and the required subroutines if they were processed at compile time. The object program is run in the following manner:

1. (a) After the message in step 20 (see page 320) of the compiling procedure has been typed, remove the object deck from the punch stacker. (Remember to Non-Process Run-Out the last card) and place the deck in the read hopper. Depress the Reader Start key and the Start key on the console. The object deck will read in.
    (b) If the object program is being run at some future time after compilation the following procedure is used.
    (1) Clear core memory to zeros.
    (2) Depress the Reset key.
    (3) Set the Overflow Check switch to "Program" and the I/O and Parity Check switches to "Stop".
    (4) Place the object deck in the read hopper.
    (5) Push the Load key. The object deck will read in.
2. After the object deck has been read in, one of the following messages will be typed and the computer will halt in the manual mode.

LOAD DATA
or ENTER SUBROUTINES, PUSH START

3. The message "LOAD DATA" will type if the subroutines were processed at compile time. If this message types omit the next three steps.
4. If the message "ENTER SUBROUTINES, PUSH START" types, place the appropriate subroutine deck in the read hopper and depress the Reader Start key.
5. Depress the Start key on the console. The subroutine deck will be read in, and the required subroutines selected and stored for use by the object program.
6. After the required subroutines have been selected and stored the computer halts in the manual mode and the following message is typed:

LOAD DATA

7. If data is being entered from cards, place the data cards in the read hopper.
8. Set margins and tab stops on the typewriter as desired. This will apply only if output is to be typed. If the output is to be punched, place blank cards in the punch hopper, and push the Punch Start key.
9. Set the program switches. Program switches 1, 2, and 3 are completely at the operators disposal at object time. If the source program contained If (Sense Switch) statements, the switches are set accordingly. Program switch 4 has a dual function at object time.

Program Switch 4 On—If trace instructions were compiled (program switch 2 on at compile time), they will be executed.

Off—Compiled trace instructions are not executed. When entering data from the typewriter (through use of the Accept statement) this switch provides the ability to correct a typing error. Switch 4 is normally off.[4] If an error is made, set switch 4 on, depress the Release and Start keys, and turn switch 4 off. The data may now be retyped.

10. Depress Start key. Program execution will begin.

TYPEWRITER ENTRY OF DATA

When data is to be entered from the typewriter, the typewriter carriage returns and control is transferred to the typewriter. Enter the data according to the formal specification. Depress the Release and Start keys on the console. Processing will continue.

ERROR MESSAGES AT OBJECT TIME

A number of error checks have been built into the Fortran subroutines. The basic philosophy that has been followed with respect to an error situation is to have an error message typed out, to set the result of the operation equal to the most reasonable value under the circumstances, and to have the program continue. Listed below are the error checks that exist in the subroutines, the error codes that are typed out, and the value to which FAC is set before the program continues. In the list it will be noted that the terms Overflow and Underflow occur several times. Overflow means that the characteristic of the result has exceeded 99. Underflow means that the characteristic of the result is less than -99.

[4] If switch 4 is on to execute trace instructions, it must be turned off prior to data entry from the typewriter. After the data has been correctly entered and the Release key has been depressed, depress the Stop/SIE key three times. Switch 4 may then be turned on again and the Start key depressed.

Error Check	Error Code	Contents of FAC
Overflow in FAD or FSB.	E1	$\overline{9}9999999\overline{99}$
Underflow in FAD or FSB.	E2	$\overline{0}0000000\overline{99}$
Overflow in FMP.	E3	$\overline{9}9999999\overline{99}$
Underflow in FMP.	E4	$\overline{0}0000000\overline{99}$
Overflow in FDV or FDVR.	E5	$\overline{9}9999999\overline{99}$
Underflow in FDV or FDVR.	E6	$\overline{0}0000000\overline{99}$
Zero divisor in FDV or FDVR.	E7	$\overline{9}9999999\overline{99}$
Zero divsor in FXD or FXDR.	E8	$\overline{9}999$
Argument in FIX ≤ -10000*	E9	$\overline{9}99\overline{9}$
Argument in FIX ≥ 10000*	E9	$\overline{9}999$
Loss of all significance in FSIN or FCOS.	F1	$\overline{9}9999999\overline{99}$
Zero argument in FLN.	F2	$\overline{9}9999999\overline{99}$
Negative argument in FLN	F3	Ln $|x|$
Overflow in FEXP or FEXN.	F4	$\overline{9}9999999\overline{99}$
Underflow in FEXP or FEXN.	F5	$\overline{0}0000000\overline{99}$
Negative argument in FAXB.	F6	$|A|^B$
Negative argument in FSQR.	F6	$\sqrt{|x|}$
Input data in incorrect form or is outside the allowable range.	F7	
Output data outside allowable range or in a form not acceptable to the applicable format specification.	F8	
Input or output card record is longer than 72 characters, or typewriter record is greater than 87 characters, or there is an element in an input or output list for which there is no specification in the corresponding Format statement.	F9	

* Floating point hardware system only.

Appendix **VIII**

The Internal Organization
of Basic 1620 Fortran

The purpose of this material is to give the student a basic knowledge of the construction of the Fortran compiler.

The heart of the Fortran system lies in the proper organization of three major tables. These are:

1. The Symbol Table
2. The Table of Encountered Operations
3. The Table of Addresses of Encountered Symbols.

THE SYMBOL TABLE

The symbol table occupies core locations 19999 to 17490 at compile time. During an initialization phase a special 10-digit field is placed in the symbol table area from its beginning to location 17499. This symbol consists of 8 zeros and 2 record marks ($\overline{0}0000000\ddagger\ddagger$). A single 10-character field, consisting of 9 zeros and a single record mark, is then located at 17489. This special symbol ($\overline{0}00000000\ddagger$) signifies the end of the symbol table.

A symbol table look-up operation occurs each time a variable, constant, or statement number is encountered. If the symbol is in the table, its object time address is determined and stored. If the symbol is not discovered to be in the table, it is placed there and its object time address is also determined and stored.

In order to determine if a symbol is in the symbol table, a brute force comparison is made with every occupant of the symbol table until (1) a successful comparison is made (the symbol was placed in the table at some previous time), (2) the symbol $\overline{0}0000000‡‡$ is encountered (this is the end of the symbol table *at present* and also the first available location for storing the symbol at hand) or (3) the symbol $\overline{0}00000000‡$ is encountered (the symbol table is full). In this fashion, mere mention of a symbol defines it.

The first 12 symbols in the symbol table are special function names of relocatable subroutines supplied with the system. A listing of these follows.

LOCATION	NAME	NUMERIC FORM
19999–19990	SIN	$\overline{6}249550000$
19989–19980	SINF	$\overline{6}249554600$
19979–19970	COS	$\overline{4}356620000$
19969–19960	COSF	$\overline{4}356624600$
19959–19950	ATAN	$\overline{4}163415500$
19949–19940	ATANF	$\overline{4}163415546$
19939–19930	EXP	$\overline{4}567570000$
19929–19920	EXPF	$\overline{4}567574600$
19919–19910	LOG	$\overline{5}356470000$
19909–19900	LOGF	$\overline{5}356474600$
19899–19890	SQRT	$\overline{6}258596300$
19889–19880	SQRTF	$\overline{6}258596346$
19879–19870	.	$\overline{0}0000000‡‡$
.	.	.
.	.	.
17499–17490	.	$\overline{0}0000000‡‡$
17489–17480	.	$\overline{0}00000000‡$

In the event that a subroutine is added to the subroutine tape or card deck, its name will appear in the symbol table after the entry of SQRTF. Should the spelling of a function name be changed, the numeric form of the symbol table entry will be altered accordingly.

The address of the special function area's last entry (19889 in our case) is retained, and any subsequent successful table look-up operation, whose object time address is greater than or equal to the retained address, is assumed to be a subroutine name as opposed to a genuine symbol.

THE TABLE OF ENCOUNTERED OPERATIONS

As operation symbols are encountered during the scan of a statement, they are stored in this table. Compilation can begin before a statement has been completely scanned and depends upon the difference of rank within a hierarchy between the operation at hand and the one previously discovered.

THE TABLE OF ADDRESSES OF ENCOUNTERED SYMBOLS

The object time address of all symbols in any statement are discovered by use of the symbol table look-up operation and are stored in this table (TAES). Each entry is a 5-digit address plus certain information about the symbol at hand (fixed, floating, and so forth).

Distinction should be made concerning the compile time address of a symbol and the object time address of a symbol since they are not necessarily the same.

THE FLOATING ACCUMULATOR

A special 10-digit location has been reserved for computational purposes. This area, known as the floating accumulator (FAC), occupies positions 51–60 of core at object time. All object time floating point arithmetic and most fixed point arithmetic is done using the floating accumulator as an intermediary device.

DETERMINATION OF CATEGORY

The presence or absence of an equal sign determines whether or not any source statement is an arithmetic statement. The only exception to this rule is the Do statement. However, a Do contains an equal sign, a comma, and *no* left parenthesis. In this way it is identified as such.

Events which Precede Determination of Category:

1. Place a record mark after the first nonblank character in a scan from right to left.[1]
2. Test for comment statement.
3. Left-justify statement by forcing out all leading blanks.
4. Process statement number if existent.
5. Force out all blanks in the statement unless a Format statement.
6. Scan for an equal sign.

CATEGORIES

Category 1 will refer to all arithmetic statements. Category 2 will refer to all statements of a nonarithmetic nature.

Certain subroutines are assumed to be at fixed object time locations. These subroutines are referenced and utilized by statements of both categories. Below is a list of all nonrelocatable subroutines by name, symbolic name, and, where necessary, function. Symbolic names marked by an asterisk will call for the relocatable EXP and LOG (base *e*) sub-

---

[1] Card system only.

routines. The size of this nonrelocatable package causes object time programs to begin at location 08300.

NAME	SYMBOLIC NAME	FUNCTION
Floating Subtract	FSB	FAC − B ⟶ FAC
Floating Add	FAD	FAC + B ⟶ FAC
Floating Multiply	FMP	FAC★B ⟶ FAC
Floating Divide Reverse	FDVR	$1/(\text{FAC}/\text{B})$ ⟶ FAC
Floating Divide	FDV	FAC/B ⟶ FAC
Floating A^{-B}	FAXBN°	$1/e^{(B \star \text{LOG}(A))}$ ⟶ FAC
Floating A^{B}	FAXB°	$e^{(B \star \text{LOG}(A))}$ ⟶ FAC
Floating A^{-I}	FAXIN	$1/(A \star A \star A \star \ldots \star)$ ⟶ FAC
Floating A^{I}	FAXI	$A \star A \star A \star \ldots \star A$ ⟶ FAC
Fixed Subtract	FXS	FAC − J ⟶ FAC
Fixed Add	FXA	FAC + J ⟶ FAC
Fixed Multiply	FXM	FAC★J ⟶ FAC
Fixed Divide Reverse	FXDR	$1/(\text{FAC}/\text{J})$ ⟶ FAC
Fixed Divide	FXD	FAC/J ⟶ FAC
Change Sign	RSGN	−FAC ⟶ FAC
Bring to Accumulator	TOFAC	B ⟶ FAC
Take from Accumulator	FRMFAC	FAC ⟶ B
Fix a Floating Number	FIX	B ⟶ J
Float a Fixed Number	FLOAT	J ⟶ B
Read Card	RACD	
Read Tape	RAPT	
Read Typewriter	RATY	
Write Card	WACD	
Write Tape	WAPT	
Write Typewriter	WATY	
Input/Output	I/O	

Category 1 Statements

The logic of scanning arithmetic statements is similar to a method employed by the Polish Logician J. Lukasiewicz. This method, sometimes termed "Polish Notation" consists of separating an algebraic statement into two stacks. One of these consists of operations and the other consists of operands. Thus, the statement A − B is written as AB−. The statement A + B★C may be written as AB + C★ or ABC + ★.

The Fortran scan builds up two tables, the combination of which simulates this notation.

These tables, described previously as the Table of Addresses of Encountered Symbols (TAES) and the Table of Encountered Operands (TEO), rely upon an order of rank in a hierarchy in arithmetic operations. Both tables may be likened to an accordion: initially closed, expanding, contracting, expanding, contracting, and finally closed. As the statement is scanned, these tables expand. But certain conditions can cause them to expel information and contract before further expansion. The expelled information becomes the compiled instructions.

Compilation of arithmetic statements relies upon the following rank in the hierarchy of operations:

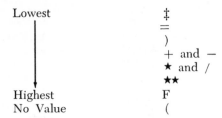

Lowest   ‡
         =
)
         + and −
         ★ and /
         ★★

Highest   F
No Value   (

The ‡ and F are not part of the programmer's repertoire of Fortran instructions and are internally generated. The record mark is generated to end a statement in the card system and appears there automatically in the tape system. The F is entered as an operation whenever an instruction requests a relocatable subroutine linkage (Sine, Cosine, and so forth).

The left parenthesis has no hierarchal value and may be considered neutral. The function of a left parenthesis is to act as a mate for the right parenthesis.

During the scan, each operation that is encountered causes investigation of the operation previously encountered. If the present operation *is of lower or equal hierarchal rank to the previous operation,* compilation begins immediately.

Thus, the statement

$$Y = A + B \star C$$

requires complete dissection before compilation is forced (by the record mark) since the operations are encountered in the following order:

       1.   =
       2.   +
       3.   ★

The statement

$$Y = A \star B + C$$

will begin compilation when the + is encountered because the operation previous to + is ★ which is of greater hierarchal rank. Note also that the statement

$$Y = A \star B + I$$

which is illegal (mixed mode), will not be noted as such until after the compilation of A★B.

Also during the scan, the symbols have their object time addresses determined by the symbol table look-up scheme. These addresses are stored in TAES. Likewise, each operation is either (1) put in TEO, (2) forces compilations and is *then* put in TEO, or (3) forces compilation and is neutralized as in the case of the right parenthesis. Often, an operation may force compilation many times before being allowed entrance into TEO, as we shall soon see. The ‡, having lowest hierarchal value, acts as a universal forcer and causes everything to be expelled from the tables into compiled form. Thus, the entry of the ‡ into TEO signals the end of compilation for a statement.

Example: X = A + B

TAES	TEO
X	=
A	+
B	

The scan routine had set up the above two tables just before the record mark was encountered. The presence of the record mark, having hierarchal rank lower than +, causes compilation.

The last element in TEO is + which requires two operands and these are chosen to be the last two entries in TAES.

The + generates two model statements which would suffice for the addition of any two floating point numbers. These statements, with addresses yet to be supplied are as follows:

```
BTM   TOFAC, _____
BTM   FAD, _____
```

These missing addresses are supplied by TAES. This generates a complete model for the addition of the floating point numbers A and B.

```
BTM   TOFAC, A
BTM   FAD, B
```

The FAD routine assumes that one argument is in FAC and that the *address* of the other has been given to it.

These two instructions, being complete, are expelled from the system and our tables are reduced to the following:

TAES	TEO
X	=
TEMP1	

The TEMP1 entry in TAES denotes two very critical items both of which seem utterly unnecessary at first glance.

1. TEMP1 is the location of a temporary storage location should it be needed during further portions of the compilation.
2. Since this temporary location is not in use (a code digit is missing in a specific location), there *must* be a previous result in FAC.

A temporary location *in use* will be denoted by underlining it in TAES. In general, an operation that causes compilation does four things:

1. Certain model statements are generated.
2. The missing operands of these model statements are filled in using addresses (always the last two) of TAES.
3. The operation and associated operands are removed from TEO and TAES permanently.
4. A notation is made in TAES which signifies that something has just been compiled and the result, at object time, will have been left in FAC.

Thus, the compiler, upon further compilation, does not know what has been done. It is only informed that *something* was done and the result has been left in FAC.

In the example, sufficient coding has been generated to handle A + B, but coding must be generated to transfer this result to X.

The record mark continues to force compilation of the program. The next element found in TEO is =, and the model statements generated are

```
          BTM   TOFAC, _____
          BTM   FRMFAC, _____
```

The required addresses are found in TAES and this yields

```
          BTM   TOFAC, TEMP1
          BTM   FRMFAC, X
```

However, since coding information in TAES tells the compiler that TEMP1 is not in use, the first statement is determined to be unnecessary and is eliminated. This yields a complete compilation of X = A + B.

```
          BTM   TOFAC, A
          BTM   FAD, B
          BTM   FRMFAC, X
```

In the same fashion,

```
     X = A − B  yields:
          BTM   TOFAC, A
          BTM   FSB, B
          BTM   FRMFAC, X

     X = A★B  yields:
          BTM   TOFAC, A
          BTM   FMP, B
          BTM   FRMFAC, X
```

X = A★★B yields:
```
BTM   TOFAC, A
BTM   FAXB, B
BTM   FRMFAC, X
```

X = A yields:
```
BTM   TOFAC, A
BTM   FRMFAC, X
```

X = −A yields:
```
BTM   TOFAC, A
BTM   RSGN
BTM   FRMFAC, X
```

I = J − K yields:
```
BTM   TOFAC, J
BTM   FXS, K
BTM   FRMFAC, I
```

I = A − B yields:
```
BTM   TOFAC, A
BTM   FSB, B
BTM   FIX
BTM   FRMFAC, I
```

Since numbers go into the symbol table just as genuine symbols do, the statement

X = 2.★.0056 yields:
```
BTM   TOFAC, 2.
BTM   FMP, .0056
BTM   FRMFAC, X
```

where the symbols 2. and .0056 represent the locations in the symbol table. At those locations, the numbers are stored as

$$\bar{2}00000000\bar{1}$$

and

$$\bar{5}600000000\bar{2}$$

Example: X = A + B★C/D

Up to the point where the ★ is encountered, the tables have been developed to the following point:

TAES	TEO
X	=
A	+
B	

When the ★ is encountered, compilation is not forced because of the hierarchal relationship between ★ and +. Thus, the tables become as follows:

TAES	TEO
X	=
A	+
B	★
C	

As the / is encountered, compilation is forced since / and ★ are of equal rank within the hierarchy. The compiled instructions are then as follows:

        BTM   TOFAC, B
        BTM   FMP, C

Our tables are reduced to:

TAES	TEO
X	=
A	+
TEMP1	

The / is now added to TEO and D is placed in TAES.

TAES	TEO
X	=
A	+
TEMP1	/
D	

The record mark (not shown) generates the remainder of the coding:

        BTM   TOFAC, TEMP1
        BTM   FDV, D

The first instruction is seen to be unnecessary by the same logic as before. This yields:

        BTM   FDV, D

This leaves the tables as follows:

TAES	TEO
X	=
A	+
TEMP1	

The following is now compiled:

        BTM   TOFAC, A
        BTM   FAD, TEMP1

Now, TEMP1, not being in use, causes a *composite* of these instructions to be generated:

        BTM   FAD, A

Our tables are further reduced.

TAES	TEO
X	=
TEMP1	

The last instructions to be generated are

```
BTM   TOFAC, TEMP1
BTM   FRMFAC, X
```

Only the second instruction is chosen and the compilation is complete.

```
BTM   TOFAC, B
BTM   FMP, C
BTM   FDV, D
BTM   FAD, A
BTM   FRMFAC, X
```

These Fortran generated instructions are equivalent to the following algebraic statement:

$$X = A + \frac{(B)(C)}{D}$$

The Fortran processor must make the assumption that at some point in the object program, the symbols A, B, C, and D will be properly defined *before* the Fortran generated coding for the statement X = A + B★C/D is encountered.

For all further examples, whenever two instructions are generated and only one is chosen, we will show only the chosen one.

Example: X = A★B + C★★D/E

The construction of the tables up to the point where the + is encountered is as follows:

TAES	TEO
X	=
A	★
B	

The + generates compilation of

```
BTM   TOFAC, A
BTM   FMP, B
```

TAES	TEO
X	=
TEMP1	

The + is now entered into TEO and C is placed in TAES.

TAES	TEO
X	=
TEMP1	+
C	

The ★★ is now encountered and placed in TEO as D is placed in TAES.

TAES	TEO
X	=
TEMP1	+
C	★★
D	

If two addresses are placed in TAES after any temporary location, *it is automatically called into use.* Since there is only one FAC, the reader will readily see that this is a necessary and sufficient condition for this action. This generates the following:

BTM   FRMFAC, TEMP1

This changes the tables to the following:

TAES	TEO
X	=
TEMP1	+
C	★★
D	

The / is encountered which generates the ★★ coding.

BTM   TOFAC, C
BTM   FAXB, D

TAES	TEO
X	=
TEMP1	+
TEMP2	

Now / may enter TEO and E may enter TAES.

TAES	TEO
X	=
TEMP1	+
TEMP2	/
E	

The record mark generates the remainder of the coding.

BTM   FDV, E

TAES	TEO
X	=
TEMP1	+
TEMP2	

BTM   FAD, TEMP1

TAES	TEO
X	=
TEMP2	

BTM   FRMFAC, X

The complete coding thus generated is:

```
BTM   TOFAC, A
BTM   FMP, B
BTM   FRMFAC, TEMP1
BTM   TOFAC, C
BTM   FAXB, D
BTM   FDV, E
BTM   FAD, TEMP1
BTM   FRMFAC, X
```

The algebraic equivalent to this statement is

$$X = \frac{C^D}{E} + (A)(B)$$

Example: The following statement is presented algebraically so that the Fortran statement can be made more meaningful.

$$X = \frac{A+B}{(C)(D)} - E(F+G)$$

$$X = ((A + B)/(C \star D)) - (E \star (F + G))^*$$

The scan proceeds until the tables appear as follows:

TAES	TEO
X	=
A	(
B	(
	+

The right parenthesis forces coding and cancels one left parenthesis.

```
BTM   TOFAC, A
BTM   FAD, B
```

This reduces the tables.

TAES	TEO
X	=
TEMP1	(

Further scanning increases the tables.

TAES	TEO
X	=
TEMP1	(
C	/
D	(
	★

---

* The extra parenthesis are in the statement for demonstration purposes.

The second operand in TAES after TEMP1 forces coding.

BTM   FRMFAC, TEMP1

TAES	TEO
X	=
TEMP1	(
C	/
D	(
	★

The encountered right parenthesis forces coding and cancels one left parenthesis.

BTM   TOFAC, C
BTM   FMP, D

The tables are reduced.

TAES	TEO
X	=
TEMP1	(
TEMP2	/

A second right parenthesis is encountered and continues to force coding.

BTM   FDVR, TEMP1

The tables are reduced.

TAES	TEO
X	=
TEMP2	

Further scanning increases the tables.

TAES	TEO
X	=
TEMP2	—
E	(
F	★
	(

The second operand in TAES after TEMP2 forces coding.

BTM   FRMFAC, TEMP2

TAES	TEO
X	=
TEMP2	—
E	(
F	★
	(

Further scanning increases the tables.

TAES	TEO
X	=
TEMP2	—
E	(
F	★
G	(
	+

The encountered right parenthesis forces coding.

```
BTM   TOFAC, F
BTM   FAD, G
```

The tables are reduced.

TAES	TEO
X	=
TEMP2	—
E	(
TEMP3	★

A second right parenthesis continues to force coding.

```
BTM   FMP, E
```

The tables are reduced.

TAES	TEO
X	=
TEMP2	—
TEMP3	

The record mark forces the remainder of the coding.

```
BTM   FSB, TEMP2
BTM   RSGN
BTM   FRMFAC, X
```

Thus, the entire compilation yields:

```
BTM   TOFAC, A
BTM   FAD, B
BTM   FRMFAC, TEMP1
BTM   TOFAC, C
BTM   FMP, D
BTM   FDVR, TEMP1
BTM   FRMFAC, TEMP2
BTM   TOFAC, F
BTM   FAD, G
BTM   FMP, E
BTM   FSB, TEMP2
BTM   RSGN
BTM   FRMFAC, X
```

INCLUSION OF RELOCATABLE SUBROUTINES

Whenever a subroutine name is encountered, the address placed in TAES is the address, less 9, where the function name *sans* terminal F is stored. Even should the programmer use the terminal F form of the subroutine name, the address is still as described above. Thus, SQRT or SQRTF generates an address of 19890 in TAES. ATAN or ATANF generates an address of 19950 in TAES, and so forth.

In addition, the operation F is stored in TEO. The programmer has no control over the F operation since it is internally generated.

During compilation, a linkage is made to the address contained in TAES. At object time, a second link, located in that portion of the symbol table which originally contained the function name, will carry us to the subroutine's actual location in core storage.

This location must be determined in the following fashion: at the end of compilation, the last location used by the object program is known through the location counter's value. Thus, if a Fortran program ends at location 12000, and relocatable subroutines have been called for, they are added, one at a time, beginning at location 12002.

Since a subroutine's length is part of the information contained in the subroutine, the last location occupied by a specific subroutine of the relocatable type can be determined. Similarly, the first location needed for the next relocatable subroutine is determined.

These *first* locations are used as the second, unconditional linkage point in the symbol table.

The address of the argument is stored, by use of a BTM command, where the function name with terminal F was stored at compile time.

Example: X = SQRT(B)

TAES	TEO
X	=
19890	F
B	(

The right parenthesis cancels the left parenthesis and the record mark generates all coding.

```
BTM    19890, B
BTM    FRMFAC, X
```

Example: X = A★SIN(B)

TAES	TEO
X	=
A	★
19990	F
B	(

The right parenthesis cancels the left parenthesis and the record mark generates all coding.

```
BTM    19990, B
BTM    FMP, A
BTM    FRMFAC, X
```

Example: $X = A + B \star SQRT(C + ATANF(LOG(D \star E) + SIN(P)))$

The following coding is generated and we leave the verification to the interested student.

```
BTM    TOFAC, D
BTM    FMP, E
BTM    19910, FAC
BTM    FRMFAC, TEMP1
BTM    19990, P
BTM    FAD, TEMP1
BTM    19950, FAC
BTM    FAD, C
BTM    19890, FAC
BTM    FMP, B
BTM    FAD, A
BTM    FRMFAC, X
```

SPECIAL NOTE ON THE SCAN

The logic employed here is sufficient even for statements of the form:

```
X = − (− A − B)
BTM    TOFAC, A
BTM    RSGN
BTM    FSB, B
BTM    RSGN
BTM    FRMFAC, X
```

However, the 1620 Fortran compiler is able to reduce this statement to its algebraic equivalent *before* compilation. This yields

```
X = A + B
BTM    TOFAC, A
BTM    FAD, B
BTM    FRMFAC, X
```

This latter coding is much more desirable because of its brevity, and this is exactly what is produced by 1620 Fortran.

In this way, a Fortran user may, from time to time, note discrepancies between the true object program he receives and the object program he expects to receive. This is due to the unary minus $(-(-A))$ and the exception given to this case in the algebraic decoding at compile time. It is this excellent feature which allows for identical compilations of such statements as

$$X = A \star B$$
$$X = (-A) \star (-B)$$
$$X = -A \star (-B)$$
$$X = -(A \star (-B))$$

```
BTM   TOFAC, A
BTM   FMP, B
BTM   FRMFAC, X
```

Category 2 Statements

I. DIMENSION

A. Single Dimensioning:

DIMENSION A(10), B(17)

The symbol for which dimensioning has been requested is placed in the symbol table at the first available location. This is most likely the first statement encountered in a source program and hence will fall immediately following the last function name entry.[2] Immediately below the symbol there are two code fields contained in *one word*.[3] The first field is five digits long and is the address of the last element in the array at object time. The second field is contiguous to the first and is a 4-digit number representing the amount of I index requested in the Dimension statement.

The above example

DIMENSION A(10), B(17)

will yield the following symbol table entries assuming that they are encountered as the first statements of a source program.

Entries	Locations
$\bar{4}$100000000	19879
0$\bar{0}$010$\bar{1}$9789	19869
$\bar{4}$200000000	19859
0$\bar{0}$017$\bar{1}$9619	19849

B. Double Dimensioning:

DIMENSION A(10, 15), BBAA(2, 7)

The symbol table entries for the double Dimension are identical with the single Dimension entries.

---

[2] It is not mandatory to have the Dimension statements as the first statement in a source program in the 1620 Fortran system.

[3] In this discussion, a word is considered to be a 10-digit symbol table entry.

The above example

DIMENSION A(10, 15), BBAA(2, 7)
will yield the following symbol table entries assuming that they
are encountered as the first statements of a source program.

ENTRIES	LOCATIONS
$\overline{4}$100000000	19879
$\overline{00}$0101$\overline{8}$389	19869
$\overline{4}$242414100	19859
$\overline{00}$0002$\overline{1}$8249	19849

The digits in locations 19860 and 19840 of both examples have no
significance. They are left-over elements. This is always true of
the high-order digit of the second word required by single or double
dimensioning.

II. GO TO n:

The Fortran location counter (called "L") is an increasing counter
which states where the Fortran statements will fall at object time. Its
initial address is 08300. If a Fortran statement generates two 12-digit
instructions, the L counter is increased by 24 and will read 08324 as the
next Fortran statement begins compilation.

The assembly of Go To statements is highly dependent upon this
counter but is totally independent of the order of encounter. Thus, the

GO TO n

may precede or follow the statement numbered n. For clarity, however,
let us first consider the case where the Go To has preceded the numbered
statement.

A symbol table look-up operation is performed on n and n is stored as a
fixed point, 4-digit number. Let us call this symbol table location Y. Thus,
n is stored at locations Y through Y–3, inclusive.

At some later point in the processing a statement with statement number n is encountered. Again a symbol table operation is performed on
the 4-digit, fixed point number n but, this time it is found to have been
stored previously at location Y. When this occurs, a 5-digit field representing the present value of the L counter is stored in the same word but
at locations Y–5 through Y–9.

Also, when the Go To statement was encountered initially, the following
statement was generated:

B   Y–9

344   The Internal Organization of Basic 1620 Fortran

At load time of the object program the field at Y–5 through Y–9 is shifted right two positions and a Branch operation code (49) is inserted at location Y–9 and Y–8. The original digits at Y–4 and Y–3 have been lost.

Thus, we have developed two successive Branch instructions. The first (B Y–9) carries us to a symbol table area where another branch takes us to the first instruction of that statement which bore statement number n. The Branch instruction generated by the Go To is only 7 digits long. Since the 1620 allows instructions to begin only at even locations, the L counter is increased by eight for every Branch instruction generated by Fortran.

Example:

1 GO TO 2
2 GO TO 1

The first available symbol table location is immediately after SQRTF. Thus, the statement number of the first statement is located in the symbol table thus:

SQRTF   19889

$\overline{0}830000\overline{0}01$ 19879

Thus, the instruction 4919860 is generated by GO TO 2. The L counter is increased by eight and the next statement is read in.

The GO TO 2 statement places the number "2" in the symbol table and generates a branch to that location minus nine.

SQRTF   19889

$\overline{0}830000\overline{0}01$ 19879

$\overline{0}000000\overline{0}02$ 19869

Thus, statement 4919860 is generated by GO TO 2. The L counter is increased by eight and the next statement is read in.

Statement 2 GO TO 1 is compiled as 4919870 and the symbol table appears as follows:

SQRTF   19889

$\overline{0}830000\overline{0}01$ 19879

$\overline{0}830800\overline{0}02$ 19869

The two generated instructions are 4919860 and 4919870.

At load time, the symbol table is altered to read (in part)

SQRTF   19889

$490\overline{8}300001$ 19979

$490\overline{8}308002$ 19969

The combination of these four branches results in the following:

08300	49	19860
19860	49	08308
08308	49	19870
19870	49	08300

III. PAUSE

The Compiler generates a Halt instruction:

48 XXXXX XXXXX

Depressing the Start key allows the program to continue.

IV. STOP

The following four instructions are generated:

```
RCTY
WATY "STOP"
H
B        ★–36
```

Depressing the Start key causes the above sequence to be repeated. **Note that "Stop" generates 44 digits as opposed to "Pause" which generates 12 digits.**

V.   IF (SENSE SWITCH i) n_1, n_2

The compiler generates two instructions.

```
BCi      STLOCn₁
B        STLOCn₂
```

where $STLOCn_j$ is the symbol table location (less nine) corresponding to the symbol table look-up on the statement numbers n_1 and n_2. A second branch is placed there in a fashion identical with that of GO TO n instructions.

VI.   IF(A) n_1, n_2, n_3

The compiler generates the following instructions:

```
BTM  TOFAC, A
BD   ★ + 20, 51
B    STLOCn₂
DORG★–3
BNF  STLOCn₃, 58
B    STLOCn₁
```

VII.   IF(I) n_1, n_2, n_3

The compiler generates the following instructions:

```
BTM    TOFAC, I
CM     FAC, 0, 8
BE     STLOCn₂
BH     STLOCn₃
B      STLOCn₁
```

VIII.   IF(EXPRESSION) n_1, n_2, n_3

The expression is evaluated and left in FAC. The rules for evaluation of an arithmetic statement have been discussed under Category 1 statements. With the argument in FAC, the instructions generated are identical with those of IF(A) or IF(I) depending upon the nature of the expression.

IX.   COMPUTED GO TO

GO TO $(n_1, n_2, \ldots, n_j)$, N

Each element in the array is treated in a fashion similar to an unconditional GO TO n. That is, an entry is made in the symbol table for each distinct statement number n_i and also for the fixed point variable N $(N = 1, j)$.

Thus, if N is 1, a branch is generated to the first symbol table entry, n_1. If N is i, a branch is generated to the i-th symbol table entry, n_i. If N is N_{max}, a branch is generated to the j-th symbol table entry, n_j. The symbol table locations which are the intermediary stopping points for these branches will have their secondary addresses filled in as the numbered statements are encountered.

A tabular array of these symbol table locations are contained in the object program but not as 5-digit addresses. The units digit of the 5-digit address is removed since all branches to the symbol table have a zero in the P_6 position.

If the i-th way branch is to be taken $(N = i)$, the i-th 4-digit set is placed in a Branch instruction of the form 49XXXX0.

Example: GO TO (1, 12, 3, 4), N

STATEMENT NUMBER	SYMBOL TABLE ENTRY
1	19859
12	19849
3	19839
4	19829

SYMBOL	SYMBOL TABLE ENTRY
N	19819

The compiled instructions are always of the following form:

```
MM      N, − 4, 10
SF      95
AM      99, ★ + 4★ N_max + 47
TF      ★ + 23, 99
TF      ★ + 17
B       XXXX0
DORG    ★ − 3
DC      4, XXXX (symbol table loc n_j)
DC      4, XXXX (symbol table loc n_{j − 1})
.
.
.
DC      4, XXXX (symbol table loc n_1)
```

Let $N = 2$ for purposes of the example.

LOCATION	COMPILED INSTRUCTIONS	
08300	MM	N, −4, 10
08312	SF	95
08324	AM	99, 8387
08336	TF	8359, 99
08348	TF	8365
08360	B	XXXX0
08368	DORG	★ − 3
08371	DC	4, 1982
08375	DC	4, 1983
08379	DC	4, 1984
08383	DC	4, 1985

Instructions 1, 2, and 3 above yield an address of 08379 in locations 95–99. Note also that location 08379 contains the first digit of the field $\overline{1}984$ which are the first four digits of the symbol table location for the statement number 12. This composite, with the aid of the two TF instructions at 8336 and 8348 produces 4919840 at location 8360. At location 19840, at object time, a second branch will then take the program to the instruction generated by that statement which bore statement number 12 at compile time.

X.   DO STATEMENTS (DO n I = J, K, L)

The following statements are generated by a Do:

```
LOC   TF(M)   I, J(, 8)        Beginning of DO
      A(M)    I, L(, 8) ⎫
      C(M)    I, K(, 8) ⎬     Outer Range
      BNH     LOC + 12  ⎭
```

The material in parenthesis refers to the use of Immediate instructions which are employed if the indices of the Do statement are fixed point constants as opposed to fixed point variables. If the L index is not specified, the first statement of the outer range is

$$\text{AM} \qquad \text{I, 1, 8}$$

Note that the outer range of the Do statement is generated immediately and *later* located at that point in the object program immediately following the instructions compiled for the statement with statement number n.

XI. CONTINUE

If a Continue statement is not associated with a Do statement, it generates nothing. If it is associated with a Do statement, it is equivalent to attaching its statement number to the instructions generated for the outer range of the Do statement. This is to circumvent the rule concerning Fortran DO-loops not ending in a branch:

$$\text{DO 1 I} = 1,100$$
.
.
.
$$\text{IF (A) 1, 2, 2}$$
$$\text{1 CONTINUE}$$
$$\text{2 . . . .}$$
.
.
.
$$\text{GO TO 1}$$
.
.
.

XII. INPUT/OUTPUT and FORMAT

Examination of the I/O statement leads one to suspect that the coding generated by any I/O must be able to find a path to the coding generated by the associated Format statement independent of the physical relationship between them. Thus, the statements

$$\text{READ1, A, B, I}$$
.
.
$$\text{1 FORMAT (F10.5, E7.4, I3)}$$

must operate at object time in a fashion identical with

$$\text{1 FORMAT (F10.5, E7.4, I3)}$$
.
.
$$\text{READ1, A, B, I}$$

and the order of encounter of these "mated" statements must be of no significance.

Format generates certain coding in the object program at that point where the Format statement is encountered. Thus, the associated I/O statement must find this information in the object program at the object level.

Consider as a first case, the I/O statement encountered before the associated Format statement.

All I/O statements use two symbol table words. If the I/O statement is encountered first, the setup in the symbol table is as follows:

$$\overline{0}0000\overline{Q}\overline{Z}ZZZ \qquad Y$$
$$\overline{0}0000\overline{Q}\overline{Z}ZZZ \qquad Y + 10$$

where Q is a code identifying an I/O-Format entry in the symbol table and ZZZZ is the statement number referencing the Format statement.

As the associated FORMAT statement is encountered, the symbol Y has more information added to it. *After* the associated FORMAT statement is compiled, the symbol Y + 10 will have more information added to it. Thus, the symbols are altered to appear as follows:

$$\overline{X}XXXX\overline{Q}\overline{Z}ZZZ \qquad Y$$
$$\overline{Y}YYYY\overline{Q}\overline{Z}ZZZ \qquad Y + 10$$

where XXXX is essentially the L counter value at the time the Format statement is encountered and YYYYY is the first *even* location in core after the material generated by the Format statement.

A third and final change is made to these symbols at the object level so that their final appearance is in the following form:

$$49\overline{X}XXXXZZZ \qquad Y$$
$$49\overline{Y}YYYYZZZ \qquad Y + 10$$

The I/O statement itself generates $N + 1$ instructions where N is the number of elements in the I/O list. The middle $N - 1$ instructions are of the form

$$\begin{aligned}
&\text{BTM} \quad \text{I/O, } A_1 \\
&\text{BTM} \quad \text{I/O, } A_2 \\
&\text{BTM} \quad \text{I/O, } A_3 \\
&\qquad\qquad \cdot \\
&\qquad\qquad \cdot \\
&\qquad\qquad \cdot \\
&\text{BTM} \quad \text{I/O, } A_{n-1}
\end{aligned}$$

The $N + 1$st instruction is of the form

$$\text{BTM} \quad \text{FINISH, } A_n$$

and the first instruction depends upon which I/O device is requested. However, it is of the general form

$$\text{BT} \quad \text{SUB, } Y - 3$$

where SUB is a specific subroutine such as RAPT WACD, etc. and $Y - 3$ is the object time address of that symbol table area where the address of the Format information may be found.

Thus, READ 1, A, B, I will generate the following:

```
BT    RACD, LOC1 − 3    (location of
BTM   I/O, A             the statement
BTM   I/O, B             number 0001 less
BTM   FINISH, I          three)
```

The statement TYPE 5, A, B, C, D, E generates the following:

```
BT    WATY, LOC5 − 3
BTM   I/O, A
BTM   I/O, B
BTM   I/O, C
BTM   I/O, D
BTM   FINISH, E
```

The only exception to the above rule is in the statement

READ 1

or another of that nature. In that case, a notation is made that no elements are in the list signifying Hollerith input or output.

When the Format statement is encountered the compiler generates one instruction and P pieces of information where P is dependent upon the Format specification.

The first information generated is an instruction of the form $B\ Y + 1$. At object time, $Y + 1$ contains a second branch which carries us around the Format coding.

The remainder of the information consists of a 5-digit code specifying the type of Format [E, F, I, / ,), (, H, X], and, if the Format is Hollerith, the actual double-digit representation of the Hollerith information.

If the FORMAT information is of the E, F, or I type, the 5-digit code is of the form

Xwwdd

where ww is the width of the field, dd is the number of decimal places after the decimal, and X is a code digit specifying E, F, or I type conversion (5, 6, and 9 respectively).

If the format information is of the Hollerith or X type, the five digit code is of the form

HHHHH

and contiguous to the code, the size of the Hollerith Field and the double-digit representation of the Hollerith information.

The 5-digit code for a left and right parenthesis will be noted as LLLLL and RRRRR respectively. Slash will be noted as SSSSS.

Thus the following material will be generated by the statement

$$5 \ \text{FORMAT} \ (4\text{HAb} = \text{bE14.8, 6HbbBb} = \text{b/F10.2})$$

B STLOC5 + 1
LLLLL
HHHHH$\overline{0}$441$\overline{0}$0$\overline{3}$3$\overline{0}$0
$\overline{5}$140$\overline{8}$
HHHHH$\overline{0}$6$\overline{0}$0004$\overline{2}$0$\overline{0}$3$\overline{3}$00
SSSSS
$\overline{6}$100$\overline{2}$
RRRRR

B STLOC5 + 1 will carry us around this Format information when it is encountered during the sequential operation of the object program.

As a further example, consider the Format statement

$$3 \ \text{FORMAT} \ (\text{I3, 10X///F7.2, 13HTHEbANSWERbIS})$$

The information generated is as follows:

B STLOC3 + 1
LLLLL
$\overline{9}$030$\overline{0}$
HHHHH$\overline{1}$0$\overline{0}$0$\overline{0}$0$\overline{0}$0$\overline{0}$0$\overline{0}$0$\overline{0}$0$\overline{0}$0$\overline{0}$0$\overline{0}$0$\overline{0}$0$\overline{0}$0
SSSSS
SSSSS
SSSSS
$\overline{6}$070$\overline{2}$
HHHHH$\overline{1}$3$\overline{6}$3$\overline{4}$8$\overline{4}$5$\overline{0}$0$\overline{4}$1$\overline{5}$5$\overline{6}$2$\overline{6}$6$\overline{4}$5$\overline{5}$7$\overline{0}$0$\overline{4}$9$\overline{5}$5

In the event that a Format statement is encountered before the corresponding I/O statement, the only difference that will occur in the construction of the output information is the setup of the symbol table words Y and Y + 10. These words will have been completely formed before the I/O statement is encountered. If the I/O statement is encountered first, symbol table words Y and Y + 10 are only partially complete when the Format is encountered and are completed therein.

Problems

For the following examples, give the proper Fortran statement needed to produce the correct algebraic result and show the coding generated by the compiler.

1. $X = A + B - C - (D)(E)$

2. $X = \sqrt{A^2 - C\,(D - E)}$

3. $X = A + B$
    $$\cfrac{}{C + D \cfrac{}{E + F \cfrac{}{G + H}}}$$

4. $Z = \mathrm{LOG}\,\sqrt{(E - F)^2}$

5. $X = \dfrac{A + B}{C - D} \quad \dfrac{(E)(F)}{G \div H}$

6. $\mathrm{ALFA} = \mathrm{BETA} + \mathrm{GAMMA} + \mathrm{RHO} - \mathrm{CHI}$

7. $\phi = a^2 + \beta^2 - 10$

8. $A = 150(\mathrm{LOG}(\mathrm{SIN}(\mathrm{COS}(A))))^{.3}$

9. $Z = \mathrm{TAN}^{-1}(G) - A - B - C - D - E - F \div G$

Given the following Fortran object programs, construct the Fortran source programs which generated the coding.

1. BTM TOFAC, A
    BTM FRMFAC, X

2. BTM TOFAC, A
    BTM RSGN
    BTM FRMFAC, X

3. BTM TOFAC, A
    BTM FAXI, I
    BTM FAD, B
    BTM FRMFAC, X

4. BTM FAC, A
    BTM FAD, B
    BTM FRMFAC, TEMP1
    BTM TOFAC, C
    BTM FAD, D
    BTM FMP, TEMP1
    BTM FRMFAC, TEMP2
    BTM TOFAC, E
    BTM FAD, F
    BTM FMP, TEMP2
    BTM FRMFAC, TEMP3
    BTM TOFAC, G
    BTM FAD, H
    BTM FMP, TEMP3
    BTM FRMFAC, X

5. 8300	TFM	I, 1, 8
8312	BT	RACD, STLOC2 − 3
8324	BTM	I/O, A
8336	BTM	FINISH, B
8348	BTM	TOFAC, A
8360	BTM	FAD, B
8372	BTM	FRMFAC, X
8384	BT	WACD, STLOC3 − 3
8396	BTM	FINISH, X
8408	AM	I, 1, 8
8420	CM	I, 100, 8
8432	BNH	8312
8444	H	
8456	B	STLOC2 + 1
	LLLLL	
	6̄0502̄	
	6̄0401̄	
	RRRRR	
8484	B	STLOC3 + 1
	LLLLL	
	HHHHH Ī0̄6̄7̄0̄0̄3̄3̄0̄0̄0̄0̄0̄0̄0̄0̄0̄0̄0̄0̄0̄0̄	
	6̄0502̄	
	RRRRR	

Glossary

Absolute Address—An instruction address in which five or fewer numeric digits are used to specify an actual 1620 core storage location. Also called actual address.

Access Time—The time required to transfer a unit of information to or from storage from or to the central processing unit.

Accumulator—A unit in a computer or hand calculator where the results of an arithmetic operation may be formed.

Acronym—A name which is formed from the initial or other letters of a phrase (for example, "SOAP" for "Symbolic Optimal Assembly Program").

Actual Address—See absolute address.

Addition Table—That area of core storage (00300–00399) which contains the table of numbers utilized during the table look-up concept of addition.

Address—A designation, usually numerical, of a location where information is stored. Also that part of an instruction which specifies the operand.

Address Arithmetic—Addition, subtraction, or multiplication performed on allowable operands of instructions or declaratives.

Alphameric—An acronym formed from the words "alphabetic" and "numeric." It signifies that data may contain both alphabetic and numeric information.

BCD (Binary Coded Decimal)—A coding system utilizing bits to represent the decimal digits (0–9). Each bit has a positional value. The decimal digit is obtained by adding the positional values of those bits in an "On" condition.

Buffer—An intermediate storage device not under programmers control which reduces to a minimum the amount of interlock time necessitated by an I/O operation.

Bug—Data processing jargon for an error in a computer program.

Chain Multiplications—The successive products of more than two data fields (for example $a \times b \times c$).

Characteristic—See scientific notation

Characteristic Overflow—A condition generated in floating point arithmetic if an attempt is made to generate a characteristic greater than 99.

Characteristic Underflow—A condition generated in floating point arithmetic if an attempt is made to generate a characteristic less than –99.

Closed Subroutine—A subroutine which may be entered from any instruction in the main program, and which provides for automatic re-entry to the main program. Also called a linked subroutine.

Compiler—A computer program which has the ability to manipulate and translate symbols into a machine language program. The compiler may generate many machine language instructions from one source statement.

Conditional Branch—A type of instruction which causes a deviation from sequential program execution if and only if a specific condition, which is being interrogated by the conditional Branch instruction, exists.

Console—That part of a data processing system that allows for operator communication with the computer.

Data Processing—A series of planned actions and operations upon information to achieve a desired result.

Data Processing Systems—The procedures and devices used to accomplish data processing.

Debugging—The process of determining the correctness of a computer program, locating any errors in it, and correcting them.

Declaratives—Statements to a symbolic processor which control the specific details of assembly.

Diagnostic Tests—Tests performed by a competent, specially trained engineer to determine if a computer is functioning properly.

Direct Address—An instruction address which is the address of data to be processed.

Direct Insert Subroutine—See "Open Subroutine."

Disk Files—A storage medium consisting of a number of rotating disks each of which is coated with a special material on which information may be stored.

Division Simulator—See "Division Subroutine."

Division Subroutine—A series of instructions which simulate division by processes such as iterative subtraction, approximation of a reciprocal through series expansion, and so forth. Also called a "division simulator."

Doubler—An internal device, used in the multiplication process, which doubles a given digit.

Equal-Zero Indicator—An internal computer indicator which is turned on if the result of an arithmetic operation is zero.

Error Messages—Messages put out by a processor, subroutine, or object program to denote a variety of error conditions.

Execution Time—The total time required to execute a given command.

Field—Data in two or more adjacent core positions to be treated as a unit. A flag is used to define the high-order position of a field.

Fixed Product Area—See "Product Generation Area."

Fixed Word Length—Condition in which all storage fields have a set length or capacity, in contrast to variable word length.

Flag Operand—The third operand of a symbolic instruction specifying which digits of the object level instruction are to be flagged.

Floating Point—A form of number representation in which quantities are represented by one number multiplied by a power of the number base.

Floating Point Arithmetic—An arithmetic system which has the ability to operate on numbers represented in floating point form.

Floating Point Subroutines—Subroutines which will handle floating point numbers as arguments.

Hang Up—Data processing jargon for the failure of a program to operate properly and to terminate for unknown reasons.

High-Positive Indicator—An internal computer indicator which is turned on if the result of an arithmetic operation is positive and not zero.

Immediate Commands—Certain specialized 1620 commands where the Q field data begins at position Q_{11} of the immediate instruction.

Indirect Address—An instruction address which is the address of a second address. This second address is the address of data to be processed. This is single-level indirect addressing. However, the second address may also be indirect giving a second level of indirect addressing. By following this concept a third, fourth, fifth, and so forth, level of Indirect Addressing may be attained.

Input—Any information which enters a computer for the purpose of being processed or to aid in processing.

Input Area—A part of storage allocated to receive information from an input unit.

Label—A symbolic name given to an instruction or pieces of data. It is generally chosen for its high mnemonic content.

Linkage—Instructions related to the entry and re-entry function of a closed subroutine.

Linked Subroutine—See "Closed Subroutine."

Load Routine—A self-contained subprogram which after loading through operator action loads an object program in entirety.

Location Counter—A program-controlled counter used by a processor to ascertain the object time address of an instruction or constant being processed. Also called origin counter.

Loop—A programming technique whereby a group of instructions is repeated with modifications of the instructions in the group and/or with modification of the data or the address of data being operated upon.

Machine Cycle—A fixed time interval in which the computer can perform a specific number of operations.

Macro-Instruction—A source language instruction which during assembly generates more than one machine language instruction.

Magnetic Core—A tiny ring of ferromagnetic material which may be easily magnetized to a negative or positive flux, and once magnetized retains the charge indefinitely unless deliberately changed.

Magnetic Core Memory—See "Magnetic Core Storage."

Magnetic Core Storage—A storage medium consisting of planes of magnetic cores. Information is represented by the magnetic state of the core. Also called magnetic core memory.

Magnetic Tapes—A storage medium consisting of specially treated tape on which information may be stored and retrieved at high speeds.

Mantissa—See "Scientific Notation."

Memory—See "Storage."

Microsecond—One one millionth of a second.

Mnemonic—A name chosen for its memory retention ability.

Module—A segment of core storage containing 20,000 addressable locations. Three such segments are available for the 1620.

Multiplication Table—That area of core storage (00100–00299) which contains the table of numbers utilized during the table look-up concept of multiplication.

Nines Complement—Given a digit x, the nines complement is defined as a digit y such that $y = 9-x$.

Noise—See "Noisy Digit."

Noisy Digit—The digit chosen to be inserted into the units position of a mantissa during left-shifting operations associated with normalization of floating point numbers. Also called "noise."

Noisy Mode—Performing floating point arithmetic with a noisy digit other than zero.

Normalized—A mantissa is "normalized" if its first digit is nonzero.

Object Program—A machine language computer program received as the result of assembling or compiling a source program.

One over One Address System—A system in which the machine language instructions utilize two addresses, one of which may reference data.

Op Code—See "Operation Code."

Open Subroutine—A subroutine which is inserted in the main line program directly where needed. Also called a direct insert subroutine.

Operation Code—The segment of a 1620 instruction occupying instruction positions O_0 and O_1. It designates the operation to be performed. Also called Op code.

Origin Counter—See "Location Counter."

Output—The results produced by a computer, usually in the form of tape, punched cards, or printed documents.

Output Area—A part of storage allocated to hold information to be written on an output unit.

Overflow Indicator—An internal computer indicator which is turned on if an overflow condition exists as the result of an arithmetic operation.

P Address—The segment of a 1620 instruction occupying instruction positions P_2 through P_6 inclusive. Also called the P operand.

P Field Data—Data whose low-order position is specified by the P address of an instruction.

P Operand—See P address.

P Record Data—Data whose high-order position is specified by the P address of an instruction.

Parallel Operation—Arithmetic or data transmission operations performed simultaneously on all digits of a data field.

Pass—One execution of the group of instructions constituting a loop.

Polish Notation—A technique attributed to the Polish logician J. Lukasiewicz which consists of treating an algebraic statement as a manipulatable string of symbols followed by a manipulatable string of operations.

Principle of Toothed Gear—A mechanical method of counting which relies on the ability of a maximum positioned gear to rotate an adjacent gear for the purpose of the propagation of carries.

Processor—A term generally given to a computer program which is an assembler or compiler.

Product Generation Area—A specific area (0080–00099) of core storage where the product in a multiply operation is developed. Also called fixed product area.

Program—*Noun:* A set of machine instructions which causes a computer to process data and to produce specific results.
Verb: To plan the method of approach and the necessary instructions to process specific data completely.

Q Address—The segment of a 1620 instruction occupying instruction position Q_7 through Q_{11} inclusive. Also called the Q operand.

Q Field Data—Data whose low-order position is specified by the Q address of an instruction.

Q Operand—See "Q address."

Q Record Data—Data whose high-order position is specified by the Q address of an instruction.

Recomplementation—An internal process which performs nines or tens complementation on the result of an arithmetic operation when required.

Record—Data in one or more adjacent core positions to be treated as a unit. A record mark is used to define the low order position of a record.

Relocatable Subroutine—A subroutine whose effect is independent of its physical location in memory, and whose object time location is determined by the processor.

Relocation—The alteration of core storage assignments (instruction locations, data areas, and so forth).

Scientific Notation—A notation in which quantities are expressed as a fractional part (mantissa) and a power of ten (characteristic).

Serial Operation—Arithmetic or data transmission operations performed one character at a time.

Solid-State Circuitry—The utilization of transistors in place of vacuum tubes in computer circuitry.

Source Program—A program written in a higher level programming language as opposed to machine language coding.

Storage—Any device into which information may be entered, held, and retrieved at a later time. Also called memory.

Storage Position—A device capable of storing one character of information.

Stored Program—A program which is located within the storage area of a computer.

Stored Program Computer—A computer whose functions are controlled by coded instructions stored in the memory device of the computer.

Subroutine—A short or repeated sequence of instructions necessary to solve a part of a problem.

Symbolic Address—A symbolic instruction address in which labels are used to reference data. This is opposed to an absolute address.

Symbolic Programming System-1620—The symbolic assembly system peculiar to the 1620.

Symbolic Assembly System—A programming system consisting of two parts: a language called the symbolic language and a computer program called a processor which translates a source program written in the symbolic language to a machine language object program.

Tens Complement—Given a digit x, the tens complement is defined as a number y such that $y = 10 - x$.

Two-Address Instruction System—A system in which the machine language instructions utilize two addresses, both of which may reference data.

Unconditional Branch—A type of instruction which causes a deviation from sequential program execution regardless of existing conditions.

Variable Word Length—Condition in which the number of positions in a storage field is completely under the control of the programmer.

Wrap Around Memory—A feature of the 1620 in which core position 00000 follows the highest allowable address when incrementing, and precedes the highest allowable address when decrementing.

Reading Reference

Alt, F. L., ed., *Advances in Computers*. New York: Academic Press, Inc., 1960.

Aronson, M. H., ed., *Computer Handbook*. Pittsburgh, Pa.: Pittsburgh Instruments Publishing Co., 1956.

Ashby, W. R., *An Introduction to Cybernetics*. New York: John Wiley & Sons, Inc., 1958.

Bell, W. D., *A Management Guide to Electronic Computers*. New York: McGraw Hill Book Company, Inc., 1957.

Berkeley, E. C., *Giant Brains*. New York: John Wiley & Sons, Inc., 1949.

Berkeley, E. C., *Symbolic Logic and Intelligent Machines*. New York: Reinhold Publishing Corporation, 1959.

Berkeley, E. C. and Wainright, L., *Computers: Their Operation and Applications*. New York: Reinhold Publishing Corporation, 1956.

Booth, A. D., *Automation and Computing*. New York: The Macmillan Company, 1956.

Booth, A. D. and Booth, K. H. V., *Automatic Digital Calculators*. London: Butterworth's Scientific Publications, 1956.

Booth, K. H. V., *Programming for an Automatic Digital Calculator*. London: Butterworth's Scientific Publications, 1958.

Bowden, B. V., *Faster than Thought*. London: Sir Isaac Pitman & Sons, Ltd., 1953.

Buckingham, W., *Automation: Its Impact on Business and People*. New York: Harper & Brothers, 1961.

Canning, R. G., *Electronic Data Processing for Business and Industry*. New York: John Wiley & Sons, Inc., 1956.

Canning, R. G., *Installing Data Processing Systems*. New York: John Wiley & Sons, Inc., 1957.

Chapin, N., *An Introduction to Automatic Computers*. Princeton, N. J.: D. Van Nostrand Company, Inc., 1955.

Crowder, N. A., *The Arithmetic of Computers*. Garden City, N. Y.: Doubleday & Company, Inc., 1960.

Culbertson, J. T., *Mathematics and Logic for Digital Computers*. Princeton, N. J.: D. Van Nostrand Company, Inc., 1958.

Doss, M.P., ed., *Information Processing Equipment*. New York: Reinhold Publishing Corporation, 1955.

Eckert, W. J. and Jones, R., *Faster, Faster*. New York: International Business Machines Corp., 1955.

Einzig, P., *The Economic Consequences of Automation*. London: Martin Secker & Warburg, Ltd., 1957.

Eustis, W., *A Primer to the Automatic Office*. Westboro: Automation Management, Inc., 1956.

Flores, I., *Computer Logic*. Englewood Cliffs, N. J.: Prentice-Hall, Inc., 1960.

Friedman, B. D., *Punched Card Primer*. New York: American Book-Stratford Press, Inc., 1955.

Gorn, S., *The Electronic Brain and What It Can Do*. Chicago: Science Research Associates, Inc., 1956.

Gotlieb, C. C. and Hume, J. N. P., *High Speed Data Processing*. New York: McGraw Hill Book Company, Inc., 1958.

Gregory, R. H. and Van Horn, R. L., *Automatic Data-Processing Systems*. San Francisco: Wadsworth Publishing, Co., 1960.

Gruenberger, F., *Diagrams in Punched Card Computing*. Madison, Wis.: University of Wisconsin Press, 1954.

Hammer, P. C., ed., *The Computing Laboratory in the University*. Madison, Wis.: University of Wisconsin Press, 1957.

An Introduction to Electronic Computers. Newark, N. J.: Prudential Life Insurance Co., 1954.

Ivall, T. E., *Electronic Computers*. London: Iliffe and Sons, Ltd., 1956.

Jeenel, J., *Programming for Digital Computers*. New York: McGraw Hill Book Company, Inc., 1959.

Leeds, H. D. and Weinberg, G. M., *Computer Programming Fundamentals*. New York: McGraw Hill Book Company, Inc., 1961.

Livesley, R. K., *An Introduction to Automatic Digital Computers*. New York: Cambridge University Press, 1957.

McCracken, D. D., *Digital Computer Programming*. New York: John Wiley & Sons, Inc., 1957.

McCracken, D. D., Weiss, H. and Lee, T. H., *Programming Business Computers*. New York: John Wiley & Sons, Inc., 1959.

Montgomerie, G. A., *Digital Calculating Machines*. Glasgow: Blackie & Sons, Ltd., 1956.

Murphy, J. S., *Basics of Digital Computers*. New York: John Francis Rider, Publisher, Inc., 1958.

National Conference on Automation, *The Challenge of Automation*. Washington: Public Affairs Press, 1955.

Postley, J. A., *Computers and People*. New York: McGraw Hill Book Company, Inc., 1960.

Richards, R. K., *Arithmetic Operations in Digital Computers*. Princeton, N. J.: D. Van Nostrand Company, Inc., 1955.

Say, M. G., ed., *Analogue and Digital Computers*. New York: Philosophical Library, 1960.

Stibitz, G. R. and Larrivee, J. A., *Mathematics and Computers*. New York: McGraw Hill Book Company, Inc., 1957.

Stifler, W. W., *High Speed Computing Devices*. New York: McGraw Hill Book Company, Inc., 1950.

Svoboda, A., *Computing Mechanisms and Linkages.* New York: McGraw Hill Book Company, Inc., 1948.

Von Neumann, J., *The Computer and the Brain.* New Haven, Conn.: Yale University Press, 1958.

Weiner, N., *The Human Use of Human Beings.* Garden City, N. Y.: Doubleday and Company, Inc., 1950.

Index

Absolute address, *see* Actual address
Accept statement, 192
Access time, 3
Actual address, 105
Add Immediate instruction, 44–46
Add instruction, 33–37
Addition, 26–27
Address arithmetic, 109
Addresses
  absolute (actual), 105
  asterisk, 106–107
  indirect, 248–252
  symbolic, 105–106
Addressing, indirect, 248–252
Algorithms, arithmetic, 26–32
Alphamerical mode, 18
Arithmetic
  algorithms of, 26–32
  floating point, 148–154
  floating point hardware, 253
Arithmetic instructions, 22, 24, 33–52, 91
Arithmetic-logical unit, 3
Arithmetic macro-instructions, 158–161
Arithmetic statements, 183–184
Assembling a program (definition of), 98
Assembly System, 98
Asterisk address, 106–107
Asterisk symbol, uses for the, 147
Automatic division feature, 13
Automatic light, 294

Branch and Transmit Immediate instruction, 64
Branch and Transmit instruction, 63
Branch Back instruction, 65
Branch instructions, 13, 22, 24, 60–73, 92
  conditional, 65–73
  unconditional, 61
  with variations, 62–65
Branch on Digit instruction 65–66
Branch on Indicator instruction, 68–70
Branch no Flag instruction, 67
Branch no Indicator instruction, 70–71

Card Read-Punch (1622), 10, 13, 74, 269–277

Cards, punched, 5–6
Central processing unit, 3–4
  arithmetic-logical unit, 3, 10
  control section, 3, 4
  1620, 10, 12
Characteristic, 150, 151, 152
Characteristic overflow, 152–153
Characteristic underflow, 152–153
Check Stop light, 294
Clear Flag instruction, 83–84
Closed subroutines, 62, 155
Coding sheet (SPS), 100–103
Comment statements, 146, 183, 216
Compare Immediate instruction, 49
Compare Instruction, 41–44
Compilation, 172
Computed Go To statement, 186–188, 346–347
Computers
  advantages of use of, 1
  characteristics of, 7–9
  parallel, 8
  1620, *see* Data processing system
  serial, 8
  "stored program," 2
Conditional branch instructions, *see*
  Branch instructions
Console (1620), 10, 13, 281–325
  indicator lights, *see* Indicator lights
  keys and signal lights, 290–295
  operating procedures, *see* Operating
    procedures
  panel, 283–288
  switches, *see* Switches
Console Typewriter, *see* Typewriter
Constants
  fixed point, 175–176
  floating point, 176–177
  Fortran system, 175–177
Continue statement, 213–215, 348
Control gate indicator lights, 284–285
Control instruction, 86–87
Control section of central processing unit, 3, 4
Control statements, 185–190
Conversions in format, 194–203

Core array (1620), 19, 20
Core plane, 18, 19

DAC (define alphameric constant) declarative, 134
DAS (define alphameric symbol) declarative, 131
Data processing
  basic considerations in, 2
  defined, 1
Data Processing System (1620)
  alphamerical mode, 18
  console, 10, 13, 281–295
    keys and signal lights, 290–295
    operating procedures, *see* Operating procedures
    panel, 283–288
    switches and indicator lights, 284–290
  expansion of basic system, 10
  field processing, 17
  input-output devices, 13, 262–280
  internal data representation, 14–18
  introduction to the, 10–21
  magnetic core storage, 18–21
  numerical mode, 18
  programming concepts, basic, 22–25
  programming systems, 13
  record processing, 17–18
Data processing systems
  data representation, 5–7
  defined, 1
  development of, in 1940's, 2
  functional units, 2–4
  input devices, *see* Input-output devices
  processing unit, *see* Processing devices
  introduction to, 1–9
  storage devices, *see* Storage devices
  stored programs, 4
Data representation, 5–7
  on cards, 5–6
  on paper tape, 6–7
DC (define constant) declarative, 122
Declarative operands, asterisk rule for, 110
Declaratives, 100
  card and tape system, 110–145
  card system only, 145–146
  DAC (define alphameric constant), 134
  DAS (define alphameric symbol), 131
  DC (define constant), 122
  defined, 98, 110
  DEND (define end), 111
  DNB (define numeric blank), 145
  DORG (define origin), 110
  DS (define symbol), 112

Declaratives *(cont.)*
  DSA (define symbolic address), 137
  DSB (define symbolic block), 138
  DSC (define special constant), 131
  DSS (define special symbol), 131
  remarks for, 104
  SEND (special end), 146
  tape system only, 146
  TCD (transfer control and load), 139
  TRA (transfer to return address), 141
DEND (define end) declarative, 111
Dictionary of machine operations, concept of, 94–98
Digit Register, 287
Dimension statement, 209–210, 342–343
Direct divide, 13, 239–247
Direct insert subroutine, 155
Display MAR key, 292
Divide feature, 239–247
Divide instruction, 241–242
Division subroutines, 33, 239
DNB (define numeric blank) declarative, 145
Do statement, 210–213, 347–348
DORG (define origin) declarative, 110
Doubler, 28
DS (define symbol) declarative, 112
DSA (define symbolic address) declarative, 137
DSB (define symbolic block) declarative, 138
DSC (define special constant) declarative, 131
DSS (define special symbol) declarative, 131
Dump numerically, 80–81

E-type Conversion, 195
Emergency off switch, 294–295
End Statement, 206–208
Equal Zero indicator, 25
Error detection, 147, 302–305, 307–308, 311–312, 314–315
Error restart procedures, 277–278
Error, procedures for handling, 303–304, 315–316
Expressions, Fortran language, 179–182

F-type Conversion, 195
Field processing, 17
Fixed word length, 9
Flag operands, 104, 107–108
Floating accumulator (FAC), 328
Floating Add instruction, 254, 255
Floating Branch and Transmit instruction, 257–258

Floating Divide instruction, 256–257
Floating Multiply instruction, 255–256
Floating point arithmetic, 148–154
Floating point hardware, 253–261
Floating point subroutines, 150, 152–153
Floating Shift Left instruction, 259–260
Floating Shift Right instruction, 258
Floating Subtract instruction, 255
Floating Transmit Field instruction, 257
Format statements, 194–206, 348–351
Fortran, 13–14, 170–220
  basic 1620, 174–220
    internal organization of, 326–353
  compiling programs on a 1620 card system, 318–325
  compiling programs on a 1620 paper tape system, 305–312
  constants, 175–177
  determination of category, 328
  expressions, 179–182
  floating accumulator, 328
  functions, 215
  introduction to, 170–173
  operations, basic, 179
  problems, 230–232
  processor control operation, 206–208
  statements, 183–206
  subscripted variables, 209–215
  subscripts, 208
  symbol table, 326–327
  table of Addresses of Encountered Symbols, 328
  table of Encountered Operations, 327
  variables, 178–179
Fortran Compiler (or Translator), 171, 174
Fortran language, 171, 174
Fortran with format, *see* Fortran, basic

Glossary, 354–358
Go To Statements, 185–188, 343–345

H-type conversion for alphameric fields, 203
Halt instruction, 84–85, 345
Head cards, 142–145
High Positive indicator, 25

I-type Conversion, 195
If Sense Switch, 190, 345
If statement, 188–189, 345–346
Indicator lights
  control gate, 284–285
  digit register, 287
  input-output, 285

Indicator lights (*cont.*)
  instruction and execute cycle, 284
  memory address register, 287
  memory buffer register, 286–287
  memory data register, 287
  multiplier, 285
  operating register, 285
  parity check, 288–289
  sense and branch, 286
Indicators
  Equal Zero, 25
  High Positive, 25
  Overflow, 25
Indirect addressing, 248–252
Information sentences, 95–97, 100
Input-output devices, 2, 3, 262–280
  Card Read Punch (1622), 10, 13, 74, 269–277
  error restart procedures, 277–278
  Paper Tape Punch (1624), 10, 13, 74, 268–269
  Paper Tape Reader (1621), 10, 13, 74, 262–267
  1620 Data Processing System, 13, 74, 262–280
  typewriter, console, 278–280, 281
Input-output indicator lights, 285
Input-output instructions, 22, 24, 74–81, 93
Input-output statements, 190–194, 348–351
Insert key, 293
Insert light, 293
Instruction and execute cycle indicator lights, 284
Instructions
  Add, 33–37
  Add Immediate, 44–46
  arithmetic, 22, 24, 33–52, 91
  Branch, 13, 22, 24, 60–73, 92
  Branch and Transmit, 63
  Branch and Transmit Immediate, 64
  Branch Back, 65
  Branch no Flag, 67
  Branch no Indicator, 70–71
  Branch no Record Mark, 68
  Branch on Digit, 65–66
  Branch on Indicator, 68–70
  Clear Flag, 83–84
  Compare, 41–44
  Control, 86–87
  Divide, 241–242
  Divide Immediate, 242
  Dump Numerically, 80–81
  Floating Add, 254–255
  Floating Branch and Transmit, 257–258
  Floating Divide, 256–257

Instructions *(cont.)*
Floating point hardware, 254–260
Floating Shift Left, 259–260
Floating Shift Right, 258
Floating Subtract, 255
Floating Transmit Field, 257
Halt, 84–85, 345
Input-Output, 22, 24, 74–81, 93
internal data transmission, 22, 24, 53–59, 92
Load Dividend, 240–241
Load Dividend Immediate, 241
machine language, 4
miscellaneous, 22, 24, 82–87, 92
Move Flag, 233–235
Multiply, 40–41
Multiply Immediate, 48–49
No Operation, 85–86
Read Alphamerically, 75–77
Read Numerically, 74–75
remarks for, 103–104
Set Flag, 82–83
Subtract, 37–39
Subtract Immediate, 46–48
Transfer Numerical Fill, 237–238
Transfer Numerical Strip, 235–236
Transmit Digit, 53–54
Transmit Digit Immediate, 56–57
Transmit Field, 54–55
Transmit Field Immediate, 57
Transmit Record, 56
Write Alphamerically, 79–81
Write Numerically, 77–79
Internal data transmission instructions, 22, 24, 53–59, 92
I/O check lights, 289
I/O check switch, 289

Label, 102–103
Light
thermal, 291
procedure to turn off, 299
Lights, *see* Indicator lights; Signal lights
Line number, 102
Linkage system, 157–158
Linked subroutines, 155
Load Dividend Immediate instruction, 241
Load Dividend instruction, 240

Machine cycles, 7–8
Machine language instruction, 4
Machine language problems, basic, 221–222
Macro-instructions, 155–169
arithmetic, 158–161
defined, 156

Macro-instructions *(cont.)*
full symbolic coding with problems, 226–230
functional, 161, 164
general information concerning, 165
list of, 157
Macroless symbolic coding problems, 223–226
Magnetic core storage, 18–21
Mantissa, 150, 151
Manual light, 294
Memory address register, 287
Memory address register display selector, 287–288
Memory Buffer Register (MBR), 19, 21, 286–287
Memory Data Register (MDR), 287
Miscellaneous instructions, 22, 24, 82–87, 92
Mnemonics, 23
Move Flag instruction, 233–235
Multiplication, 27–29, 40–41
Multiply instruction, 40–41
Multiplier 5-light register, 285
Multiply Immediate instruction, 48–49

No Operation instruction, 84–86
Noise, 167–169
Normalization, 167
Numerical mode, 18

Open subroutine, 155
Operands, 104–108
Flag, 104, 107–108
P, 104–107
Q, 104–107
Operating procedures, console, 296–325
assembling SPS programs on a 1620 card system, 318–325
assembling SPS programs on a 1620 tape system, 299–305
clear core storage to zeros, 297
compiling Fortran programs on a 1620 card system, 318–325
compiling Fortran programs on a 1620 paper tape system, 305–312
instruct the computer from the typewriter, 296
print core storage data on typewriter, 298
program alteration and/or data entry, 298
program entry from the typewriter, 297
single instruction execution of program, 299
to turn off thermal light, 299
Operation register indicator lights, 285

Output devices, *see* Input-output devices
Output statements, 192–194
Overflow check switch, 289–290
Overflow indicator, 25
Overflow lights, 290

P address, 22
P operand, 104–107
Page number, 102
Paper tape, punched, 6–7
Paper Tape Punch (1624), 10, 13, 74, 268–269
   loading the, 268–269
Paper Tape Reader (1621), 10, 13, 74, 262–267
   components, 263–264
   loading the, 264–266
   operating keys, switches, and lights, 264
   tape handling tips, 267
Parallel computers, 8
Parity check indicator lights, 288–289
Parity check switch, 288
Pause statement, 206, 345
Pick subroutines, 166
"Polish Notation," 329
Power On light, 290
Power Ready light, 290–291
Power switch, 290
Print statement, 193
Problems, 221–232
   basic machine language, 221–222
   Fortran, 230–232
   full symbolic coding with macro-instructions, 226–230
   macroless symbolic coding, 223–226
Processing devices, 2, 3–4
Program switches, 290
Programming concepts, basic, 22–25
Programs, 4
   stored, 4, 10
Punch, *see* Paper Tape Punch and Card Read Punch
Punch check error, restart procedure, 278
Punch No Feed light, 292
Punch statements, 192
Punch Tape statement, 193
Punched cards, *see* Cards, punched
Punched paper tape, *see* Paper tape, punched

Q address, 22, 25
Q operand, 104–107

Read Alphamerically instruction, 75–77
Read check error, restart procedure, 277–278

Read Numerically instruction, 74–75
Read statement, 191–192
Reader, *see* Paper Tape Reader and Card Read Punch
Reader check error, restart procedure, 277
Reader No Feed light, 292
Record processing, 17–18
Register
   digit, 287
   memory address, 287
   memory buffer, 19, 21, 286–287
   multiplier, 285
   operation, 285
Release key, 293
Reset key, 291
Restart procedures, 277–278
   punch check error, 278
   read check error, 277–278
   reader check error, 277

Save key, 292–293
Self-checking devices, 2
SEND (special end) declarative, 146
Sense and Branch indicator lights, 286
Serial computers, 8
Set Flag instruction, 82–83
Signal lights
   Automatic, 294
   Check Stop, 294
   Insert, 293
   Manual, 294
   Power On, 290
   Power Ready, 290–291
   Punch No Feed, 292
   Reader No Feed, 292
   Save, 293
   Thermal, 291
Source Program, 171
Source statement, 171
Start key, 293
Statement numbers, 184–185
Statements
   Accept, 192
   Accept Tape, 192
   arithmetic, 183–184
   comment, 183, 216
   Computed Go To, 186–188, 346–347
   Continue, 213–215, 348
   control, 185–190
   Dimension, 209–210, 342
   Do, 210–213, 347–348
   End, 206–208
   Format, 194–206, 348–351
   Fortran, 183–206
   Go To, 185–188, 343–345
   If, 188–189, 345–346

Statements *(cont.)*
  If Sense Switch, 190
  input-output, 190–194, 348–351
  Pause, 206, 345
  Print, 193
  Punch, 192
  Punch Tape, 193
  Read, 191–192
  specification, 194–206
  Stop, 206, 345
  Type, 193–194
  Unconditional Go To, 185–186
Stop SIE key, 294
Stop statement, 206, 345
Storage devices, 2, 3, 170
"Stored program" computers, 2
Stored programs, 4, 10
Subroutines
  closed (linked), 155
  floating point, 150, 152–153
  open (direct insert), 155
  Pick, 166
Subscripted variables, 209–215
Subscripts, 208
Subtract Immediate instruction, 46–48
Subtract instruction, 37–39
Subtraction, 27
Switches
  emergency off, 294–295
  I/O check, 289
  overflow check, 289–290
  parity check, 288
  power, 290
  program, 290
Symbol Table, 326–327
Symbolic address, 104, 105–106
Symbolic Programming System (SPS), 13, 23, 88–147
  assembling on a 1620 card system, 312–318
  assembling on a 1620 tape system, 299–305
  coding sheet, 100–104
  declaratives, *see* Declaratives
  error detection, 147, 302–303, 307–308, 314–315
  introduction to, 88–99
  operands, 104–108

Table of Addresses of Encountered symbols, 328, 329
Table of Encountered Operations, 327, 329
Tape handling tips, 267
TCD (transfer control and load) declarative, 139
Thermal light, 291
  procedure to turn off, 299
TRA (transfer to return address) declarative, 141
Transfer Numerical Fill instruction, 237–238
Transfer Numerical Strip instruction, 235–236
Transmit Digit Immediate instruction, 56–57
Transmit Digit instruction, 53–54
Transmit Field Immediate instruction, 57
Transmit Field instruction, 54–55
Transmit Record instruction, 56
Truncation errors, 168
2-address instruction system, 24–25
Typewriter, console, 278–280, 281
  instructing the computer from the, 296
  print core storage data on, 298
  program entry from the, 297

Unconditional branch instructions, *see* Branch instructions
Unconditional Go To statement, 185–186

Variable word length, 9
Variables
  fixed point, 178
  floating point, 178–179
  subscripted, 209–215

Word length
  fixed, 9
  variable, 9
Write Alphamerically instruction, 79–81
Write check error, 278
Write Numerically instruction, 77–79

X-type conversion for blank fields, 202